# Civil Strife in Latin America

# Civil Strife in Latin America:
# A Legal History of U.S. Involvement

William Everett Kane

Published under the auspices of
the American Society of International Law

THE JOHNS HOPKINS UNIVERSITY PRESS
BALTIMORE AND LONDON

# Contents

# Foreword

As a principal element in its program of continuing education and re-search, the American Society of International Law convenes study panels on a variety of subjects of concern to the international lawyer. These subjects are often of interdisciplinary interest. The panels include there-fore scholars and practitioners of other crafts, as well as lawyers.

The study panels are determined by the Society's Board of Review and Development. This body has twenty members, at least three of whom are known for their contributions to disciplines other than law. The range of subject matter covered by the score or more of panels has been a wide one, from telecommunications to China, to trade, to human rights, to the inter-national movement of national art treasures.

One has addressed itself to what is perhaps the most important con-temporary challenge to international peace and security: the civil war. More particularly, this panel has dealt with the international law of civil war. As its first chairman, Professor Richard A. Falk, has said, the purpose of the panel was "to clarify current patterns of state practice bearing on the relevance of law to civil-war types of situations and to illuminate the policy problems that arise when a particular conflict exhibits an interplay of domestic violence and external participation." (*Infra*, p. xvi.)

The panel's members, whose names are set out on page ix, represent a diversity of opinion and experience. Through a series of meetings, they hammered out considerations to guide their inquiry, and then commis-sioned studies of particular civil wars. The panel used these studies to inspire its own lively efforts toward a more general theoretical reinterpre-tation of the modern relevance of international law to civil war.

Such labors deserve a purpose broader than the private instruction of the panel. So the panel recommended to the Board of Review and Develop-ment that several of the studies be published. Six, together with an intro-duction and a summary, appeared in a single volume under the Society's auspices, *The International Law of Civil War*, Richard A. Falk, editor (The Johns Hopkins Press, 1971).

In addition, the panel recommended this study by William Everett Kane as worthy of independent publication. Not only does the volume contribute importantly to the scholarly literature of international law, it sheds some dazzling new light as well on our own national record of rough and ready intervention in the civil troubles of the peoples to the south of us.

It is clear enough that conventional principles of international law have yet to contain domestic political violence, or foreign meddling in it. One hopes that the international law of civil war may someday be reformulated in such a way as to have genuine influence on national policy choices. If so, the effort must begin with just such inquiries as the panel's and with just such scholarship as this volume.

WILLIAM D. ROGERS

*Washington, D.C.*
*January, 1972*

# AMERICAN SOCIETY OF INTERNATIONAL LAW

*Panel on The Role of International Law in Civil Wars*

Wolfgang Friedmann, Columbia University School of Law, *Chairman*

John Norton Moore, University of Virginia School of Law, *Rapporteur*

Richard J. Barnet, Institute for Policy Studies

Thomas Ehrlich, Stanford Law School

Richard A. Falk, Princeton University

Tom J. Farer, Rutgers University School of Law

Edwin B. Firmage, University of Utah College of Law

G. W. Haight, of the New York Bar

Eliot D. Hawkins, Milbank, Tweed, Hadley & McCloy

Brunson MacChesney, Northwestern University School of Law

Myres S. McDougal, Yale Law School

Louis B. Sohn, Harvard Law School

Howard J. Taubenfeld, Southern Methodist University School of Law

Lawrence R. Velvel, University of Kansas School of Law

Burns H. Weston, University of Iowa College of Law

# Civil Strife in Latin America

# I.

# Introduction

IF ONE HAD TO CHOOSE a one-word characterization of U.S.–Latin American relations since the turn of the century, "intervention" would probably be the choice of a majority of Latin American scholars. If, on the other hand, legal scholars were forced to make a similar single-word choice to describe the inter-American system, "nonintervention" would appear to be a likely candidate. Fortunately, the decisions of statecraft, unlike toothpaste, are not sold in the market place on the basis of what leading doctors prescribe; but the discrepancy between U.S. actions and U.S. legal commitments in the Western Hemisphere is a real one. From the beginning of the Pan-American movement during the Wilson administration, to the good neighbor policy, to the Charter of the Organization of American States (O.A.S.), the United States has renounced, in increasingly inclusive terms, all interference in the affairs of its southern neighbors.[1] But both in the past and in recent years, the United States has shown a

[1] The most inclusive commitment to date is found in Articles 15, 16, and 17 of the O.A.S. Charter, which read as follows:

"15. No State or group of States has the right to intervene, directly or indirectly, for any reason whatever, in the internal or external affairs of any other State. The foregoing principle prohibits not only armed force but also any form of interference or attempted threat against the personality of the State or against its political, economic, and cultural elements.

"16. No State may use or encourage the use of coercive measures of an economic or political character in order to force the sovereign will of another State and obtain from it advantages of any kind.

"17. The territory of a State is inviolable; it may not be the object, even temporarily, of military occupation or of other measures of force taken by another State, directly or indirectly, on any grounds whatever."

1

surprising tendency to disregard even the minimum prohibition against the use of armed force. Through subsequent interventions in Guatemala, Cuba, and the Dominican Republic, it has become increasingly difficult, even for special pleaders, to square the realities of U.S. intervention with the nation's legal commitments to nonintervention.[2] In fact, one statement by the legal adviser to the Department of State with regard to the Dominican intervention suggests that legal considerations are to be sacrificed to policy in such situations:

> It will surprise no one here if I say that international law which cannot deal with facts such as these, and in a way that has some hope of setting a troubled nation on the path of peace and reconstruction, is not the kind of law I believe in. . . .
> We recognize that, regardless of any fundamentalist view of international law, the situation then existing in the Dominican Republic required us to take action to remove the threat and at the same time to avoid nuclear war. In the tradition of the common law we did not pursue some particular legal analysis or code, but instead sought a practical and satisfactory solution to a pressing problem.[3]

Had Mr. Meeker been speaking of a situation in which general international law was applicable, his point of view, however heretical, might have been tenable. But he was speaking of an area protected by the prescriptions of both the U.N. Charter and Articles 15 and 17 of the O.A.S. Charter.[4] The American House of Representatives was less equivocal than Mr. Meeker, but it was more legalistic. On September 20, 1965, the congressmen passed a resolution declaring the communist "subversive domination or any threat of it" violates the Monroe Doctrine; in such a case, any American state "may, in the exercise of individual or collective self-defense, which could go so far as resort to armed force . . . take steps to forestall or combat intervention, domination, control, and colonization in any form."[5] The resolution went far beyond anything that our treaty commitments could be interpreted to allow, but congressional resolutions

---

[2] For a well-structured attempt to legitimize U.S. actions in the Cuban missile crisis of 1962, see Abram Chayes, "The Legal Case for U.S. Action on Cuba," Department of State, *Bulletin* no. 47 (November 19, 1962), pp. 763-5.

[3] Quoted in Wolfgang Friedmann, "United States Policy and the Crisis of International Law," *American Journal of International Law* 59 (October 1965): 868.

[4] According to some writers, the U.N. Charter alone would be sufficient to prohibit any form of forceful intervention. "There is no question that the applications of armed force prohibited by the Charter include both the comprehensive and relatively milder exercises often described in the past as 'measures short of war.' " Myres S. McDougal and Florentino P. Feliciano, *Law and Minimum World Public Order* (New Haven: Yale University Press, 1961), p. vii.

[5] H. Res. 516, *Congressional Record*, vol. 3, no. 173, 89 Cong. 1 sess. (September 20, 1965), p. 23458.

are not noted for their solid foundations in international law. What is more important is the emphasis upon action taken in "individual self-defense." There is nothing peculiar about the individual right of self-defense; but here it is defined to mean prevention of communist control in any American state.

Both Mr. Meeker's statement and the congressional resolution imply a dramatic expansion of the territorial area that is considered inviolable if American security is to be maintained. Or is it really an expansion? American intervention in Latin America is not exactly a new phenomenon. From 1898 to 1933 there were few members of the marine corps who had not visited Latin America, at some point, as a member of an expeditionary force. American historians have even provided the modern generation with ready terms, such as "big stick" and "dollar diplomacy," to bestow a sort of instantaneous castigation upon the interventionist policies of certain administrations. But the fact of the matter is that American intervention in Latin America is and has been a completely nonpartisan activity. President Wilson, for whom there is no catchy label, was the greatest interventionist of all American presidents. Likewise, it would be difficult to distinguish between Eisenhower's C.I.A. (Central Intelligence Agency) in Guatemala and Kennedy's Cuban refugees in the Bay of Pigs, unless one cares to distinguish between degrees of exposure. What is new, therefore, is not the American interventions, but the American commitment to nonintervention.

## Strategy, Intervention, and International Law

"Intervention," in the broadest sense of the word, might be considered the conceptual anonym for the "absolute sovereignty of the nation-state." Fashioned in this manner, the concept of "nonintervention" is virtually meaningless. "In an interdependent world it is inevitable and desirable that states be concerned with and try to influence the actions and policies of other states."[6] But used in this sense, the word "intervention" is at best descriptive and connotes a range of conduct along a spectrum of varying degrees of coercion and violence. While it is true that this descriptive use of the term is most frequently applied to indicate the use of substantial military power to influence political outcomes in foreign nations, it is just as accurately applied to less coercive attempts to influence outcomes. Thus, during the 1960 presidential campaign in the United States, statements by the Soviet premier on American politics were said by some to constitute an intervention into domestic politics.

[6] Edward McWhinney, "The 'New' Countries and the 'New' International Law," *American Journal of International Law* 60 (January 1966): 23.

"Intervention" as a juridical concept falls into a class with "pacific blockade" and "reprisals"—terms traditionally included under the general rubric of "measures short of war." Doctrines related to measures short of war were devised in the context of the nineteenth century balance of power among European nations. Their purpose was to localize the coercion and violence employed by the advanced industrial nations against weaker and less developed states. In general, "the rules on 'measures short of war' restricted the lawful application of limited coercion to cases in which a prior unlawful act, or a culpable failure to perform international obligations was attributable to the state against which coercion was applied."[7] Primary among the motivations for specific instances of armed interventions in the nineteenth and early twentieth centuries was the enforcement of financial obligations.

It is only against this traditional tolerance for limited coercion that the principle of nonintervention can be assessed. That principle found one of its first important expressions in the Covenant of the League of Nations, which bound signatory states to "respect . . . the territorial integrity and existing political independence" of one another. But because the Covenant's limitations upon the "resort to war" could be circumvented by the use of the verbal symbology of "measures short of war," the Kellogg–Briand Pact attempted to limit the area of permissible coercion even more by binding states to renounce war as an instrument of national policy and to seek the settlement of their disputes by "pacific means." But it remained for the Charter of the United Nations to settle the question of the permissibility of "measures short of war."

The most comprehensive commitment of the United States to nonintervention is contained in the Charter of the Organization of American States. That commitment might be considered the logical extreme of the doctrine of nonintervention:

> No State or group of States has the right to intervene, directly or indirectly, for any reason whatever, in the internal affairs of any other State. The foregoing principle prohibits not only armed force but also any other form of interference or attempted threat against the personality of the State or against its political, economic, and cultural elements.

As a practical matter, Article 15, in its strict interpretation, is the legal equivalent of a moral imperative to walk through a wall. The massive political, economic, and cultural influence of the world's greatest power cannot help but permeate the Western Hemisphere. In the economic sphere,

---

[7] McDougal and Feliciano, *Minimum World Public Order*, p. 137.

for example, it has been said that "when the American economy sneezes, Latin America comes down with pneumonia." In the cultural realm the middle-class Latin American goes to American movies, wears American clothes, and reads American trash-novels in translation. In a number of Latin American countries the "man-in-the-street" is more likely to know the name of the current U.S. president than he is to know the name of his own head of state. In short, U.S. compliance with the nonintervention norm, taken literally, is an impossibility. It might be added that "literally" is precisely the way the Latin Americans usually read Article 15.

For those who view the country's international legal commitments as primarily important as expressions of our intentions toward other countries, all of this can be easily put to one side. There is a vague sense in which both our own heads of state and the Latin Americans "understand what these commitments *really* mean"; and no one seriously contemplates the withdrawal of United States Information Agency (USIA) libraries and American movies from Bogotá. But what cannot be put to one side is a history of U.S.–Latin American relations, extending on into recent years, that is littered with occasions of military and paramilitary operations carried on by U.S. government agencies for and against incumbent Latin American governments, diplomatic arm-twisting and threats far beyond accepted norms of diplomatic intercourse, and economic boycotts levied against disfavored Latin American regimes—conduct which clearly lies on the prohibited side of the intervention/nonintervention line however it might be drawn. Few would deny, for example, that the operations of the C.I.A. in Guatemala in 1954 and the landing of 15,000 troops in the Dominican Republic in 1965 were clear violations of inter-American legal commitments—the Latin American press and diplomatic corps were unanimous on this issue and Mr. Meeker's statement would suggest that even the U.S. State Department was in near agreement.

It is a matter of common observation that in the international system as a whole the legal circumscription of armed intervention has not been generally effective. In the Cold War context internal conflicts have shown a disturbing tendency toward internationalization, while the "revolution of rising expectations" in emerging nations seems to have increased the frequency of internal conflicts. The reasons for this development are so numerous as to preclude their discussion here, but the general problem is well stated by Professor Richard Falk: "This congeries of capability, risk, goal, and necessity places great emphasis upon the strategic manipulation of intrastate violence by groupings of nations contending for dominance in the world today. If empire once depended upon the extent of colonial occupation, it now increasingly depends upon the capacity to influence the outcome of important internal wars."[8] To date, the international community has been unable to fashion an alternative to the intervention and counterinterventions of major Cold War rivals in the internal conflicts of less powerful nations. The old terminology of "measures short of war" has found new use as a vocabulary for a dialogue between intervening powers and between potential interveners, for the purpose of avoiding major confrontations. Nor has this process of symmetrical intervention been confined to the so-called "gray areas" of nonaligned nations. Latin America, with its explosive revolutionary potential and its history of animosity toward the United States, in many ways constitutes a kind of backyard Vietnam for U.S. policy.

The peculiarity of the problem of U.S. intervention in Latin America is twofold. On the one hand, given the extensiveness of our hemispheric commitment to nonintervention, even relations and activities that would be otherwise normal between friendly nations can rapidly come to be perceived as legally interventionary with only slight changes in the context within which those relations take place. Thus, minor diplomatic disputes between the United States and Brazil result in a charge of "cultural intervention" levied against the U.S. ambassador for his criticisms of Brazilian literature. A dispute between the President of Colombia and American economists of the International Monetary Fund (IMF) is accompanied by a bombing of the USIA cultural center and much semiofficial discussion of the interventionary nature of U.S. cultural centers. On the other hand, there is a problem in identifying the kind and degree of activity that constitutes intervention under the O.A.S. Charter, even if the diplomatic context is held constant—a problem which the inter-American system shares with the international system as a whole, but in dramatically enlarged proportions. For example, the United States supplies arms and counterinsurgency experts to the incumbent government in La Paz, for the purpose of suppressing a guerilla war which has gone on for years, in which the guerillas control large portions of territory and in some cases have set up viable local governments, and in which U.S. support of the incumbent government has been the determining factor in the government's remaining incumbent. Even in the context of the traditional distinction between rebellion, insurgency, and belligerency, there remains a serious question as to whether or not U.S. support of the incumbent government would be interventionary. In the context of our inter-American commitments, that support should probably be characterized as illegal. The truth is that neither international law nor the inter-American system have

[8] Richard A. Falk, "Janus Tormented: The International Law of Internal War," in James M. Rosenau (ed.), *International Aspects of Civil Strife* (Princeton: Princeton University Press, 1964), p. 189.

developed categories of identifiable conduct that is per se interventionary. In short, once it is recognized that the "paper commitments" are untenable, the nonintervention norm takes on a fluidity far in excess of that which characterizes the international system as a whole.

The problem of formulating normalogical thresholds for the identification of certain activities as interventionary is further complicated by the natural tendency of legal writers to focus upon interventionary acts, as opposed to interventionary intentions and motivations. Much has been written, for example, from the premise that the violation of territorial sovereignty by armed forces would in itself be intervention. But we live in a world of the over-flight. A U.S. military plane violating Cuban airspace may be doing so for the purpose of bombing Havana, of collecting military intelligence, of air-dropping supplies or paramilitary groups, or because the pilot missed the beacon lights at Miami. By the same token, an American ambassador may criticize Brazilian literature as part of an overall attempt to undercut a local traditionalist movement, in order to express semiofficial displeasure at some group of local authors, or because he is an economist by training, a political appointee, and does not know any better. In both of the cases mentioned the intention behind the act is as important as the act itself for purposes of characterizing the activity as interventionary or noninterventionary. With these criteria in mind, an attempt has been made in subsequent chapters to apply the prescriptive label of intervention only to those cases of U.S. involvement in Latin American civil strife in which there would exist widespread agreement that interventionary acts coincided with interventionary intent. Second, an attempt has been made to use only those cases of Latin American civil strife which had factually gone beyond mere rebellion and would be easily classified by an impartial observer as either insurgency or belligerency. Even after the field is so narrowed, there remains sufficient evidence to support the proposition already suggested: that the United States has historically acted as an outlaw with respect to civil strife in Latin America. Guatemala, Cuba, and the Dominican Republic are the most recent examples and probably gather disproportionate emphasis from their recency and their abruptness. But the history of U.S.–Latin American relations in this century is, in large part, the chronicle of such examples.

In the study which follows, great emphasis has been placed upon the development of strategic doctrines in the United States and their acceptance by civilian leaders as a source of explanation for U.S. interventionary practice. It is contended that since the 1890's nonintervention has not been compatible with dominant American strategic doctrine. The American commitment to nonintervention resulted from an atypical absence of any external threat between the two world wars, when strategy took a back seat to other political considerations. And it will be contended that the conmitment to nonintervention effectively collapsed when the security of the hemisphere was again threatened by the Axis and, later, by what was perceived by U.S. policymakers as the threat of international communism.

This strategic emphasis is not designed to deny the relevance of other considerations in U.S. interventions. There is little doubt, for example, that national attitudes toward the desirability of foreign markets and toward the role and destiny of the United States in world affairs created— particularly in the early part of the century—an atmosphere that was not conducive to respect for the individual sovereignty of weaker nations. Rather, the emphasis on strategic doctrine is an attempt to specify the realm in which alternatives to armed intervention could and can operate.

Compliance with an individual norm of international law, such as nonintervention, implies an *immediate* sacrifice of other values—in this case, that of national security. In such an instance it is always necessary for the advocate of legal order to evaluate the relative "essentiality" of the particular interest involved. It may be that the establishment of a viable system of minimum public order will prove to be the only alternative to global annihilation— that is a possibility that the future will ascertain or deny. But it is a matter of common observation that the necessity for world order is rarely perceived in such crucial terms. In the eyes of most national decisionmakers world order remains one instrument, among others, for the achievement of national goals. But because of its instrumental nature, world order cannot require the sacrifice of interests perceived by national decisionmakers to be essential to national security. This study's emphasis upon strategic doctrines is merely one way of identifying the perceptions of "national security interests" dominant at a given point in time.

# II.

# The United States and Latin American Independence

PRIOR TO THE DECADE of the 1890's, U.S. interests in the Caribbean and in the rest of what is now called Latin America were primarily of a commercial nature and, therefore, severely limited in scope. Before the French Revolution began the long decline of Spain's colonial commercial monopolies with the colonies, the trade ties between the newly independent United States and the crown colonies were, at best, illegal. U.S.–Latin American relations could well be said to have begun in Haiti; for it was here that enterprising New Englanders built up a flourishing trade in French-made military supplies with even more enterprising French colonials.[1] The extent of U.S. contraband trade with the colonies is almost impossible to estimate accurately, but some idea of the figure may be gained from the fact that contraband trade is sometimes estimated to have accounted for about 90 percent of total Latin American trade in the two decades preceding the close of the eighteenth century.[2] Of course, the great majority of this trade was of Dutch and English origin, but the Americans of the period were not known for letting a potential market go untended. Even so, as late as 1796, when Spain's grip on the colonies was notably slipping in the commercial area, U.S. exports to Latin America still accounted for only 3 percent of total U.S. exports.[3]

---

[1] Edwin Lieuwen, *U.S. Policy in Latin America: A Short History* (New York: Frederick A. Praeger, 1965), p. 4.

[2] See, R. F. Nichols, *Hispanic American Historical Review* 13 (1933); and C. L. Chandler, *Hispanic American Historical Review* 2 (1919).

[3] Arthur Preston Whitaker, *The United States and the Independence of Latin America* (Baltimore: The Johns Hopkins Press, 1941), p. 38.

9

Significant commercial ties between the United States and the Spanish colonies had to await the royal order of November 18, 1797, by which warring Spain, unable to wrest maritime control from Britain, threw the colonies open to neutral trade. In a single stroke Spain began the growth of U.S.–Latin American trade that was to continue apace despite all subsequent attempts by the Spanish Crown to call it to a halt. By 1806 exports to Latin America accounted for 12 percent of total American exports,[4] but, of more importance, Latin America served as a middle station and source of specie for the growing American Eastern trade with China, the East Indies, and Smyrna. The growing importance of this trade led to the establishment of the first U.S. government agencies in the area. These quasi-consular establishments later "provided both a pretext and part of the personnel for the establishment of quasi-diplomatic relations with the revolutionary governments of that region."[5] The Ordinance of Free Commerce was revoked with the restoration of peace in 1802. But the subsequent restrictions were not enthusiastically enforced by the colonials, and by 1804 Spain was again involved in the war between England and France.

The main impediment to the expansion of U.S.–Latin American commercial ties in the era preceding the War of Independence was not the Spanish Crown, but the British. Britain's free-port system in the Caribbean, combined with the Spanish Crown's continued dependence upon her maritime ally in Europe, gave Britain an overwhelming advantage in the pursuit of the colonial trade, while British restrictions upon neutral commerce in Latin America provided a serious handicap for U.S. shipping. It was here—in the struggle for commercial advantage—that the conscious Anglo–American rivalry that was to color U.S.–Latin American relations for more than a century began. Behind the forthright commercial rivalry always lurked the possibility that England would take the colonies from the faltering hands of a weakened and declining Spain—a possibility that threatened not only American trade but also the very existence of the young nation. Thus, from the beginning, U.S. policy toward Latin America was faced with a dilemma that was to become a constant refrain in Latin American relations: any change in the status quo might result in the transfer of the colonies to a more powerful and dangerous master, while the maintenance of the status quo—in this case, the Crown monopolies—was intolerable.

When the War of Independence finally came, Latin America became a virtual danger zone for the United States. The creation of the Holy

---

[4] *Ibid.*
[5] *Ibid.*, p. 2.

Alliance in Europe provided the United States with one driving purpose for its Latin American policy: that the Europeans be kept out of the hemisphere.

## First Moves toward Independence

The War of Independence actually began in Latin America with the breakdown of the Crown monopoly. Latin America was sporadically thrown open to both new ideas and new products—both of which spelled final doom for Spanish dominion. But the first physical stirrings of the independence movement came with Napoleon's invasion of the Iberian Peninsula and the subsequent refusal of the Latin American creoles to submit to the rule of the upstart Joseph, whom Napoleon had placed on the Spanish throne. In Bogotá, Quito, Buenos Aires, and Santiago, the creole *cabildos* ousted the Crown officials and declared their continued allegiance to the deposed Ferdinand VII. But this new freedom proved heady wine for the Latin Americans, and never again was the Spanish Crown able to regain control of the situation. From 1810 to the decisive battle of Ayacucho, in 1824, the former Spanish colonies were in a constant state of internal strife.

The initial American reaction to the upheavals in Europe and in the colonies was one of concern lest the colonies fall into the hands of Britain or France. The general malaise was expressed by Jefferson in a letter to Governor Claiborne of Louisiana: "If they (the Spaniards) succeed, we shall be well satisfied to see Cuba and Mexico remain in their present dependence, but very unwilling to see them in that of France or England, politically or commercially. We consider their interests and ours as the same, and that the object of both must be to exclude all European influence from this hemisphere."[6] In short, even at this early date the basic tenets of the Monroe Doctrine—the exclusion of European influence from the hemisphere—were already being articulated by American statesmen. But the United States in 1808 was hardly in a position to attempt to expand its own influence in the hemisphere much less talk of excluding the Europeans. The one possibility available to the Americans was the active support of those Latin American revolutionaries who shouted for complete independence from a French-influenced Spain. So it was that in October 1808 agents of the United States were authorized by the President and his cabinet to pass the following message on to influential persons in Mexico and Cuba: "Should you choose to declare your independence, we cannot now commit ourselves by saying we would make common cause with you, but reserve ourselves to act according to the then existing circumstances;

[6] Isaac J. Cox, "The Pan American Policy of Jefferson and Wilkinson," *Mississippi Valley Historical Review* 1 (1914): 212–39.

but in our proceedings we shall be influenced by friendship to you, by a firm feeling that our interests are intimately connected, and by the strongest repugnance to see you under subordination to either France or England, either politically or commercially."[7]

Parenthetically, it should be noted that these instructions did not simply indicate U.S. support of the Spanish patriots; they were instead an invitation to the Latin American insurgents to go even farther than they had already gone and to declare for complete independence from any Spanish government—Ferdinand VII, notwithstanding. All of which was quite in line with prevailing American policy. It is often forgotten that during this period "the United States was, in the eyes of many Europeans, as radical a threat to the existing order as is the regime of the Kremlin today."[8]

But at no time during the War of Independence did the promise of American support for the insurgents ever materialize, and even U.S. recognition of the insurgents as the rightful governors of Latin America was greatly delayed by the exigencies of international politics. The first blow to the policy of 1808 was struck before the policy itself was articulated. It came in the form of Jefferson's embargo on American commerce, which was not repealed until February of 1809. The embargo seems to have intensified opposition to all things Jeffersonian, including his Latin American policy. But, of more importance, at the critical moment of the Iberian invasion, the embargo effectively cut all but illegal communications with the Spanish colonies. "Thus at the very time when the relations of the United States with Latin America most needed to be multiplied, the administration stubbornly adhered to a measure which, if enforced, would have severed them almost completely."[9] The real winner in the embargo game was, of course, Britain—who used the time gained to get British commercial expansion into Latin America well underway. When commercial relations were renewed with Latin America after 1809, the Americans were to find the British firmly entrenched on both sides of the Atlantic. The danger of the situation was, however, well recognized in the United States. In a speech to Congress on December 13, 1808, New York Representative Barent Gardenier warned that if Napoleon were to conquer Spain, the Spanish colonies would ally with Britain: "We shall have in them, of consequence, hostile and dangerous neighbors; while Great Britain will monopolize their trade, and if our present difficulties continue, perpetually instigate them to hostility against us. All this might have been prevented, if, in relation to Spain only our government had pursued

---

[7] Quoted in Whitaker, *Independence of Latin America*, p. 42.

[8] Dexter Perkins, *The United States and Latin America* (Baton Rouge: Louisiana State University Press, 1960), p. 45.

[9] Whitaker, *Independence of Latin America*, p. 49.

the proper course. . . . It is not perhaps even now too late to retrieve the advantages the Administration have overlooked. A change of conduct may regain us the affections and friendship which have been unnecessarily lost."[10]

When the embargo was ended in 1809 it was already clear that the United States had to work fast in Latin America or face intensified British influence in the hemisphere. Uppermost in the minds of American statesmen was the fear that some of Spain's colonial possessions might be transferred to Britain. The No-Transfer Resolution, adopted by Congress in January 1811, resulted more from the fear that Britain might acquire Florida than it did from sympathy for the Latin American rebels. Hence, 1809 marked the first effort on the part of the United States to extend its agencies in Latin America. The government used three types of agents—special agents, agents for commerce and seamen, and consuls—in its first serious attempt to influence the Latin American political situation.

The agents for commerce and the consuls were identical as to purpose and function—the former term being used where consuls were not allowed. The original instructions of William Shaler (Havana) and Joel Roberts Poinsett (Buenos Aires, Chile, and Peru) show that their primary duty was to foster U.S. commercial interests.[11] But a firm government eye was kept on the possibility that Spanish America might "dissolve altogether its colonial relations to Europe," and the agents were therefore to "diffuse the impression that the United States cherish the sincerest good will towards the People of Spanish America as Neighbors" and that it would "coincide with the sentiments and policy of the United States to promote the most friendly relations, and the most liberal intercourse between the inhabitants of this hemisphere." The special agents were more specifically interventionary. In 1809 General James Wilkinson stopped off in Havana to inform the captain-general of Cuba that the United States would take steps to prevent the military use of Cuba by any of the European belligerents except Spain.[12] And in 1811 General George Mathews and Colonel John McKee were authorized to accept that part of West Florida remaining in Spanish hands, if the Spanish Government would cede it peacefully, and to seize East Florida forcibly, if a foreign power seemed likely to occupy it.[13]

The Congress cooperated in the effort to expand U.S.–Latin American ties. In the latter half of 1811 the House of Representatives voted a relief appropriation of $50,000 for Venezuela—actuated, as one congressman

[10] *Annals of Congress*, 10 Cong., 2 sess., pp. 848–89.
[11] Whitaker, *Independence of Latin America*, p. 65.
[12] *Ibid.*, p. 63.
[13] *Ibid.*

explained, "by a regard to the interests of the United States, which peculiarly required them to cultivate amity with and conciliate the South American provinces."[14] Unfortunately the supplies fell into the hands of the royalists upon the collapse of the Venezuelan revolutionary government.

Finally the Madison administration began to allow Spanish American revolutionary agents to reside in and buy arms in the United States. And there is every indication that the complicity of the American government went a little farther than merely turning its back upon private sales of arms. The case of the Buenos Aires agents Diego de Saavedra and Juan Pedro de Aguirre is particularly illustrative.[15] In March 1811 Joel Poinsett recommended one William G. Miller for a post as resident consul in Buenos Aires. Three months later Saavedra and Aguirre arrived in New York with Miller's draft on John Allen of Philadelphia for $3,515. The two agents proceeded to Philadelphia where they made their final purchase through a mercantile house with the most conspicuous name of Miller and Van Beuren. In May 1812 the two returned to Buenos Aires accompanied by a cargo of 1,000 muskets and 372,050 flints. However, with regard to this story and others like it, it is necessary to add the caveat that the degree of the U.S. government's involvement in these affairs remains indeterminate. "The consular agents, both regular and disguised, received no salary but only the fees of the office, with the result that such posts usually had to be filled with men who had business interests in Latin America."[16] Agents such as Poinsett and Miller inevitably worked in dual capacities as official representatives and private businessmen with specific political alignments. The result is that it is impossible to fix the blurred line between official action and private interests. A second result that was to become more important later was that American decisionmakers were to become highly dependent upon their naval officers for information about Latin America.

Whatever the degree of official complicity in their machinations, U.S. agents were generally successful in rivalry with their British counterparts. Throughout the War of Independence, British commerce enjoyed preferential treatment from royalists and insurgents alike.[17] In the first place, Jefferson's embargo gave the British an important headstart in the region. Second, the British free-port system was much more favorable to the insurgents than was the unofficial American head-turning. Colombian

---

[14] *Ibid.*, p. 86.

[15] *Ibid.*, pp. 67–69.

[16] *Ibid.*

[17] German Cavelier, *La Politica Internacional de Colombia* (Bogota: Editorial Iqueima, 1959), Tomo I, pp. 47–67.

agents of Bolivar operated quite freely in the London arms and money markets, and a large expeditionary force of British volunteers even served in the Granadine army.[18] In short, initial American attempts to compete with the British ended in defeat, with the result that the Madison administration exhibited a marked tendency to cooperate with France in the cause of Latin American independence.[19] This exacerbated even more the Anglo–American rivalry that finally ended in the War of 1812.

The War of 1812 itself served a near fatal blow to U.S.–Latin American relations. With almost complete naval control in the region, the British were given the opportunity to consolidate their commercial position in the Spanish American colonies, while U.S. contacts in the area were cut to a minimum. Meanwhile U.S. incursions into Spanish Florida—an inevitable by-product of the war—caused the deterioration of U.S.–Spanish relations. Since the United States could scarcely afford Spanish entrance into the war, she was forced to walk softly where relations with the rebellious Latin Americans were concerned.

Thus by 1815 when peace was finally restored in Europe it was clear that the United States had lost the first round in the struggle for influence in Latin America. In Brazil British control over the House of Braganzas meant excessive preferential advantages for British commerce. In the Spanish American colonies similar preferences were exacted by the British as the price for not allowing restoration of Crown rule. On the other hand, American commerce suffered under a large number of restrictions which were not applied to British trade.[20] Nor was the American government disposed to seek special favors for its commerce. The official government policy was one of reciprocity and the open door,[21] and it would have been particularly difficult to maintain another stand with respect to Latin America. Finally the Latin Americans were in a position of almost complete dependence upon British naval power for the preservation of what autonomy they had gained.

## Neutrality and the War of Independence

After the War of 1812 and the peace of 1815 what had hitherto been an Anglo–American rivalry in Latin America was expanded in scope. The creation of the Holy Alliance seemed to make the intervention of the European powers in Latin America inevitable—an intervention that could well have threatened the very existence of the United States as an independent

[18] *Ibid.*, p. 53.
[19] Whitaker, *Independence of Latin America*, p. 55.
[20] *Ibid.*, p. 124.
[21] See, Vernon G. Setser, *The Commercial Reciprocity Policy of the United States, 1771–1829* (Philadelphia, 1937).

nation. In fact, at several points during his mission, Onis, the Spanish minister in Washington proposed to Ferdinand VII in Madrid that the principle of legitimacy required the restoration of Louisiana to the Spanish Crown.[22] At the same time, the continuing U.S.–Spanish negotiations over Florida made the United States circumspect in its relations with Spain.[23] U.S. policy, therefore, was essentially a negative one of not provoking the intervention of the European allies in Spanish America. The general attitude toward the conflict in Spanish America was well expressed by Monroe in a letter to Andrew Jackson, dated December 1818: "I think that the proof which is now in possession of the Government, is satisfactory, that the policy, which was then, and has been since pursued, in regard to Florida, and to Spain and the Colonies in South America, has contributed essentially to produce the decision of the Allies at Aix-la-Chapelle, not to interfere in favor of Spain against the Colonies, or against us. By this policy we have lost nothing, as by keeping the Allies out of the quarrel, Florida must soon be ours, and the Colonies must be independent, for if they cannot beat Spain, they do not deserve to be free."[24]

Undoubtedly, implicit in U.S. fears of full-scale intervention by the Holy Alliance was a gross underestimation of the conflict of national interests within the alliance that prevented any wholesale restoration. Britain, for example, could not allow the restoration of the monarchist commercial monopolies in Spanish America, and when the cards were down at Aix-la-Chapelle, she vetoed a restoration attempt. But reality in this case is not nearly so important as the Americans' perception of it. And so strong was the current of Anglophobia that ran through America after the War of 1812 that it was difficult for the Americans to distinguish between British commercial designs and the monarchal machinations of the members of the alliance. As late as August 13, 1823, Robert Walsh, editorializing in the *National Gazette*, described British intentions in this manner:

> Indeed, deeming them, as we do, scarcely less the enemies of "essentially republican" systems than the members of the Holy Alliance, we do not find extravagant the idea that they may connive at the attempts of France to bring the late Spanish colonies again under the yoke of European monarchy, as they have at her crusades against the free institutions and national independence of Portugal. . . . The distracted condition of Mexico and Peru will enable them to accomplish much in those countries with a comparatively small force. . . . Let the people of our Union be on their guard against such neighbors. This subject is fruitful and *momentous*.

[22] Whitaker, *Independence of Latin America*, p. 22.
[23] Cavelier, *Politica Internacional*, p. 13.
[24] Quoted in Whitaker, *Independence of Latin America*, p. 211.

And earlier, in June 1817, the *Aurora* was warning that Buenos Aires could become a base in this hemisphere from which Britain could menace the United States, as it was already threatening China from its Bengal base.[25]

But if American policy walked in fear of European intervention, it also walked in sympathy with the Latin American revolutionaries. Apart from the strong sentimental appeal of republican revolutionaries fighting monarchist restoration, sympathy for the Latin American cause was potentially profitable. This coupling of idealism and profit was well expressed by one Isaac Briggs, while addressing a committee of Congress in 1817: "But where shall we find a market for our manufactured cotton and woolen goods? I answer, in Mexico and South America. . . . I am not an advocate for an improper interference in the concerns of another nation; but I wish for the rational freedom of the human race. I think we ought to stand prepared to avail ourselves of a passing good, when it can be *lawfully* offered to our acceptance. We shall have a jealous and watchful rival. A *first* possession will be a very strong point—those whom I address can understand me."[26] Second, the current Anglophobia was nimbly played upon by advocates of Latin American independence.[27] Most simply stated their argument was that if the United States did not help the revolutionaries the British would and, thereby, gain the everlasting gratitude of the Latin Americans. Finally, American sympathy for the revolutionary cause was useful in U.S.–Spanish negotiations over Florida. The ever-present possibility that the United States would recognize the revolutionary governments was a small but important stick over Spanish heads.

The neutrality doctrine proclaimed by the United States in September of 1815 clearly evidenced the ambivalence present in American policy. The proclamation of 1815 merely confirmed the liberal definition of neutral rights contained in the Pickney–Godoy Treaty of 1795 and previous American legislation of 1794 and 1797. These earlier acts prohibited sale of war materials to "any belligerent prince or state," but it made no provision for such sales to insurgents—hence, the latter remained legal.[28] Second, although a citizen of the United States could not send a ship out of the

---

[25] *Ibid.*, p. 166.

[26] *Ibid.*, p. 111.

[27] One of the most effective propagandists for the Latin American cause was Captain David Porter, USN. In a letter to Poinsett, dated October 23, 1817, he described the gist of the propaganda line: "We want to make it appear that the interests of the U.S. are jeopardized by the machinations of England through their agents, that we are the *natural* allies of S. America, that unless we aid them they will throw themselves into the arms of our worst enemy (our natural enemy), that no time is to be lost, that England has been long at work to effect her object" (quoted in Whitaker, *Independence of Latin America*, p. 164).

[28] Richard W. Leopold, *The Growth of American Foreign Policy* (New York: Alfred A. Knopf, 1964), pp. 29–40.

country for use by a belligerent, there was nothing to keep him from selling such a ship to the belligerent's agent in this country. In practice, both these loopholes operated heavily in favor of the Latin American revolutionaries. By March 1817, when new neutrality legislation was enacted, relations with Spain were deteriorating almost to the point of war. The Neutrality Act of March 3, 1817, served to placate the Spaniards, but it still left large holes in favor of the revolutionaries. In fact, the congressional debate that accompanied the act featured Henry Clay's impassioned appeal for action in favor of the insurgents—an appeal that launched the congressional campaign for recognition of the rebel governments. Whatever legal advantages the Spaniards gained in 1817 they lost in April of 1818, when the acts of 1794 and 1817 were combined into a single statute that remained the law of the land until 1889. The new statute prohibited Spain from augmenting the force of its ships of war in U.S. ports; but, more importantly, the legislation carefully omitted that part of the act of 1797 which attempted to prevent the arming of American vessels beyond the limit of territorial waters for hostile actions against a power with which the United States was at peace. From 1818 on it was possible for revolutionary agents to buy an unarmed ship in the United States, take it outside the three-mile limit, and there take on all the necessary armaments.

American neutrality doctrine during this period was a harbinger of future problems related to internal strife. In point of fact, the Act of 1817 moved American doctrine a step closer to the traditional point of view that: "A neutral Power is not bound to prevent the export or transit, for the use of either belligerent, of arms, ammunition, or, in general, of anything which could be of use to an army or fleet."[29] Early partial treatment of the Latin American insurgents resulted from the fact that prolonged colonial insurgency on this scale was a relatively recent phenomenon, not contemplated by traditional international law. But it is important to remember that the American government was forced into this position of relative impartiality by (1) continued negotiations with Spain over Florida; (2) the ever-present possibility of an Anglo–Spanish alliance against the United States itself; and (3) the bad showing of the Latin American insurgents in the field during this early stage of the war. Just as important was the necessity of protecting U.S. commerce in the area. In effect, the United States was forced to toe a British line with respect to neutrality if it was to maintain any commerce at all. But time was to prove that the desire to protect commerce could cut both ways, as soon as the balance of power between the Latin American insurgents and the Spanish royalists began to tip the other way.

[29] Article 7, Hague Convention XIII of 1907, was actually a codification of a practice over a century old in Western Europe and America.

## The Question of Recognition

The question of U.S. recognition of the Latin American insurgents illustrates the intimate triangle between the United States, Europe, and Latin America. From the early days of the independence movement, American public opinion and, from time to time, the actual political situation in Latin America exerted strong pressures upon the U.S. government for the recognition of the insurgents. At the same time, U.S.–Spanish negotiations over Florida made the United States timorous of endangering the negotiations by precipitate action. So while recognition made an important threat to hold over the heads of the Spaniards, it was more important as a threat than as a fait accompli. In 1818 the United States did take the initiative in proposing joint recognition to the British, but this move was closely related to the Anglo–American rivalry for the sympathy and trade-favors of the insurgents. And the ease with which the whole project was abandoned indicates some lack of seriousness on the part of the North Americans.[30]

Toward the end of 1820, however, the situation had altered drastically. In the autumn of 1818, Britain checked the plans of the Holy Alliance for intervention in Spanish America, leaving Spain in the position of minimizing her losses rather than looking forward to a total recovery of her American territory. The American occupation of East Florida emphasized the improbability of that particular piece of territory being left under Spanish dominion.[31] Accordingly, on February 22, 1819, the Onis–Adams Treaty (John Quincy Adams, secretary of state) conceding the Florida territory to the United States was signed. Still the Spaniards withheld ratification in hopes of obtaining further concessions from the United States. The Vives mission, which arrived in Washington early in 1820, conditioned ratification on (1) strict American neutrality in the War of Independence; (2) a formal guarantee of the integrity of other Spanish possessions in the New World; and (3) a formal American promise not to recognize any of the rebellious colonies.[32] Adams rejected the Spanish conditions, and the negotiations might well have ended there. But in the autumn of 1820 the Riego revolution in Spain put the Crown in a highly precarious position, and in October the King signed the treaty. The Florida question was thus removed from the problem of recognition.

Meanwhile, several factors favoring the recognition of the Latin American insurgent governments began to take on greater importance in American foreign policy. The intermittent successes of the insurgents made it imperative to assure future good relations in the event that the rebels

[30] Cavelier, *Politica Internacional*, pp. 48–49.
[31] *Ibid.*
[32] *Ibid.*, p. 49.

should win. The solidarity of the Holy Alliance exhibited at Troppau revived fears of European intervention in the Western Hemisphere, and, as always, such intervention was understood to involve a possible attempt to suppress free governments everywhere—even in the United States.[33] And, importantly, recognition was perceived as one way of protecting American commerce in the area.

Protection of U.S. commerce was always an important goal of American diplomacy during the 1800's, but the ever-changing balance of power in Latin America made such protection particularly difficult. American commerce suffered at the hands of rebels and royalists alike; but whereas diplomatic representation was possible at least in theory to the Spaniards, little could be officially done about the depredations of the rebels. Thus as early as January 1819 Adams was pointing out to the British that one argument for recognition was that "only by recognizing them could other nations compel them to observe the ordinary rules of international law in their intercourse with the civilized world."[34] The same protection policy led the United States to follow the example of France and Britain and to station warships in Latin American waters to protect the lives and property of U.S. citizens. By act of Congress of March 3, 1819, U.S. warships were given the right to convoy U.S. merchant vessels on the high seas and to retake U.S. vessels "which may have been unlawfully captured upon the high seas."

It is important to remember in this respect that shortly before 1819 the United States fought a war with Britain in which one of the principal questions had been that of the doctrine of effective blockade. Only seven years later the United States was faced with a situation in which neither of the belligerents could mount an effective blockade but both continued to prey spasmodically upon U.S. ships. The problem was most acute on the west coast of South America, where the conflict between Chilean patriots and Peruvian royalists endangered not only U.S. trade with the local area but also U.S. trade with Asia. The ultimate American reaction was to force both sides to withdraw their blockade orders and to enforce that withdrawal with a Pacific naval station, which was established in 1821.[35] Since the Spaniards received a higher proportion of their logistical supplies from abroad, this American prohibition of "paper blockades" tended to be most detrimental to the insurgents. Needless to say, such an outcome was not publicly popular in the United States. This was, after all, a period in which important political figures, such as Henry Clay, were advocating

[33] See, Whitaker, *Independence of Latin America*, pp. 317–43.
[34] *Ibid.*, p. 275.
[35] *Ibid.*, pp. 295–98.

U.S. support of the Latin American cause "by all means short of actual war."[36]

The American frame of mind was well expressed by Adams in a speech delivered in the House of Representatives on the Fourth of July, 1821.[37] In his address and the letters which followed it, Adams developed the twin principles of the illegitimacy of colonial regimes and the necessity of U.S. abstention from foreign wars, even in the defense of liberal principles. In a later letter to Edward Everett, Adams applied his anticolonial principle to the South American revolution: "It settles the justice of the struggle of South America for independence, and prepares for an acknowledgment upon the principle of public law of that independence, whenever it shall be sufficiently established by the fact."

What is important about Adams's anticolonial principle is that, on the one hand, it fielded a justification for the recognition of the Latin American insurgents and, on the other hand, it asserted a new principle of international law. The doctrine of legitimacy, accepted at that time by most European nations, implied nonrecognition of merely de facto governments, such as those that were coming and going with great rapidity during the War of Independence. Largely for reasons of its own history, the United States had long maintained the legitimacy of revolutionary regimes. As early as November 7, 1792, Thomas Jefferson, as secretary of state, had written: "It accords with our principles to acknowledge any Government to be rightful which is formed by the will of the people substantially declared."[38] And in March 1793 Jefferson again spoke out on the subject: "We surely cannot deny to any nation the right whereon our own Government is founded—that every one may govern itself according to whatever form it pleases, and change those forms at its own will."[39] The problem, of course, was in determining what the "will of the people substantially declared" really was; and the very fact of a civil war going on in South America made a determination in favor of either the insurgents or the royalists at least questionable. Also, internationally, American recognition of the Latin American rebels was contraindicated; "for it had long been and still was the almost unanimous opinion of European authorities that recognition of a belligerent during the course of hostilities was an unneutral act. The opposite rule supported by the United States was therefore an innovation upon the generally accepted rules of international

---

[36] *Ibid.*, p. 345.

[37] I have used the account of Adams's speech found in Whitaker, *Independence of Latin America*, pp. 348–54; but I do not subscribe to Whitaker's interpretation of the importance of the speech.

[38] Leopold, *American Foreign Policy*, p. 56.

[39] *Ibid.*

law."[40] The negotiations over Florida forced the United States to toe the line until 1821; but once those negotiations were terminated, there were no bases in reciprocity or in sanction for U.S. conformity to traditional rules of recognition. On the other hand, there was a strong motive for early recognition in the Anglo–American competition for the hearts and the markets of the Latin Americans.

In a special message of March 8, 1822, President Monroe declared that Colombia, Chile, the united provinces of the Plata, Peru, and Mexico were in full exercise of their independence and that their governments had acquired full rights to recognition.[41] That the move had very little to do with the fervent republicanism of the President was amply demonstrated by the fact that the Latin American government recognized by the United States was the Iturbide monarchy in Mexico. In fact, the main emphasis of Adams's instructions to the first American ministers sent to the newly recognized republics was on the necessity of counteracting European influence in the area.[42] Said Adams: "With relation to *Europe*, there is perceived to be only one object, in which the interests and wishes of the United States can be the same as those of the South American nations, and that is that they should all be governed by republican institutions, politically and commercially independent of Europe."[43] This was in effect a return to the policy of 1808—namely, the exclusion of European influence from the hemisphere—and a precursor to the Monroe Doctrine of one year later.

*The Monroe Doctrine and the Post-Independence Period*

It was a very short step from recognition of the Latin American states— with an eye toward excluding European influence—to the enuciation of the Monroe Doctrine—with an eye toward excluding European military intervention.[44] In 1823 France's lightning restoration of the Spanish monarchy revived fears of a possible mobilization of the Holy Alliance for military activity in the Western Hemisphere. In the meantime it had become clear that England was unlikely to side directly with the Alliance, but it was generally thought that England did have designs on Cuba. Finally, ideological considerations played a large role in Monroe's thinking and,

---

[40] Whitaker, *Independence of Latin America*, p. 360.

[41] Cavelier, *Politica Internacional*, p. 52.

[42] Whitaker, *Independence of Latin America*, pp. 412–15.

[43] Quoted in *ibid.*, p. 415.

[44] For our present purposes, a full exposition on the formulation and promulgation of the Monroe Doctrine is quite unnecessary. Those interested can find an exemplary treatment in Dexter Perkins, *A History of the Monroe Doctrine* (Boston: Little, Brown & Company, 1955).

thus, in the formation of the policy that bears his name.[45] With these factors in mind, President Monroe delivered his famous statement of December 2, 1823, in which he said: "We owe it, therefore, to candor, and to the amicable relations existing between the United States and those (European) powers, to declare that we should consider any attempt on their part to extend their system to any portion of this hemisphere as dangerous to our peace and safety."

Monroe's statement marked the culmination and the turning point of U.S. relations with the Latin American states. Even at the time it was made, France had already informed Britain that she was abandoning any intentions of using armed force against Spain's rebelling colonies.[46] Within a few short months the military situation in South America was such that even Spain was forced to admit defeat. In a sense the Monroe Doctrine became an anachronism within a few years after its pronunciation. It fell into almost immediate disuse and, with a few exceptions which will be discussed below, was scarcely heard from again until the late 1800's. In effect the United States entered a period of isolationism that was not to end until well after the Civil War.[47] When the Monroe Doctrine was revived in the late 1800's it was to be revived as a Caribbean doctrine, applying only to that restricted part of Latin America.[48]

In no area was the U.S. policy of noninvolvement more apparent than in her intermittent and unenthusiastic participation in the so-called Pan-American movement that grew out of Bolivar's attempt to unite the newly freed Spanish colonies. In large part, of course, hesitant U.S. participation can be attributed to Bolivar's own reluctance to accept the already powerful "colossus of the North" as a viable partner in a union based upon communality of culture and language. So far as the "Great Liberator" was concerned, even the common cultural and political interests of the Latin American states were a limited foundation for consolidation. "It is a grand conception," he said in his famous Jamaica letter of September 6, 1815, "to consolidate the new world into a single nation with a single bond uniting all its parts. Since the different parts have the same origin, language, customs, and religion, they ought to be confederated into a single state; but this is not possible because differences of climate, diverse conditions, opposing interests and dissimilar characteristics divide America."[49] What

[45] See, Perkins, *The United States and Latin America*, pp. 47–48.

[46] This was done by means of the famous Polignac Memorandum which was not known in the United States until much later. See for example of content, Cavelier, *Politica Internacional*, pp. 55–56.

[47] Lieuwen, *U.S. Policy in Latin America*, pp. 12–18.

[48] Perkins, *The United States and Latin America*, p. 18.

[49] Lucio Pabon Nunez, *El Pensamineto Politico del Libertador* (Bogota: Instituto Colombiano de Estudios Historicos, 1955), p. 49.

Bolivar attempted instead was to achieve some kind of loose union between the states primarily for purposes of mutual defense. The Colombian treaties of union, which laid the groundwork for the Pan-American conference at Panama in 1826, were of the nature of mutual defense treaties. They committed the signatories to "unite, league, and confederate" in order to sustain their independence from foreign domination—in particular, that of Spain.[50] Five nations entered into such treaties with Colombia between 1822 and 1825, and only one failed to ratify.[51] Bolivar's lieutenant, Santander, was convinced, after hearing of Monroe's pronouncements, that the United States could make "a powerful ally for Colombia in the event that her independence and liberty should be threatened by the allied powers."[52] But when Salazar, the Colombian minister in Washington, attempted to sound out Adams on the willingness of the United States to enter into such an alliance, he was told that the United States would remain neutral with regard to use of Spanish forces in Latin America and that any future problems would have to be referred to the Legislature.[53] Thus, the U.S. government was already backing away from the foreign commitment implied by the Monroe Doctrine.

Bolivar's efforts culminated in the Panama Conference of 1826, to which the United States was ultimately invited. But Secretary Clay's instructions to the U.S. delegates clearly indicate that the United States was interested in nothing more than an expansion of trade relationships and a Latin American commitment to a liberal policy toward U.S. neutrality, in the event of a renewed war with Spain. There was a decided effort to avoid anything that hinted of mutual security. The delegates were not even to discuss the war with Spain, except in those areas which pertained to maritime neutrality and the preservation of peace. In spite of widespread popular support for Cuban independence, the delegates were to oppose any attempt to free Cuba from the Spanish Crown, lest a weak Cuba provoke intervention by some other European power. Most important, for our purposes, the Monroe Doctrine was to remain a unilateral policy of the United States. The American delegates were to propose a joint declaration "that each American state, acting for and binding only itself, would allow no European colonies to be established within its territory."[54]

[50] Antonio Jose Uribe, *Anales Diplomaticos & Consulares de Colombia* (Bogota: Imprenta Nacional, 1917), Tomo VI.

[51] *Ibid.* Nations entering into treaties with Colombia were Chile (October 21, 1822), Peru (July 6, 1822), Buenos Aires (March 8, 1823), Mexico (October 3, 1823), and Central America (March 15, 1825). Chile failed to ratify.

[52] Cavelier, *Politica Internacional*, p. 57.

[53] *Ibid.*, p. 58.

[54] J. Lloyd Mecham, *The United States and Inter-American Security, 1889–1960* (Austin: University of Texas Press, 1961), pp. 36–38.

Apparently the United States was attempting to substitute diplomacy for a competitive navy.

The attempt in 1826 to design a system of mutual security was a resounding failure.[55] The U.S. delegation did not even arrive in Panama City until several days after the conference had been adjourned. Judging from the record of attendance, it is doubtful that the Latin American states took the meeting very seriously, and not one of the treaties signed at the Panama conference was subsequently ratified. Two considerations precluded the creation of an inter-American organizational structure such as that envisioned by Bolivar. In the first place, the Latin American nations themselves were unable to settle an infinite number of political differences that the War of Independence had served only to obscure. The internecine strife that was to divide and redivide both South and Central America was only slightly below the unified front that Bolivar was attempting to show to Spain. Second, the hemisphere's largest power, the United States, was militarily incapable of assuring her own continental security, much less that of her southern neighbors. The brutal fact was that even the much-heralded Monroe Doctrine was enforceable only in the territories contiguous to the United States, and it was enforceable there only when the military threat came in the form of land forces.[56] In 1825 a French fleet was sent to Haiti to exact indemnities for recognition without U.S. protest.[57] England seized the Bay Islands and the Falkland Islands in 1833, with immunity from American protest or military action.[58] And as late as 1838 British and French troops were operating in northern Mexico with total impunity.[59] In the light of her intrinsic military weakness, the United States could attempt nothing more than an expansion of export trade by means of the preferential tariff.

By 1845 an expanding and strengthened United States did begin brandishing the Monroe Doctrine, but then only in relation to the North American continent.[60] But that extension was brought to an abrupt halt by the American Civil War. By 1865, with the failure of the French experimental monarchy in Mexico, the embryonic Pan-American movement entered a

[55]Latin American writers tend to give a somewhat more optimistic interpretation of the significance of the Panama Conference. Those whose tastes run toward diplomatic history of the romantic school can read J. M. Yepes, *Del Congreso de Panama a la Conferencia de Caracas, 1826-1954* (Caracas: Gobierno de Venezuela, 1955); and Francisco Cuevas Cancino, *Del Congreso de Panama a la Conferencia de Caracas, 1826-1954* (Caracas: Gobierno de Venezuela, 1955).

[56] Lieuwen, *U.S. Policy in Latin America*, p. 18.

[57] *Ibid.*, p. 14.

[58] *Ibid.*, p. 15.

[59] *Ibid.*

[60] Dexter Perkins, *Monroe Doctrine* (2nd ed. rev., 1941), p. 18.

period of suspended animation.[61] When it was revived in 1889, its doctor was an American Secretary of State whose support came largely from commercial interests desirous of finding new export markets.[62] From the vigorous assertion of the Monroe Doctrine which resulted in the final withdrawal of French troops from Mexico in 1867, to the Spanish–American War in 1898, American interest in Latin American territory or problems was, at best, minimal. West European nations continued to threaten the area, even in the nearby Caribbean; but an industrializing nation involved in the immediate problems of postwar reconstruction could not be concerned with the problems of her Latin American neighbors, so long as the major powers of Europe did not attempt territorial aggrandizement too close to home.[63]

In large part, the decline of American interest in Latin America was the result of a general disgust with Latin Americans after independence was gained. As Professor Perkins puts it: "Without any tradition of self-rule, with ignorant and illiterate populations, with wide social cleavages between the governing class and the mass of the people, with the ascendancy of the military classes which had been responsible for the success of the revolutions, many, indeed most, of the Latin American states sank into disorder, or came under the sway of military despots. These general conditions naturally reduced enthusiasm in the United States for the new republics, and they were accompanied, oftentimes, by diplomatic controversies which did not improve the atmosphere."[64] Intra-elite fighting became the order of the day, and interstate meddling was not uncommon. As the new states began to fragment, boundary questions were often connected to internal squabbles over control of the government. A tradition of intra-Latin American intervention continued particularly strong in the Central American states. Constant disorder was a danger to the lives and property of foreigners and nationals alike, and to deal with the problem two legalistic practices came into being: internal diplomatic asylum[65] and limited intervention.

Until the Spanish–American War, U.S. policy regarding intervention in Latin America is probably best characterized as the use of force for the protection of the life and property of American citizens, but not for the enforcement of the international financial obligations of the Latin American states. Thus on July 13, 1854, Captain George N. Hollins of the *Cyane*

---

[61] Arthur Preston Whitaker, *The Western Hemisphere Idea: Its Rise and Decline* (New York: Cornell University Press, 1954), pp. 56–60.

[62] Perkins, *The United States and Latin America*, pp. 57–58.

[63] Harold and Margaret Sprout, *The Rise of American Naval Power, 1776–1918* (Princeton: Princeton University Press, 1946), Chap. XII.

[64] Perkins, *The United States and Latin America*, pp. 50–51.

[65] See below.

bombarded part of San Juan del Norte in Nicaragua in retaliation for unredressed outrages against American citizens and their property.[66] In 1858 President Buchanan sent an expedition to Paraguay to obtain redress for various injuries, including a firing upon an American naval vessel. But the final redress covered only a fraction of the cost of the expedition.[67] On the other hand, the U.S. government declined the invitations of the British and French to participate in the interventionary enforcement of Mexico's financial obligations in the first half of the nineteenth century. With respect to intervention, the United States was far behind her European counterparts, who were making liberal use of their naval and marine forces in Africa, Asia, and the Caribbean. Interventions on the part of the major European powers increased notably in the late nineteenth century, as a function of the renewal of European imperialistic expansion, which continued down to World War I.

There are, however, three exceptions to the general rule of American indifference to Latin America that should be treated: the annexations of Mexican territory; U.S. concern over Cuba; and the Mallarino–Bidlack Treaty of 1846 with Colombia. The annexations of Mexican territory had very little to do with the general Latin American policies of the U.S. government. They were, instead, a part of the westward expansion of the United States that was to be glorified with the label of manifest destiny. Civil strife on both sides of the border was a major factor conditioning the relative ability of each state to effect an outcome to its liking, but it was rarely at the center of attention in the nineteenth century. Consequently U.S. intervention in Mexico—and, for that matter, Mexican intervention in the United States—was most often part of a larger game of peaceful and not-so-peaceful "negotiation" by which the territorial domain of the United States was extended to its present southern reaches. Says Howard Cline, "it may be noted that transfers involved real estate, not peoples. Before the Texas revolution of 1836 and after the Gadsden Purchase of 1853, the population of Mexico remained at about 8,000,000."[68] Second, U.S.–Mexican disputes during this period were not entirely one-sided. "Centralist Mexican leaders during the Mexican War with the United States had a standing army several times as large as that of the United

[66] Leopold, *American Foreign Policy*, p. 98.

[67] *Ibid.*, p. 97. Leopold also cites some of the comic opera cases of individual actions that were interventionary but not official. One example was the capture of Monterey in October 1842 by Commodore Thomas Catesby Jones who, through his own impeccable channels of information, had mistakenly learned that war had broken out.

[68] Howard F. Cline, *The United States and Mexico* (rev. ed.; New York: Atheneum, 1965), p. 11.

States, and were sanguine enough in 1847 to expect that perhaps they would dictate a conqueror's peace from Washington."[69]

Cuba, too, was an exception to the general Latin American policy of the United States. Throughout the nineteenth century, U.S. leaders lived in fear of the transfer of Cuba to England. To prevent such a transfer American statesmen seemed willing to go much further than they would have gone or did go in the protection of the rest of Latin America. Adams believed that Cuba had "an importance in the sum of our national interests, with which that of no other foreign territory can be compared, and little inferior to that which binds the different members of this Union together."[70] Accordingly, when the crisis arose in Europe in 1823, he instructed his new ambassador to Spain to inform the Spanish government that the transfer of Cuba to England could not be permitted, since it would infringe upon the rights of the Cubans and would injure vitally important interests of the United States. He further suggested that if such a transfer were to be attempted the Cuban people would be justified in declaring their independence and that the United States would be justified in aiding them in attaining it.[71] Said Adams: "The question both of our right and our power to prevent it (the acquisition of Cuba by England), if necessary, by force, already obtrudes itself upon our councils, and the administration is called upon, in performance of its duties to the nation, at least to use all the means within its competency to guard against and forfend it."[72] Adams referred to discussions held during Monroe's administration on the possibility of annexing the island by supporting friendly revolutionary groups.[73] In the end it was decided that forcing Spain to maintain the status quo in Cuba was the safer course, and this was the policy followed by the United States in the Panama Conference, when it decided to attempt to discourage Latin American attempts to free Cuba. But this was also the policy that was to come up for revision when internal pressures for Cuban independence outran Spain's ability to suppress them in 1898.

In retrospect, the most important deviation from the general policy of noninvolvement during the nineteenth century was the Treaty of 1846 with Colombia. It will be remembered that during the 1830's and 1840's Britain was intervening freely in Central America and in Colombia, which at that time included the Isthmus of Panama.[74] After taking the Falkland Islands in 1833, Britain took over Roatan in the Gulf of Honduras in 1838. San

[69] *Ibid.*
[70] Whitaker, *Independence of Latin America*, p. 400.
[71] *Ibid.*, pp. 406–7.
[72] *Ibid.*, p. 400.
[73] *Ibid.*, p. 401.
[74] See, Cavelier, *Politica Internacional*, pp. 195–210.

Juan del Norte in Nicaragua was occupied in 1841, and the frontier of Belize was expanded several times during the 1830's. When a British protectorate was extended over the Mosquito Coast and Las Bocas del Toro in the 1840's, New Granada, fearing for its sovereignty over the Isthmus, began looking around for a powerful ally.[75] The Colombians looked first to France, who agreed to undertake the construction of the canal but not to guarantee its neutrality or continued Colombian sovereignty over the canal. It was then that the Colombians turned to the United States. For its part, the United States was greatly disturbed by the growing superiority of the British in the Caribbean; and, in order to establish a controlling hand in any future isthmian communications route, the United States agreed to guarantee both the neutrality of any future communications and Colombian sovereignty over the Isthmus. It was the first time in Latin America that the United States violated the famous dictum of Washington to avoid foreign entanglements, and it was the last time it was to do so in the nineteenth century.[76]

With the signing of the Treaty of 1846, the Monroe Doctrine, which had lain in disuse and had even been reduced in scope by President Polk, once again came into play—but this time as a strictly Caribbean doctrine. It was alleged against Britain several times before the Civil War, but only for incursions that seemed to threaten the balance of control of the isthmian route—which, in turn, gained in importance for the United States in proportion to the growing American activity on the west coast of the United States. By 1850 constant Anglo–American bickering had brought their relations near the breaking point. It was then that a sort of stalemate was recognized in the Clayton–Bulwer Treaty of 1850. By that document the United States and Britain agreed to share in the construction of any future canal and not to "occupy, or fortify, or colonize . . . or exercise any dominion over Nicaragua, Costa Rica, the Mosquito Coast, or any part of Central America."[77]

[75] *Ibid.*, pp. 213–41.
[76] *Ibid.*, p. 217.
[77] See more complete discussion of the treaty below.

# III.

# Intervention As Strategy

UNTIL THE 1880's the United States was practically a negligible factor in international military relations. She possessed an outmoded strategy and an outmoded navy to match, and in the nineteenth century, military power meant naval power. The prevailing U.S. strategic doctrine in 1890 was conservative in the extreme. It consisted of two elements: commerce raiding, or the *guerre de course*, and a passive coastal defense.[1] Commerce raiding as understood in the nineteenth century was little more than maritime guerrilla warfare. It offered the advantage of requiring a minimum naval force and was, therefore, cheap. Coastal defense was primarily the job of stationary fortifications—to which warships were merely added reinforcement. Such reinforcement had the subsidiary political advantage of dispersing the small national fleet among the greatest possible number of constituencies. It was vaguely recognized that "military control of the Caribbean, as well as of the Atlantic and Pacific approaches to the United States, might be imperatively necessary to render the continental homeland of the American people invulnerable to external pressure and armed aggression";[2] but it was to require a major revolution in both naval strategy and technology to make that necessity a militarily feasible objective.

By the mid-1880's the technological half of that revolution was well under way. The sail and mast were rapidly giving way to coal and steam, the steel cruiser had made its advent upon the international naval scene,

[1] Harold and Margaret Sprout, *The Rise of American Naval Power, 1776–1918* (Princeton: Princeton University Press, 1946), Chap. XII.
[2] *Ibid.*, p. 24.

and the perfection of the explosive shell capable of being launched for great distance was just over the horizon. At the same time, innovations in artillery ballistics were rendering passive fortifications for populated areas potentially ineffective. In terms of naval composition, these developments produced an unprecedented differentiation of ship-types. Because it was impossible to combine heavy armor, speed, and gun power in a single ship, these elements were combined in different proportions for a multiplicity of specialized purposes. The battleship, the armored cruiser, the protected cruiser, and the small, fast gunboats that were constructed to carry the newly invented automotive torpedo were all children of the growing specialization in military equipment.

These technological changes, of themselves, had an important effect on strategic thinking. It was recognized—if only begrudgingly admitted—that the potential radius of large-scale naval operations had been severely narrowed by the new developments. Dependence upon steam instead of wind meant that operations could never be attempted very far from coaling stations. And the increased use and complexity of machinery multiplied the necessary logistical support for naval operations many times over. The movements of the new fleets were in fact "extremely hampered, and their scope restricted, by the very elements to which they owe much of their power."[3] Within this completely altered technological context previous concepts of naval strategy were about as effective as classical physics in explaining the movements of elementary particles. In the 1890's, amidst the technological revolution going on in naval armaments, several new theorists stepped in to fill the intellectual vacuum of predominant naval strategy, but none stepped so decisively as Captain Alfred Thayer Mahan. With the publication of *The Influence of Sea Power Upon History, 1660-1783*, Mahan began the series of books and articles through which he was to revolutionize strategic thought. Mahan held that national power and security depended upon the accumulation of wealth in larger proportions than that provided by the development of national resources alone. Consequently an active foreign commerce was necessary to great national power. That commerce, reasoned Mahan, required a large merchant marine; and in light of the competition evident among international powers that merchant marine would have to be protected by safe havens at each end of the routes of commerce and by a strong navy in between trade outlets. As Mahan said, in relation to the British experience: "The needs of commerce, however, were not all provided for when safety had been

[3] Alfred Thayer Mahan, "Blockade in Relation to Naval Strategy," *Proceedings of the United States Naval Institute* 21 (November 1895): 863. Quoted in Sprout, *Toward a New Order of Sea Power: American Naval Policy and the World Scene, 1918–1922* (Princeton: Princeton University Press, 1946), p. 6.

secured at the far end of the road. The voyages were long and dangerous, the seas often beset with enemies. . . . Thus arose the demand for stations along the road . . . not primarily for trade, but for defence and war."[4] Mahan bitterly criticized American policy for its apparent ambivalence toward the acquisition of overseas bases. American ships, said the strategist, "are like land birds, unable to fly far from their shores."[5]

But Mahan was no simple naval enthusiast, arguing for an expanded navy and merchant marine; he was a geopolitical theorist of the highest caliber and he followed the implications of his arguments to their logical extremes. Control of commercial routes, he continued, is not simply a matter of protecting ships en route. Control must be maintained of the high seas in the area of commerce; the commercial route itself is no more than an "interior line of communications." Dominion of the high seas meant that the nation must have a naval force capable of sweeping the enemy from the area, and such a force cannot be accumulated by dividing the fleet into separate portions, as American practice tended to do. Mahan borrowed the principle of "concentration of force" from the principles of land warfare. It was a principle to be echoed later by President Theodore Roosevelt, when he urged his successor "never under any circumstances to divide the American fleet between the Pacific and Atlantic Oceans."[6]

On the basis of this doctrine, Mahan added his voice to those of the advocates of the proposed trans-isthmian canal. The migration of the American population westward and the rapid development of natural resources on the west coast had already made the trans-isthmian railway an important communications link for the country. Mahan further insisted that the United States must increase its trade with the Far East and contended that the construction of the canal was a vital link in the development of that trade.[7] But it followed that the construction of the canal would dramatically alter the relationship between the United States and the Caribbean. The United States would have to develop a powerful naval force in order to insure its commercial intercourse from encroachment by outside powers. On this latter point Mahan has been much criticized for not realizing that the Caribbean, unlike the Mediterranean, was not bordered by any hostile powers,[8] but this criticism underestimates the po-

---

[4] Alfred Thayer Mahan, *The Influence of Sea Power Upon History, 1660–1783* (Boston: Little, Brown and Company, 1928), pp. 27–28.

[5] Margaret Tuttle Sprout, "Mahan: Evangelist of Sea Power," in Edward Mead Earle (ed.), *Makers of Modern Strategy* (Princeton: Princeton University Press, 1941).

[6] *Ibid.*, p. 431.

[7] Richard D. Challenger, "unpublished notes and manuscript on the meetings and war plans of the General Board of the Navy and the Joint Board from 1900 to 1918," I: 10. Hereafter noted as "Challenger." Professor Challenger was kind enough to allow me to use this valuable material which he has gleaned from the National Archives.

[8] See Sprout, "Mahan," p. 426; and Dexter Perkins, *A History of the Monroe Doctrine* (Boston: Little, Brown & Company, 1955).

tentialities of British seapower in the Caribbean at the turn of the century. The British held bases in Bermuda, throughout the West Indies, and in the Falkland Islands. The British navy was fully capable of blocking American commerce through the Caribbean; and extensive American commercial competition in the Far East could be expected to give them the political motivation to do so. In any case, all American military planning of the period was based on the idea of Britain as a possible aggressor in the Western Hemisphere. Just how tenacious this concept was to prove is indicated by the fact that in 1919 the naval advisory group that accompanied Wilson to Paris was still attempting to convince the President that with Germany prostrate, Britain was the nation to be feared.[9]

Secondarily, Mahan based his support of the projected canal upon the principle of concentration of force. An isthmian canal route would cut U.S. fleet requirements for guarding the coasts of continental North America almost in half. As the United States became more deeply involved in Asia, this consideration was to grow ever more important.

Once again Mahan carried the implications of his doctrine to their logical conclusion. He recognized that the construction of the canal would greatly enhance the military value of the Caribbean area. He warned that the great states of Europe would attempt to block the commercial expansion of the United States by attempting to establish control of the trade routes through the Caribbean. To counter such moves the United States had no other alternative than to build its own naval stations in the Caribbean, to secure the approaches to the canal in the Pacific, and to create a powerful naval establishment.

That Mahan's ideas should have become immediately popular with American navalists is no surprise. Their complete acceptance of the Mahan thesis is best indicated by a comment, attributed to a later secretary of the navy, that, "to the average American Naval officer, the United States Navy was the only True Church, Neptune was God, and Mahan was His Prophet."[10] It is a tribute to the influence of Mahan that at the first official meeting of the General Board of the Navy—which, as we shall see, was to play an all important role in the formulation of U.S.-Latin American policy—the members of the Board agreed that their first project should be a list of desired naval stations in the Caribbean and the Pacific. In fact, the writing of the bases proposal that was presented to Secretary Hay in July 1900 was largely the work of Captain Henry C. Taylor, the man who had persuaded Mahan to give the series of lectures at the Naval War College that culminated in the publication of his first book in 1890.[11]

---

[9] Challenger, I: 14.
[10] *Ibid.*, p. I–10.
[11] *Ibid.*, p. I–6.

The rapidity with which Mahan's influence became apparent among civilian policymakers was likewise incredible. The annual report of the secretary of the navy in 1889 relied so heavily upon Mahan's thinking that some writers have concluded that parts of the report may have been written by Mahan himself.[12] Secretary Tracy informed the House of Representatives that the United States needed a fleet capable of diverting a hostile fleet from our coasts "by threatening his own, for a war, though defensive in principle, may be conducted most effectively by being offensive in its operations." The Secretary then proceeded to request that the Congress appropriate money for beginning the construction of twenty high-speed battleships and sixty light-armor cruisers.[13] This sudden turnabout in civilian naval thinking came about through the chance conjunction of Mahan's arrival on the policymaking scene with a historical accident. In the winter of 1888–89 the interest of the American navy in a coaling station in the Samoan Islands brought about war rumors of a clash with German and British forces.[14] A few days later three American ships were destroyed or disabled by a hurricane in the harbor of Apia—which event left the United States without a Pacific fleet.[15] The sudden attention that was given to the inferiority of the American navy, no doubt, had a great deal to do with the new found navalism of the Congress.

The Naval Appropriations Act of 1890 constituted a revolutionary departure in the country's system of naval defense. It began the creation of an offensive fighting fleet capable of commanding the seas within a 5,000 nautical-mile radius of established coaling bases.[16] The 5,000 mile limitation is important, for it meant that serious control even of the Caribbean could be accomplished only by securing naval bases further south than the continental United States. Second, the endurance and speed of these ships meant that the problem of shifting the fleet from the Atlantic to the Pacific by way of Cape Horn was complicated by greater coaling requirements. Consequently the technical aspects of the new fleet increased the desirability of the trans-isthmian canal.

It is also notable that the navy was cognizant of this problem and had so informed the Congress. In January 1889 six naval officers, appointed to study the country's naval requirements after the Samoan disaster, issued their report. In general, Mahan's formula for battleships was followed closely, but the officers suggested that ships with a cruising radius of 13,000 knots (15,000 miles) were more appropriate to the navy's needs.[17] Unfor-

[12] Sprout, *American Naval Power*, p. 207.
[13] *Ibid.*
[14] *Ibid.*, p. 206.
[15] *Ibid.*
[16] U.S., *Congressional Record*, 51st Cong., 1st sess., 28, p. 3193.
[17] U.S. Congress, Senate, *Senate Executive Document No. 43*, 51st Cong. 1st sess., p. 11.

tunately the navalist zeal of the young officers was all too apparent in their proposals, and a general public outcry against "naval fanaticism" caused the Senate to cool on the whole idea of increased naval strength.[18] However, pushed by Representative Charles A. Boutelle of Maine, the House Naval Affairs Committee remained "selectively" receptive and introduced that part of the naval proposals which attempted to establish battleship-fleet control of the U.S. coastline and the Caribbean into the Act of 1890. The so-called "battleship clause" provided an appropriation for "three sea-going, coastline battleships designed to carry the heaviest armor and most powerful ordnance upon a displacement of about five thousand knots."[19] The result was that the country got the worst of all possible worlds. The fleet that the Congress began to build in 1890 would be able to operate in the Caribbean only with the support of a large network of overseas naval bases. This was to become painfully apparent in 1898, when the United States went to war with Spain. It is a kind of ironic justice that one of the ships constructed under the appropriation of 1890 was the *Oregon*, whose voyage around Cape Horn to join the Atlantic fleet during the war with Spain was to provide overwhelming public support for the construction of the Panama Canal.

But military strategy is rarely a simple question of existing technology. It is definitively shaped by the nature of the challenges emanating from other units of the international system and by the perceived capability for dealing with those challenges militarily. That is to say, military strategy is but one element in the "package deal" called foreign policy, and its importance in that "package" can vary widely. We have already seen how the lack of military capability played an important role in the aloofness of the United States from the early alliances of the new Latin American republics. It will now be shown how alterations in the power and identity of the perceived enemy in the Caribbean later increased U.S. willingness to involve itself in the internal problems of the Caribbean republics.

Until the turn of the century American statesmen and militarists could give an unequivocal answer to the question of who was to be feared in the Caribbean—it was Great Britain. The Clayton–Bulwer Treaty, ratified in 1850, was little more than a tribute to the commanding power of the British Caribbean squadron. Under the terms of this agreement control of any future isthmian railway or canal would be under the joint tutelage of Great Britain and the United States, the neutrality of any such trans-isthmian communications was guaranteed, and equal transit tolls for the

---

[18] *New York Herald*, January 31, 1890, quoted in Sprout, *American Naval Power*, p. 211. Sprout further concludes, from a reading of the subsequent hearings on the naval bill, that Secretary Tracy and the senators began to treat the commission's proposals like the political "plague."

[19] *Ibid.*

citizens and subjects of both parties were assured. It was further agreed that neither power would fortify the canal or its vicinity, nor colonize Central American territory, nor establish dominion over any Central American country. The treaty continued: "[Nor] will the United States or Great Britain take advantage of any intimacy, or use any alliance, connection, or influence that either may possess, with any State or Government through whose territory the said Canal may pass, for the purpose of acquiring or holding,—directly or indirectly, for the citizens or subjects of the one, any rights or advantages in regard to commerce or navigation through the said Canal, which shall not be offered on the same terms to the citizens or subjects of the other."[20] In spite of the noncolonization commitment, Great Britain refused to abandon her protectorate over the Mosquito Indians and declared the Bay Islands to be a British colony, in 1852. To a large extent then, the treaty, unsupported by American naval power equivalent to that of the British, constituted a hopeless effort to substitute diplomacy for guns. But the pact does mark something of an equilibrium point at which the powers were successfully nullifying each other with respect to hegemony in the Caribbean. It is telling that one of the most authoritative historians of Colombian foreign policy considers the Clayton–Bulwer Treaty a triumph of Granadine diplomacy, in that "it established a praiseworthy principle which would have the consequence of impeding the exclusive preponderance of a single power in Panama."[21]

By the turn of the century, however, this situation was changing rapidly. The reconstruction of the American navy, which was accelerated by the influence of Mahan and his followers in the 1890's, placed increasing strains upon British naval requirements in the Caribbean. Meanwhile the rise of German naval power in Europe and Japanese expansion in the Far East threatened the dominant British position in the eastern Atlantic and the western Pacific. The British Admiralty was faced with a choice of enemies and opted to maintain its positions in Europe and the Far East at the expense of its Caribbean dominion. "Only by progressively strengthening its overseas squadrons could the British Admiralty have preserved even a semblance of its former primacy in American and Far Eastern waters. And whatever the desires and inclinations of British naval authorities, developments nearer home soon rendered such a course practically impossible."[22] Besides the growing Anglo–German naval rivalry, Britain's disputes with France over conflicting interests in African colonization and

---

[20] Samuel Flagg Bemis, *The Latin American Policy of the United States: An Historical Interpretation*, (New York: Harcourt, Brace and Company, 1943), p. 106.

[21] German Cavelier, *La Politica Internacional de Colombia* (Bogota: Editorial Iqueima, 1959), p. 226. (Translation my own.)

[22] Sprout, *Toward a New Order of Sea Power*, p. 20.

the even more absorbing South African War pushed Great Britain toward greater dependence upon American cooperation in the Caribbean.

The diminishing danger of British encroachment in the New World was reflected in the thinking of American military strategists. Mahan, writing to Roosevelt in 1906, gave a rosy picture of the future of Anglo–American relations: "British interests are not American interests, no. But taking the constitution of the British Empire and the trade interests of the British islands, the United States has certainty of a very high order that the British Empire will stand substantially on the same line of world policy as ourselves; that its strength will be our strength; and the weakening of it injury to us."[23] By 1906 the documents of the General Board were filled with references to "parallel" British and American interests in the Western Hemisphere and the value of Britain as "the strongest hook in the jaws of Germany."[24] The army shared the navy's enthusiasm for America's new ally. In 1904, speaking for the Army War College, Tasker Bliss informed the Joint Board that as far as the college's research staff was concerned war with Britain was the "least probable of all possible conflicts."[25]

But this new-found friendship was not quite a sentimental expression of the solidarity of the English-speaking peoples. Apart from the somewhat forced diminution of British military power in the Caribbean, military strategists seem to have come to a belated recognition of the role of Canada as the hostage of the United States against British aggression in the Caribbean.[26] As Bliss put it, somewhat euphemistically, it was always possible for the United States "to reimburse ourselves by more desirable property near home to replace that which we should have lost further away."[27] Nor did military planners ever assume British aid in possible conflicts with other European powers. Naval war plans for a possible conflict with Germany always included the assumption of British neutrality.[28]

American diplomacy was not loath to make good upon the decline of British power in the Caribbean and the increased desire for American cooperation on the other side of the Atlantic. In 1899 Secretary of State John Hay began negotiations with the British for a revision of the Clayton–Bulwer Treaty of 1850, by which both governments had renounced unilateral control of any future isthmian canal. That treaty had rested upon

[23] Challenger, I: 24–25.
[24] *Ibid.*, I: 25.
[25] *Ibid.*, I: 26.
[26] This point has been almost universally overlooked by historians of Anglo–American relations in the Caribbean. Samuel Bemis, in his *Latin American Policy of the United States*, seems to be the first such historian to realize the importance of Canada as a hostage. See Bemis, pp. 97, 99, 106, 108, 111, 142, 159, 386.
[27] Challenger, I: 26.
[28] *Ibid.*, I: 27.

conditions of military equilibrium that did not exist by the turn of the century. The final results of the Hay–Pauncefote negotiations was a complete victory for the American secretary. The Hay–Pauncefote Treaty, promulgated in November 1901, guaranteed free passage to vessels of all nations in time of peace or war, but left open the possibility of American fortification of the proposed canal.[29] The treaty then was a turning point in Anglo–American relations, for it constituted an implicit recognition by the British of American hegemony in the Caribbean.

The internal upheavals that wracked the United States in the mid-nineteenth century served to delay the extension of American hegemony in the Caribbean, but not to stop it. American public opinion soon followed the conclusions of the American strategists with respect to the decline of the threat of British seapower. Several events in the 1890's and early years of the twentieth century served to direct the attention of both the American public and the strategists away from the British and toward the Germans. Not the least important of these incidents was the Venezuelan border crisis of 1895–96. The immediate dispute in this case was over the demarcation of the boundry between Venezuela and British Guiana. The full details of the case can be found elsewhere,[30] suffice it to say that the United States intervened quite strongly in favor of submitting the dispute to third-party arbitration.[31] After initial rejection of the American demands the British agreed to submit the dispute to arbitration, and this capitulation of the British, coupled with a strong anti-American reaction in the German press,[32] seems to have pacified American public opinion with respect to the danger of British encroachments in the Caribbean.[33] On the other hand, "apprehension regarding Germany increased, and within a few years the German government's intentions regarding America became almost the sole object of American distrust."[34] Within a short time the American press and political leaders achieved admirable agreement upon suspicion of Germany. Particularly as the projected isthmian canal moved ever closer to reality, "it was supposed that Germany had designs upon half a

[29] Dana Munro, *Intervention and Dollar Diplomacy in the Caribbean, 1900–1921* (Princeton: Princeton University Press, 1951), pp. 37–38.

[30] See accounts in Perkins, *Monroe Doctrine*, pp. 171–86, and in J. Fred Rippy, *The Caribbean Danger Zone* (New York: Putnam's Sons, 1940), pp. 26–29.

[31] A note sent by Secretary of State Richard Olney to Lord Salisbury, demanding submission of the dispute to third party arbitration, was to become one of the most quoted documents in the history of the Monroe Doctrine. (*Foreign Relations, 1895*, pp. 545–62.) Olney's assertion that "the United States is practically sovereign on this continent, and its fiat is law upon the subjects to which it confines its interposition" remained a sore spot in U.S.–Latin American relations for years.

[32] See below.

[33] Rippy, *Danger Zone*, p. 29.

[34] *Ibid.*

dozen naval strongholds from which the projected interoceanic canal might be dominated. Among these were Curaçao, Dutch Guiana, the Danish West Indies, Margarita, and harbors off the coast of lower California."[35]

Some Latin American historians have argued that to explain American actions in the Caribbean by reference to German expansionism is the ploy of the imperialists and Wall Street.[36] Nothing in the now open German archives, it is argued, will support the contention that Germany was attempting to secure bases in the Caribbean area. But this critique misses the essential point that what is important is the threat that was perceived, whether actually existent or not. And in the years that closed the last century and began the present one, Americans were given a plethora of evidence that German intentions in the Caribbean were not entirely of a peaceful nature. The German press was violently anti-American and pro-expansionist,[37] statements of German political leaders were filled with anti-American bias and references to world empire,[38] and Germany sided heavily with Spain during the Spanish–American War.[39] If German aggression in the New World would have become feasible with the acquirement of naval bases in the Caribbean, then American diplomats and military men had every reason to attempt to forestall German lodgement.

But Americans did not have to read the German press to realize that American and German interests were in conflict in Latin America. German material interests in the Latin American countries increased dramatically after the turn of the century. In 1896 there were only 400,000 people of German descent in Latin America; by 1913 there were between 600,000 and 700,000.[40] In those same sixteen years German investment in Latin America increased from $500 million to $2 billion, and her trade with Latin America grew from $146 million to $470 million.[41] At the same time, members of the "big navy" movement in Germany began to take an interest in Caribbean bases. In 1896 Ernst von Halle called attention to the desirability of the Danish West Indies, and during the Spanish–American War, Admiral von Tirpitz was suggesting to Chancellor von Bulow that the time was ripe for acquiring a Caribbean base.[42] In the American mind the increasing German economic activity in Latin America and the drive

[35] *Ibid.*, p. 30.
[36] Dexter Perkins, *The United States and Latin America* (Baton Rouge: Louisiana State University Press, 1960), pp. 12–19.
[37] Rippy, *Latin America in World Politics* (New York: Alfred Knopf, 1923), pp. 143–44, 147.
[38] *Ibid.*
[39] *Ibid.*
[40] *Ibid.*, pp. 142–43.
[41] *Ibid.*
[42] Perkins, *Monroe Doctrine*, p. 209.

of the German Naval Office for bases became undeniably linked in the fall of 1899. The event that convinced Americans of the subversive intent of German activity in the Caribbean was known as the Christmas Affair.

In the latter months of 1898 a German trading company was formed for the ostensible purpose of exploiting the trade potential of the island of St. John in the Virgin Islands. In reality, the purpose of the organization was to effect the eventual transfer of the territory to Germany. It is, in fact, possible that the main stimulus for the plan came from the German Naval Office.[43] Through the treason of one of the conspirators, an intriguing figure by the name of Captain Christmas, the plot became known in America. The result was a remarkable outburst of war fever at high governmental levels. By April 1900 Elihu Root was ominously warning of war.[44] On May 11 Senator Lodge pointed out to his colleagues in the Senate that possession of the Danish islands would give control of the projected canal. "Such an act by any European power," he said, "would mean war."[45]

Fear of a confrontation with Germany over the question of the Virgin Islands prompted intensive activity in the State Department, directed toward the "preclusive"[46] acquirement of the Danish property. The object of the treaties of 1902 and 1916, which ultimately resulted in the purchase of the islands for $25 million, was not to acquire bases for ourselves but to prevent Germany from acquiring stations in the Caribbean area. In fact, the State Department received little support from the military strategists on the more positive grounds that the United States needed a base in these islands. In September 1898 Admiral Royal B. Bradford wrote to Hay concerning the projected purchase: "The proposition for purchase is made in order to prevent them from falling into the hands of Germany. . . . In accordance with the principles of the Monroe Doctrine this country would be forced to object to their acquisition by Germany. . . . It appears to be a good business proposition to buy rather than risk war on their account."[47] This thought was reiterated by Admiral George Dewey in December 1915, while the second treaty for the purchase of the islands was under consideration. (The first treaty was not ratified by the Danish parliament.) Dewey summed up the conclusions of the General Board of the Navy by saying that while the United States had no need for bases in the Danish islands, their purchase might be desirable to preclude Germany's acquiring them.[48]

---

[43] Ibid.

[44] Ibid.

[45] Ibid., p. 210.

[46] William L. Langer, "Farewell to Empire," Foreign Affairs, 41 (October 1962): 115–30. Professor Langer suggests a theory of "preclusive imperialism" as the best explanation of European imperialism in Asia and Africa. The similarity of this idea to my treatment of American intervention in Latin America should be apparent.

[47] Rippy, Danger Zone, p. 128.

[48] Ibid., p. 129.

The Christmas Affair has been described at length because it offers a clear illustration of the development of what might be called a preclusive mentality that had previously been obvious only in relation to the protection of trans-isthmian communications. By the turn of the century it had become apparent to military and diplomatic officials alike that the security of the canal implied American dominion in the Caribbean. In the case of Britain little could be done. British lodgment in the Caribbean was a fact, and dislodgment could only be accomplished at the cost of war. So long as British military resources were pinned down in Europe and the western Pacific and Canada could be held as hostage against British designs elsewhere, dislodging Britain from the Caribbean was scarcely worth contemplating. Germany, however, presented quite a different story. German lodgment in the Caribbean would have constituted a decided threat to American security interests; but, in opposition to the British case, such lodgment could be aborted by the United States.

Fear of Germany continued to obsess American military planners right up to World War I. In 1906 the General Board of the Navy rendered an official opinion as to Germany's intentions in the Caribbean: "Germany wants to expand her colonial possessions. Especially it is thought that she is desirous of obtaining a foothold in the Western Hemisphere, and many things indicate that she has her eyes on localities in the West Indies, on the shores of the Caribbean, and in parts of South America. It is believed in many quarters that she is planning to test the Monroe Doctrine by annexation or establishment of a protectorate over a portion of South America, even going to the extent of war with the United States when her fleet is ready."[49]

The assumption that a German attack upon the Western Hemisphere would proceed by way of the Caribbean was explicit in prewar American military planning. To an ever-increasing extent the possibility of a direct German attack upon the continental United States was abandoned and replaced with the assumption of a two-stage operation whereby the Germans would strike first in the Caribbean, in order to gain naval bases, and only later at the continent. Granting primary-target status to the Caribbean was nothing more than a recognition of the fact that technological and logistical problems made a continental attack impossible, except under the most unusual of circumstances. As one naval memorandum pointed out in 1910, "Any European power, other than England, must conduct operations against the continental portions of the United States by oversea expeditions pure and simple—expeditions so monumental that their transport and maintenance will be exceedingly difficult under the most

---

[49] Challenger, I: 27.

favorable circumstances."[50] After 1905 the assumption of a primary German attack in the Caribbean was the basis of defense planning at the Naval War College.[51] "The role of the American fleet was to take the strategic defensive against these German moves—that is to say, to prepare itself to wage in the Caribbean the decisive encounter which would defeat the Kaiser's navy."[52]

Concern with Caribbean security was most forcibly expressed in the so-called "color" plans, which formed the basic parameters for all American military planning from 1900 to 1914. Only Germany and Japan were honored by the General Board to the extent of having specific defenses designed to counter their attack; but between the two, Germany was clearly favored as the most probable aggressor. The Orange Plan (against Japanese attack), in fact, assumed that the Pacific attack would find the American fleet concentrated in the Atlantic—presumably, guarding against European aggression.[53] The Black Plan, designed to counter German aggression, stated clearly that "Black (Germany) will insist upon the occupation of Western Hemisphere territory under the Black flag, and Blue (United States) will then have to defend her policy by force, or acquiesce in the occupation."[54] The exact nature of the planned defense against German attack changed at different times from 1900 to 1914, but the basic assumption that Germany would first have to establish naval stations in the area remained unchanged.

The assumption of the primacy of the European threat, coupled with the technological limitations upon a European attack, led quite naturally to the conclusion that the most probable war would occur in the Caribbean. In 1904 the leading officers of the General Board and the army staff, meeting for the first time as the Joint Board, agreed that the most probable source of war would be a European threat to the "policy enunciated by President James Monroe."[55] Furthermore, all war planning "assumed that the United States could not possibly be defeated unless an enemy first secured a base for operations in the Western Hemisphere and that the only possible area in which such a base could be located was in the Caribbean."[56] The inevitable conclusion was that European lodgment—especially, German lodgment—would constitute an intolerable alteration of the strategic position of the United States. In the first place, European lodgment would constitute a danger to the continental security of the United States; and second, such lodgment would make it impossible for the navy

[50] *Ibid.*, I: 32.
[51] *Ibid.*, I: 28.
[52] *Ibid.*
[53] *Ibid.*, I: 30–2.
[54] *Ibid.*, I: 28.
[55] *Ibid.*, I: 35.
[56] *Ibid.*

to assure the neutrality of the projected Panama Canal. From the beginning of the American republic, Cuba had been recognized as a particularly dangerous area with respect to the possibility of foreign lodgment; and the growing importance of trans-isthmian communications only served to enhance its strategic importance to the United States. It would seem quite natural therefore that the first American intervention clearly outside of the existing norms of the international law of the times should occur there.

## The Spanish–American War

The Spanish–American War is the name usually given to the first "illegal" armed intervention of the United States in Latin American affairs. Earlier troop landings for the protection of life and property, and even for debt-collection, had been opposed on the grounds of a lack of necessity in the particular case. But rarely, if ever, had even Latin Americans argued against such incursions as violations of international law. American purposes for intervening and much of the on-going dialogue on the real motivation for the American intervention must be set aside as essentially sterile attempts to reduce a multi-causal political phenomenon to a uni-causal event. It is sufficient for our purposes to point out that continued control of Cuba by a European power, and especially by a weakened power, would not only have endangered the continental United States but also would have made secure American control of isthmian communications impossible. Control of Cuba (and Puerto Rico) meant control of the naval communications between the Atlantic and the Caribbean and, therefore, between the Atlantic and the Pacific. "If those Spanish islands could be annexed, or even made independent under the protection of the United States," says Samuel Bemis, "that nation would be in a position hence-forth to gainsay a European attempt to dominate a region of the seas so vital to the mastery of the future Isthmian canal; that is, to the defense of the Continental Republic which was the supreme achievement and the very basis of American nationality."[57] Spain, to be sure, was not considered to be a major military threat to the United States. But the real danger to U.S. security lay in Spain's weakness. This much had been apparent even to John Quincy Adams, and it was equally as evident to Cleveland and McKinley. Furthermore, this fear that Spain's weakness might lead to the domination of Cuba by a more imposing European power was seem-ingly justified early in 1898, when the Queen Regent of Spain issued en-treaties of aid to the other monarchal powers of Europe—including Germany.[58]

---

[57] Bemis, *Latin American Policy*, p. 123. Bemis, in fact, argues that the isthmian ques-tion lay behind the U.S. entry into the war.

[58] *Ibid.*, p. 134.

The fear of foreign intrusion into an island of such close proximity to the continental United States would have been sufficient motivation of itself, once the United States was militarily capable of confronting the Europeans, but added to the strategic motivation was the tremendous popularity of the Cuban independence movement in the United States. The "yellow press" made a lavish play upon the miseries of the Spanish concentration camps, and the victorious Republican campaign platform of 1896 had cited Cuban independence as a prime tenet. The policy undertaken by Cleveland to maintain U.S. neutrality laws and to attempt to collect damages for the destroyed property of U.S. citizens was particularly galling in the light of the traditional procrastination of the Spanish government. Then on the night of February 15, 1898, the American battleship *Maine* was blown up in Havana harbor with a loss of 260 members of her crew. The cause of the *Maine* tragedy was of very little import, since American public opinion, already vociferously anti-Spanish, simply assumed that the Spaniards were responsible. Under these circumstances what is surprising is not that McKinley decided to intervene but that he waited as long as he did.

Accordingly McKinley's war message to the Congress was a peculiar mixture of national security interests and high humanitarian ideals.[59] It, in fact, established a major precedent for one of the most unfortunate characteristics of American interventionist policy—the tendency to seek justification and public support in broad idealistic terminology.[60] The President's resort to "humanitarian intervention" was even more unfortunate in light of the fact that it was entirely unnecessary in order to square the nation's coming action with the international legal norms of the period. In 1898 the right of intervention to abate a general nuisance or grievance was generally recognized by international law and international custom. Humanitarian norms with respect to intervention in civil strife were not nearly as well developed.

Nevertheless, the core of the President's message was an appeal to the national security interests. Much of his justification for armed intervention rested upon the probability that both sides would be weakened by the conflict. McKinley said:

> The war in Cuba is of such a nature that short of subjugation or extermination a final military victory for either side seems impracticable. The alternative lies in the physical exhaustion of the one or other party, or perhaps of both. . . . The prospect of such a protraction and conclusion of the present

[59] *Foreign Relations, 1898*, pp. 750–60.

[60] Perkins, *The United States and Latin America*, "American statesmen have believed, and acted upon the belief, that the best way to rally public opinion behind their purposes is to assert a moral principle" (p. 19).

strife is a contingency hardly to be contemplated with equanimity by the civilized world, and least of all by the United States, affected and injured as we are, deeply and intimately.[61]

The President also mentioned the "cause of humanity" and the protection of the life and property of citizens of the United States, but he gave primary importance to the fact that the existing conditions in Cuba constituted "a constant menace to our peace" and, inasmuch as these conditions required the United States to remain on a "semiwar footing," they entailed an "enormous expense" upon the government.[62]

The predominance of security interests in America's involvement in the war was even more apparent in the negotiations for the Treaty of Paris and the Treaty of Reciprocity which, respectively, ended the war and provided for the withdrawal of American troops from the Cuban island. On the eve of the meeting of the peace commissioners in Paris the Navy Department issued a set of confidential orders to Admirals Sampson and Schley, who were then commanding the American naval forces in the Caribbean. The admirals were given priority orders to occupy all naval stations and naval property that were left behind by the Spaniards. Immediate action was said to be essential.[63] The desire for naval bases was also apparent in the Peace of Paris, signed in December 1898. By virtue of that document Spain ceded the Philippine Islands, Guam, and Puerto Rico to the United States in turn for a payment of $20 million.[64] Cuba was placed under a trusteeship, in spite of Spain's expressed desire that the United States should annex the island.[65] "The peace settlement clearly revealed that the United States Government's interests were broader than mere liberation for Cuba. Equally important was the desire for strategic bases."[66]

But the two documents that most clearly evidence the purposes of the United States in the Spanish–American War are the Platt Amendment and the Reciprocity Treaty of 1903. The Platt Amendment to the Cuban Constitution of 1902—the adoption of which was prerequisite to the withdrawal of the American protectorate—reserved to the United States the right to intervene in Cuba for the "protection of life, property, and individual liberty." This much was generally conceded by the international law of the era. But the Platt Amendment went further; it assured the United States the right to intervene for purposes of its own defense—

---

[61] *Foreign Relations, 1898*, p. 754.
[62] *Foreign Relations, 1898*, pp. 757–58.
[63] Challenger, III: 300.
[64] Edwin Lieuwen, *U.S. Policy in Latin America: A Short History* (New York: Frederick A. Praeger, 1965), p. 34.
[65] Bemis, *Latin American Policy*, p. 136–38.
[66] Lieuwen, *U.S. Policy, in Latin America*, p. 34

including the defense of naval bases on the island. These naval bases were, in turn, assured by Article VII of the Platt Amendment:

> To enable the United States to maintain the independence of Cuba, and to protect the people thereof, as well as for its own defense, the Government of Cuba will sell or lease to the United States lands necessary for coaling or naval stations, at certain specified points, to be agreed upon with the President of the United States.

The amendment also gave recognition to the possible use of the external debt of other European powers to acquire a foothold on the island. The traditional international law did, after all, recognize the right of military intervention for the collection of pecuniary claims. Hence, by the terms of Article I the Cuban government was forbidden to enter into any compact with any foreign powers which would impair her independence or permit lodgment for military or naval purposes. This same concern with possible lodgment of foreign powers was carried into Article II, by which Cuba was barred from accumulating a foreign debt beyond her ability to finance. In other words, Cuba was tied by law to a balanced budget.

Probably the best historical interpretation of the purposes of the Platt Amendment is that given by the author of the document, Secretary of War Elihu Root. Root insisted upon the traditional policy of the United States, as laid down in the no-transfer principle, of not allowing any other foreign power to acquire the island.[67] Then he went on to stress the security considerations that were the underpinnings of that policy: "It would be a most lame and impotent conclusion, if after all the expenditure of blood and treasure by the people of the United States for the freedom of Cuba, and by the people of Cuba for the same object, we should, through the constitution of the new government, by inadvertence or otherwise, be placed in a worse position in regard to our own vital interests than we were while Spain was in possession."[68]

The Cuban Reciprocity Treaty, which followed close upon the heels of the Platt Amendment, supports the case made here for the predominance of security interests, inasmuch as it belies the case of those who argue that the Platt Amendment was a disguised attempt to subjugate the Cubans to the interests of American investors.[69] The treaty, signed on December 11, 1902, gave a 20 percent advantage to Cuban imports over similar imports from other countries; a similar advantage was given to U.S. imports in Cuba. But greater reductions in tariffs were given on a list of special

[67] Bemis, *Latin American Policy*, p. 139.
[68] *Ibid.*
[69] *Foreign Relations, 1903*, pp. 375–81. See also, U.S. Tariff Commission, *Effects of the Cuban Reciprocity Treaty* (Washington: GPO, 1929).

items, and these reductions were decidedly in Cuba's favor. On an *ad valorem* basis, U.S. reductions averaged nearly twice as much as those made by Cuba.[70] Nor is there any indication that the restoration of a colonial status for Cuba or aid to American investors played any role in the formulation of the treaty.[71] In fact, in 1903 only 20 percent of the Cuban sugar crop was American-owned, and the beet growers in the United States actually lost by the treaty.[72] Some important American products with correspondingly powerful congressional lobbies, such as tobacco, received no tariff reduction in Cuba.[73]

In general, the prosperity of the island in its first years of independence is directly attributable to the Reciprocity Treaty. Tobacco and sugar were the island's principal exports, and the stable market provided by the treaty could not help but to be a boon to the Cuban economy. That the long-range result of the new commercial relationship between Cuba and the United States was a monocultural economy on the island and the extensive penetration of American capital into the island's economy does not invalidate the integrity of the original intent of this "dollar diplomacy." In the absence of a structure for direct capital transfers, American diplomats, seeking capital to stabilize the Cuban economy, had no other recourse than to American private investors. "Conceivably, political and social conditions in the island would be healthier today if the reciprocity treaty had not been adopted, but it is difficult to say that the statesmen who were dealing with the situation in 1902 could or should have chosen to risk an immediate economic and political collapse in the hope that a more balanced economy would develop."[74]

As we shall soon see, the Spanish–American War and the assumption of a semiprotectorate over Cuba established methods which were to be repeated elsewhere in Latin America during the early twentieth century. Treaty arrangements for U.S. intervention were subsequently established in Panama, Nicaragua, and Haiti. But the effects of the war upon American naval strategy were even more far-reaching and, in the end, equally as important as its effects upon American diplomacy. For the strategists the main lessons of the war lay in the technological realm. In the first place, the experiences of the war dramatically underlined the limitations that the modern steam technology placed upon the effective operating radius of naval vessels. The extreme dependency of the furnaces and machinery of the modern vessels upon ready access to fuel, drydocks, machine shops,

---

[70] U.S. Tariff Commission, *Cuban Reciprocity Treaty*.
[71] Munro, *Intervention and Dollar Diplomacy*, pp. 32–33.
[72] *Ibid.*
[73] Bemis, *Latin American Policy*, p. 139.
[74] Munro, *Intervention and Dollar Diplomacy*, p. 33.

and ammunition supplies forcefully carried the implication of the need for developing an overseas network of naval bases. Some feeling for how vivid this lesson must have been in the minds of the naval men can be gained by considering the implications of even the war's most successful campaign—that of Commodore Dewey in the Manila Bay. The Asiatic squadron, consisting of four cruisers and two gunboats, sailed from Hong Kong to the harbor in the Philippines, where they destroyed the anchored Spanish force. Had Dewey lost at Manila and been cut off from the British bases by a pursuing Spanish fleet his ships would have foundered in the Pacific for lack of coal.

Second, the war dramatized the problems of shifting ships between the Atlantic and the Pacific and thereby accentuated the need of an isthmian canal. The sixty-eight-day voyage of the *Oregon* from San Francisco to Key West, in order to join the forming Caribbean fleet, held the center of public attention for several days.[75] One can be certain that the future members of the General Board of the Navy were no less interested. America's new territorial acquisitions in the Pacific and the Caribbean likewise accentuated the problems of interoceanic transfer. The United States new latitudinal line of defense ran from Puerto Rico in the east to the Philippines in the west. Assuming attack upon only one area at a time, there were two possible ways in which these positions could be defended: (1) the United States could maintain fleets in both oceans that would be capable of dealing with the expected local aggressor; (2) a single fleet capable of defending against any possible aggressor could be maintained and rapid transfer potential be established by the construction and control of an isthmian canal. The idea of a two-ocean fleet had been the pipe-dream of naval men from John Paul Jones to Thayer Mahan. But there was no more chance of achieving that dream in the early 1900's than there was in 1890, when a three-ship authorization bill had been considered chauvinistic. In the first place, there was no effective leadership in the Congress that would push for naval expansion. And second, even the postwar spurt of shipbuilding authorizations that culminated in the Naval Bill of 1900 gave way to the pacifist opposition of the Progressives in the next Congress. Consequently, the military men—then as now the servants of the politically feasible—agitated for the canal and for bases to defend it. In this area, at least, the militarists had the support of the Eastern merchants and exporters who, enchanted with the prospect of new trade outlets in the Far East, "quite understandably became advocates of a much shorter water route to Pacific markets."[76]

[75] *Ibid.*, p. 233.
[76] Lieuwen, *U.S. Policy in Latin America*, p. 38.

Another important consequence of the war was an increased concern with military organization. In particular, concern that the Congress was evidencing a surprising lack of sympathy for building American ships with a larger cruising radius resulted in the formation of the General Board of the Navy in 1900.[77] The timing of the Board's creation, however, is indicative of something more than concern with the technical incompetence of the men on Capitol Hill. The U.S. navy, even in 1900, had lived long enough with incompetence to suspect that it was endemic. It is much more likely that the actual purpose of the Board was to provide a "realist" criticism of the idealistic foreign policy to which the Progressives were beginning to devote such a large portion of the *Congressional Record*. Whatever the original motivations behind the creation of the Board, it did, in fact, give an increased voice to the dispositions of the U.S. navy toward the formulation of American foreign policy. Such was particularly the case after Roosevelt's accession to the presidency in 1901.

The pervasive influence that Mahan exercised over the General Board has already been pointed out, but it remains to indicate what effects the war had upon the Board's specific view toward Caribbean naval defense strategy. There can be no doubt that the war greatly stimulated the navy's desire for overseas naval bases. Mahan's "strategy board" of 1898 had already informed the secretary of the navy that the United States would now *have* to acquire naval bases and stations outside the continental United States.[78] In the Caribbean the area of vital concern with respect to naval bases was the Windward Passage between Cuba and Santo Domingo. This is the route through which all commercial traffic bound to and from the Isthmus must pass.[79] Said the Mahan group, "No solution of the problem of coaling and naval stations can be considered satisfactory which does not provide for military safety upon that route."[80] Immediately upon its establishment, the General Board took up the same chorus. Some of the Board's "advice" to the secretary of the navy and the Congress has been mentioned earlier, but the prospect of actually securing the key bases in Cuba and Puerto Rico stimulated particularly enthusiastic lobbying on the part of the navalists. In 1902 the Board prepared and submitted a consolidated report on Caribbean naval stations.[81] Guantanamo Bay was the principal goal of the naval men. It was the one location that was "indispensable to the efficiency of the naval force in the West Indies."[82] Said the

[77] Sprout, *American Naval Power*, p. 247.
[78] Challenger, I: 38.
[79] *Ibid.*
[80] *Ibid.*
[81] *Ibid.*, III: 102.
[82] *Ibid.*

Board: "Our right to establish ourselves at that point should be obtained at the earliest moment, irrespective of the future status of Cuba—whether it remain independent, or be annexed by request."[83] Equal emphasis was given to the protection of the Isthmus, and a request was made for additional bases on the Isthmus of Panama.[84] Then the Board gave the most penetrating analysis to that date of what would be required for the security of the future canal. The Board laid down the position—from which they were not to deviate until after World War I—that it would not be sufficient merely to provide fortified bases at the termini of the proposed canal.[85] Canal security rested upon absolute American control of the Caribbean. The Caribbean, so far as the navy was concerned, had to remain an "American lake." Because the Caribbean was virtually landlocked and access to the area could be controlled by securing the Windward Passage, the security of the canal, as well as the security of the continental United States, depended upon the navy's ability to put a "cork" upon the Caribbean bottle. And as one member of the General Board phrased it, "one cork is alone necessary for this bottle."[86] What the "cork" strategy meant was the absolute necessity of obtaining the Guantanamo base, but it also goes far toward explaining the almost paranoid concern which was evidenced with respect to European intervention in Haiti or the Dominican Republic. It should also be added that as technological advances made land fortifications ever less efficient the necessity of maintaining the "cork" intact would become ever more imposing. This was, in fact, the strategy which lay behind the bold attempt of the secretary of war to secure the Guantanamo base by means of the Platt Amendment.

A number of conclusions could, therefore, be drawn by military strategists at the turn of the century. Primary among them was that the United States could permit no European lodgment in the Caribbean and especially in the Windward Passage from the Isthmus to the northwestern tip of Haiti. British lodgment in Jamaica was at least tolerable due to (1) the relations existing between Britain and the United States; (2) the vulnerable position of Canada; and (3) British preoccupation with the growing German navy. Second, immediate construction of the isthmian canal was essential to the defense of the western seaboard and the newly acquired American outposts in the Pacific. And the security of that canal was equally essential, if it was not to become more a liability than an asset. But the corollary conclusion, and the one to which American statesmen and strategists came only by necessity, was that no situation which was

[83] *Ibid.*, I: 38.
[84] *Ibid.*, III: 103.
[85] *Ibid.*
[86] *Ibid.*, III: 106.

conducive to European lodgment in the Caribbean could be tolerated by the United States.

At the same time that these conclusions were being reached, a new tenor of public opinion was emerging in the United States—one that would impose few restraints upon government administrations, Democratic or Republican. A business community strongly interested in foreign commercial markets combined with a general public evidencing a missionary faith in the benefits of American institutions and American abilities to govern effectively to produce an atmosphere in which later interventionists would find little organized opposition.

# IV.

## Intervention As Policy

IN THE DECADE FOLLOWING the Spanish–American War the type of armed intervention upon which that war was initiated became the express policy of the U.S. government. During those years the United States slowly established an incontestable control over the Caribbean area by means of a system of de facto protectorates[1] into the affairs of which the United States intervened militarily and diplomatically as a matter of course. In a majority of cases American armed intervention took place by virtue of treaty arrangements similar to those formulated in the Platt Amendment. But in other cases—i.e., those of the Dominican Republic and Haiti—U.S. intervention took place without the benefit of legal justification.

In the conventional wisdom of the academic world this growing tendency to intervene has often been ascribed to economic considerations. Indeed, anti-Yankee Latin American writers have often picked up this refrain, with no little success in the Latin American popular mind. But these considerations have been given little notice in the present study for a number of reasons. In the first place, a careful analysis of the State Department's records for the period of the active interventionist policy (from 1901 to 1921) does not support the charge of complicity with the business com-

---

[1] In keeping with common historical practice, the word "protectorate" has been used in this study in a descriptive rather than legal sense. While this usage may be somewhat confusing, it was a common practice at the time, and it probably comes as close as any other word in suggesting the congeries of claims, treaty commitments, and practice that constituted U.S. domination of the Caribbean nations.

munity.[2] Second, the importance of American foreign investment in the formulation of the intervention policy can be called into serious question by a brief comparison of investment statistics with a map. The policy of armed intervention was for the United States a Caribbean policy and did not extend to those areas of Latin America in which vital American security interests were not involved. In 1900, 2 percent of total American foreign trade was with the Caribbean area, compared with 1.6 percent of that trade with South America.[3] However, by 1927 American trade with South America had grown to 10.5 percent of the total, while trade with the Caribbean countries had increased to only 5.5 percent.[4] The obvious reason behind this relative decline in Caribbean trade was the very political instability that motivated the disembarcation of U.S. troops. If American "imperialism" was founded on the desire to expand markets, one would have to conclude that the imperialists were not adept economists.

U.S. direct investment, which comprised about 80 percent of total U.S. investment in Latin America, was concentrated largely in Cuba and Mexico—thus lending some support to the Marxian thesis. The thesis runs into problems, however, with respect to both size and distribution of that investment. The 1914 U.S. aggregate investment in Latin America as a whole is generally estimated at about $1.6 billion, or about 45 percent of the estimated United Kingdom investment in the same region. Most of this money flowed first into Mexico and then into Cuba, largely as an extension of U.S. enterprises at home—i.e., agriculture, mining, and petroleum extraction. In the Central American republics, Haiti, and the Dominican Republic, U.S. investment was relatively small, even in terms of aggregate Latin American investment.

---

[2] By far the best study of those records to date is Munro's *Intervention and Dollar Diplomacy in the Caribbean, 1900–1921* (Princeton: Princeton University Press, 1951) On the basis of his study, Munro concludes: "It would be impossible to deny that many of the American government's actions were ill-judged and unfortunate in their results. As we look back on the story, however, it seems clear that the motives that inspired its policy were basically political rather than economic. What the United States was trying to do, throughout the period with which this study has dealt, was to put an end to conditions that threatened the independence of some of the Caribbean states and were consequently a potential danger to the security of the United States. Revolutions must be discouraged; the bad financial practices that weakened the governments and involved them in trouble with foreigners must be reformed; and general economic and social conditions, which were a basic cause of instability, must be improved. The Platt Amendment was an effort to achieve these purposes in Cuba, and the Roosevelt Corollary to the Monroe Doctrine meant that the United States would seek to achieve them in other Caribbean states" (p. 531).

[3] Henry Kittredge Norton, "The United States in the Caribbean," in Jones, Norton, and Moon (eds.), *The United States and the Caribbean* (Chicago: University of Chicago Press, 1929), *passim*.

[4] *Ibid.*

Of course, these figures have little meaning without some sort of detailed breakdown of the personality of individual investments and some notion of what influence specific personalities may have had on the formulation of U.S. policy. And data with this degree of specificity is almost impossible to come by, given the inadequacy of statistical records for this period in most of the Latin American nations. What may be said with regard to this influence, however, is that (1) it is little in evidence in available records (with one or two exceptions) and (2) under both Wilson and Roosevelt the degree to which the President exercised personal control over U.S.–Latin American policy makes such a sinister interpretation unlikely. What must be recognized, however, is that growing American business interests in the Latin American region, combined with a generalized faith in the expansion of foreign commerce as a panacea for a number of domestic ills, undercut potential opposition to the foreign involvement of the United States in the Latin American area.

But perhaps the strongest argument against any simplistic Marxian interpretation of American intervention in Latin America is found in the attempts of American diplomats to provide some pacific alternative to direct intervention that would prevent the internal disorders that inevitably carried with them the specter of foreign lodgment. Primary among these attempts was the determined effort of American diplomats, beginning in 1889, to create a multilateral system for the settlement of disputes in the Americas. In the first meeting of the International Conference of American States, in 1889, U.S. support was given to an arrangement for compulsory arbitration of disputes that would have undoubtedly have had the effect of mitigating the policy of intervention.[5] Even as late as 1901 the American delegation to the Second International Conference of American States was supporting a more limited arrangement for the compulsory arbitration of pecuniary claims.[6] But by 1906 the United States was backing away from any such compulsory arbitration commitment.[7] At the same time, the U.S. government was in the process of promulgating and implementing an exclusive unilateral claim to the right to intervene in the internal affairs of the nations of the Western Hemisphere. By the 1920's the United States claimed treaty rights to a veto power in the international financial dealings of Cuba, the Dominican Republic, and Haiti. And it claimed the right to forcefully maintain the public order in every nation in the Caribbean area.

[5] J. Floyd Mecham, *The United States and Inter-American Security, 1889–1960* (Austin: University of Texas Press, 1961), p. 55.
[6] *Ibid.*, p. 61.
[7] *Ibid.*, pp. 64–65.

The period that followed and ended with World War I was to see other attempts to substitute multilateral peace-keeping arrangements for the policy of unilateral intervention. But in every instance the tension between national security interests and respect for the sovereignty of the Latin American nations was to be resolved in the end in favor of national security. The failures of these attempts at pacific solutions to the dilemma can be attributed in large part to two causes. Foremost was the intense nationalistic hostility that the Latin American republics exhibited toward each other, as well as toward the United States. Second was the unavoidable fact that the United States could not absolutely renounce the right of intervention in certain cases unless all other potential aggressor nations did so as well.

### Roosevelt and the Caribbean

"During the greater part of his first term, Roosevelt himself directed American policy in the Caribbean."[8] Consequently the policy initiated in 1901 can be ascribed in large part to the prejudices and analyses of the American chief executive. And there can be little doubt that the President's vociferous nationalism served to make him highly sensitive to the security demands of the country. While still governor of New York, Roosevelt had sounded the death knell for national isolation: "We cannot sit huddled within our own borders and avow ourselves merely an assemblage of well-to-do hucksters who care nothing for what happens beyond. Such a policy would defeat even its own ends; for as the nations grow to have ever wider and wider interests and are brought into closer and closer contact, if we are to hold our own in the struggle for naval and commercial supremacy, we must build up our power without our own borders. We must build the Isthmian canal, and we must grasp the points of vantage which will enable us to have our say in deciding the destiny of the oceans of the east and the west."[9] This was as pure a statement of the Mahan doctrine as could be offered by any military leader of the period, but the similarity is not in the least surprising, for the President had long been a devoted student of the "Father of Modern Sea Power." Roosevelt's interest in naval affairs went back to his undergraduate days at Harvard, where he began work on his first book, *The Naval War of 1812*. Published in 1882, this short work on naval strategy demonstrated a remarkable similarity between Mahan's philosophy of sea power and Roosevelt's own conclusions on the subject. In 1894 Roosevelt wrote a highly complimentary

[8] Munro, *Intervention and Dollar Diplomacy*, p. 112.
[9] Theodore Roosevelt, address before the Hamilton Club (Chicago: April 10, 1900). Quoted in Howard C. Hill, *Roosevelt and the Caribbean* (Chicago: University of Chicago Press, 1927), p. 1.

review of Mahan's first two books,[10] and afterwards he maintained an extensive correspondence with Mahan, even during his term as President.[11] In 1897 the future President became assistant secretary of the navy and in that capacity played a large role in the naval strategy of the Spanish–American War.[12] Notably, President McKinley evidenced some uneasiness upon the entry of Roosevelt to his administration.[13] Roosevelt, as an advocate of "a big navy, an aggressive foreign policy, and, in particular, armed intervention in Cuba and territorial expansion," was hardly compatible with the peaceful McKinley.[14] And in February of 1900, shortly before his accession to the presidency, Roosevelt was complaining to his friend Mahan about the first Hay–Pauncefote Treaty: "I do not see why we should dig a canal if we are not to fortify it so as to insure its being used for ourselves and against our foes in time of war."[15]

As we have pointed out, the strategic situation which presented itself to Roosevelt when he assumed office in 1901 gave compelling arguments for the development of the canal. Foreign naval powers were growing rapidly on both of the exposed seaboards of the continent. So far as Roosevelt was concerned there was an absolute necessity for maintaining the American fleet in the Caribbean and the Atlantic areas. As president, Roosevelt displayed an almost paranoid alarm over both German and Japanese sea power,[16] but whenever it was a question of the choosing of enemies, the Germans won. "The specter of German aggression in the Caribbean or elsewhere in Latin America became a veritable nightmare with him. He was absolutely convinced that the Kaiser would one day start trouble somewhere in this hemisphere."[17] In light of the political infeasibility of developing adequate fleets in both the Atlantic and the Pacific, the canal was of first priority in the President's eyes. But Roosevelt was by no means alone in his desires. Public opinion was solidly behind an isthmian passage, "built by the United States, owned by the United States, controlled by the United States, and governed by the United States."[18] It is evidence of Roosevelt's intense concern that one of his first acts as President was to take direct control of the negotiations then in progress for the second

[10] *Political Science Quarterly* 9 (March 1894).

[11] Joseph Bucklin Bishop, *Theodore Roosevelt and His Time Shown in His Own Letters*, 2 vols. (New York: Charles Scribner's Sons, 1919, 1920).

[12] Harold and Margaret Sprout, *The Rise of American Naval Power, 1776–1918*, pp. 224–30.

[13] *Ibid.*, p. 226.

[14] *Ibid.*

[15] Bishop, *Theodore Roosevelt*, I: 143.

[16] Sprout, *American Naval Power*, p. 225.

[17] *Ibid.*, p. 253.

[18] Hill, *Roosevelt and the Caribbean*, p. 32.

Hay–Pauncefote Treaty, which would allow the United States to fortify the future canal.[19]

The two most popular debates regarding American–Latin American relations during Roosevelt's administration are those centering around the political machinations of Philippe Bunau-Varilla in assuring the choice of the Panamanian canal route and those attempting to prove the degree of involvement or noninvolvement of the United States in the separation of Panama from Colombia. The details behind the choice of the Panamanian route, in effect, involve nothing more sinister than the triumph of Colombian diplomacy over that of the badly organized Nicaraguans. Both sides had lobbyists in Washington, as was standard practice for the Latin American republics even in 1900; but the Colombians had the benefit of the aid of several experienced French promoters.[20] Likewise, the degree and course of U.S. involvement in the Panamanian revolution is an interesting and much debated issue, but its relevance to this discussion is limited to this: at a time when U.S. security interests were felt to be at stake the American government was willing to violate its treaty commitments and so accepted norms of international law.[21]

As early as 1846, as we have seen, the isthmian route was considered to be sufficiently important to justify the first American assurance of a foreign power's sovereignty. Likewise, we know that Roosevelt felt the construction of the canal to have been "imperative" for military reasons.[22]

[19] *Ibid.*, p. 34.

[20] For those interested in this aspect of canal politics, any of the general references in the bibliography for this period will contain the essential details. Especially notable is Hill's *Roosevelt and the Caribbean* and Munro's *Intervention and Dollar Diplomacy.* The most recent materials on the subject are surveyed in Charles D. Ameringer, "The Panama Canal Lobby of Philippe Bunau-Varilla and William Nelson Cromwell," *American Historical Review* (January 1963); and "Philippe Bunau-Varilla: New Light on the Panama Canal Treaty," *Hispanic American Historical Review* (February 1966).

[21] A word of explanation is, perhaps, in order for the failure to include a more detailed analysis of the Panamanian controversy in a study of American involvement in Latin American civil strife. In accordance with the policy announced in the Introduction, I have attempted to choose my examples, as much as possible, from relatively uncontroversial historical material. The degree of U.S. official involvement in the *origin* of the revolt in Panama is a matter that may remain forever hidden in a private conversation between Bunau-Varilla and Roosevelt; hence, there is great uncertainty as to whether Bunau-Varilla acted with Roosevelt's assurances or whether he acted upon his own assessment of what the Americans were likely to do. What is certain is that American warships were ordered to prevent the landing of government troops, if that was necessary to prevent interruption of isthmian traffic, and the United States recognized Panamanian independence rather than assuring Colombian sovereignty over the isthmus. Hence, U.S. treaty commitments were violated, regardless of the interpretation given to the origin of the revolt.

[22] Theodore Roosevelt, *Autobiography* (New York: Charles Scribner's Sons, 1913), p. 523.

Finally, with "canal fever" at its highest and with Panamanian separation-
ism at a boiling point, the Colombian congress attempted to hold up the
American government for larger indemnities.[23] The result was almost inevitable. There is no doubt that American warships did prevent the re-
establishment of Colombian control over the territory. This much was
granted by Under Secretary of State Bassett Moore, who made an ex post
facto attempt to interpret the Treaty of 1846 between the United States and
New Granada as justifying American interference.[24] But by the explicit
terms of the Treaty of 1846, the United States was obligated not only to
maintain freedom of passage but also to assure the continued sovereignty
of New Granada over the territory. This was, in fact, the understanding of
President Polk, under whose administration the treaty was ratified. As
Polk explained it to the Senate: "The guaranty of the sovereignty of New
Granada over the isthmus is a natural consequence of the guaranty of its
neutrality, and there does not seem to be any other practicable mode of
securing the neutrality of this territory. New Granada would not consent
to yield up this province in order that it might become a neutral State;
and if she should, it is not sufficiently populous or wealthy to establish and
maintain an independent sovereignty."[25]

The United States violated its commitments to the government of New
Granada when, in the opinion of the U.S. leaders, the control of the
isthmian property became a military necessity. Five years earlier the
nation had gone to war to assure dominion over the Cuban island. Panama,
which was equally important in a strategic sense, cost a good bit less. Time
was to prove that the same strategy that dictated the construction and
fortified control of the canal by the United States would lead to ever more
extensive intervention in Caribbean affairs in order to assure continued
American domination of the canal area.

The first step in the expanding intervention policy was the reduction of
Panama to the status of a protectorate. This was largely accomplished by
the Bunau-Varilla–Hay Treaty which was proclaimed in February 1904.[26]
By virtue of the first article of the treaty, the United States guaranteed and
pledged itself to maintain the independence of Panama, and Article VII
gave the United States the right to intervene in the cities of Panama and
Colon to maintain public order, "in case the Republic of Panama should
not be, in the judgment of the United States, able to maintain such order."[27]

[23] German Cavelier, *La Politica Internacional de Colombia* (Bogota: Editorial Iqueima,
1959), III: 11–34.
[24] Hill, *Roosevelt and the Caribbean*, p. 45.
[25] Quoted in *ibid.*, p. 41.
[26] *Foreign Relations, 1904*, pp. 543–51.
[27] *Ibid.*, p. 546.

Taken together, these grants could justify almost any intervention of the United States in Panamanian affairs. Within the ten-mile-wide canal zone the United States was to act as "If it were the sovereign of the territory . . . to the entire exclusion of the exercise by the Republic of Panama of any such sovereign rights, power or authority."[28]

With the canal under construction, the necessity of preventing enemy lodgment in the Caribbean became a primary position in American policy. Here the danger lay in the stormy politics of the Central American and Caribbean countries. At the turn of the century these countries had not had the benefit of the British and American capital which had produced a period of relative political and economic stability in South America. Political and economic affairs were usually dominated by tightly knit oligarchies of landholders, who vied among themselves for control of the government—which was another way of saying control of the customs revenues. Political divisions usually took the form of allegiance to a particular leader. And the primary weapon in the political arena was not the ballot box, but the revolution—à la palace coup. The result in almost all of the Caribbean island countries and in Central America was a continuous state of siege. Parties in power had to suppress the latest revolution being planned by the parties out of power. Suppression made life even more intolerable for the great mass of the people and eventually provided sufficient support for the success of the next revolution.

Caribbean political leaders attempted to consolidate their power in three ways: (1) by purchasing the loyalty of their military leaders at the expense of the public treasury; (2) by maintaining friendly governments in power in neighboring countries; and (3) by trading valuable strategic and commercial assets for the protection of a more powerful foreign benefactor. It was this last tendency which had earlier resulted in the promulgation of the no-transfer principle as a corollary to the Monroe Doctrine. As J. Fred Rippy explains that principle:

> This readiness to barter away strategic assets or grant control over important phases of national economic life caused restless uneasiness among great powers that were competitors and rivals all around the world. It was especially disturbing to the United States. The alienation of such economic and strategic advantages might have jeopardized the national security of the United States as well as that of its Caribbean neighbors. It was therefore necessary for the Washington authorities to inform the dictators that there was only one market for such asset: the United States of America. In fact they were informed more often than otherwise that there was only one market and even that market was closed—at least temporarily.[29]

[28] *Ibid.*, p. 544.
[29] J. Fred Rippy, *The Caribbean Danger Zone* (New York: Putnam's Sons 1940), p. 12.

But by the early 1900's Latin American politicians had learned that American concern lest strategically located territory fall into European hands was worth substantial additions to the national exchequers. There is little doubt that much of the American anxiety over the attempts of the Germans to secure Caribbean bases originated in Quito, Bogotá, and Santo Domingo—not in Berlin. Negotiations for naval bases in the Galapagos is a particularly comic illustration of this point.[30] Ecuadoreans were able to keep an overly active American minister in an almost constant state of panic for five years by conjuring tales of German and French intrigues to secure control of the islands. In retrospect it is readily apparent that "Ecuador's principal interest was a virtual raid on the U.S. treasury and that the most ardent enthusiasts for the Galapagos were the employees of John Hay"[31]—not the German Naval Office.

The problem of mutual Latin American interference in neighboring governments was particularly acute in Central America. Here the dream of a federal arrangement for the Central American states inspired both idealists and dictators alike. It was in this area that American diplomats first sought to substitute a regional security arrangement for the interventionist policy. Certain Latin American political figures, as we shall see, were also striving for unification of the area—only they looked forward to unified domination rather than federal cooperation.

Before leaving this general description of Caribbean politics at the turn of the century, one additional contribution to the chaos must be identified—the general incompetence of the American diplomats sent into the region. Before the Rogers Act of 1924, able diplomats simply did not find their way to Caribbean posts. In a foreign service characterized by political appointees, the Caribbean posts were usually considered the least desirable.[32] The result was that "incompetent diplomatic representation was a major factor in many of the most unfortunate episodes in our Caribbean policy."[33]

The constant state of political disorder in the Caribbean was generally regarded by American military strategists with something approaching horror. Important members of the General Board regarded the endemic revolutions as "nothing more nor less than struggles between the different crews of bandits for the possession of the customs houses—and the loot."[34] And Charles Sperry probably reported the prevailing opinion of the Board when he stated that the bankruptcies and debt repudiations at-

[30] Full accounts of these negotiations can be found in Rippy, *ibid.*, and in Challenger, III: 133–41.
[31] Challenger, III: 133.
[32] Munro, *Intervention and Dollar Diplomacy*, p. 23.
[33] *Ibid.*
[34] Challenger, I: 18.

tendant to the political chaos furnished "the simplest and readiest pretext" for European intervention and lodgment.[35] The navy's preliminary answer to the situation of unrest was to back up diplomatic protestations with evidence of military power. In the autumn of 1902 the Navy Department established its permanent Caribbean squadron. Its purpose was to act as a visual reminder of American power. According to the Navy Department, the squadron was to be "utilized to exert our influence towards maintaining order in those regions where disorder would imperil the lives and property of our citizens. This is a duty which naturally devolves upon this government because of its well defined policy towards those countries."[36] This was the policy which the Roosevelt Corollary was to elevate to the status of a national obligation.

As is well known, the Roosevelt Corollary—the name usually given to the American assertion of a unilateral right of intervention in the Caribbean—was first enunciated to justify American intervention in the Dominican Republic. But its real roots go back to 1902, when a joint Anglo–German intervention was threatened in Venezuela. The Venezuelan dictator, Cipriano Castor, had defaulted on both private and public debts, and aliens were generally unable to gain any just settlement in the controlled Venezuelan courts. The American government had at first acquiesced in an Anglo–German attempt to obtain redress, if necessary, by force. German participation in the scheme was solicited by the British, and at several points in the negotiations which preceded intervention the United States was informed of Anglo–German intentions and assured that no territorial aggrandizement was contemplated by either power.[37] Nevertheless, in the midst of the intervention, Roosevelt sent off strong ultimatums to the governments involved that the matter should be submitted to arbitration. This was, in fact, the ultimate result, but confusion and prolongation of the intervention caused frayed nerves on all sides.

Why Roosevelt had first acquiesced in the intervention and later forced the Anglo–German withdrawal is still unclear. The President's explanation does not follow the actual chronology of events, but he was probably telling the truth when he said, "I became convinced that Germany intended to seize some Venezuelan harbor and turn it into a strongly fortified place of arms, on the model of Kiauchau, with a view to exercising some degree of control over the future Isthmian Canal, and over South American affairs generally."[38] What is important in the Venezuelan case is that the President promoted the settlement of the affair by means of international arbitration.

[35] *Ibid.*
[36] *Ibid.*, I: 20.
[37] The account is based upon Hill, *Roosevelt and the Caribbean*, pp. 106–47.
[38] Quoted in Dexter Perkins, *The United States and Latin America* (Baton Rouge: Louisiana State University Press, 1960), p. 13.

He did so at the suggestion of Secretary Hay that submission of the case to the Hague Court would "promote the cause of international arbitration."[39]

Ultimately, a series of mixed claims commissions was set up to deal with the various national claims against Venezuela (ten nations held Venezuela in default), and 30 percent of Venezuelan customs revenues were to be set aside for settlement of adjudicated claims. But one important question remained. By a special protocol Venezuela and several of the creditor nations came before the Hague Permanent Court of Arbitration to settle the question of whether or not the nations which had initiated the intervention were entitled to a prior claim upon the specified assets for settlement.[40]

While the Court was considering the question of priority another ominous situation developed in the Dominican Republic. The assassination of Dominican strongman Ulysses Heureaux, in 1899, had left that country in economic and political chaos. A succession of short-lived presidents continued to increase the size of the foreign debt and the threat of European intervention. The efforts of American diplomats to reorganize Dominican finances, in the end, did no more than increase the number of private claims against the defaulting governments which passed through Santo Domingo.[41] For the United States the situation was further complicated by constant rumors of German attempts to secure naval bases on the island. Acting upon the investigations of two junior officers, the General Board concluded: "It is certain that Germany has recently taken steps to acquire concessions in Santo Domingo; she failed because the President failed. Another time the one with whom she deals may be more successful."[42] The fear of the General Board was confirmed by the American minister to the republic W. F. Powell in March 1903.[43] The naval opinion is particularly important in this case, since Roosevelt, frustrated by the morass of diplomatic intrigue involved in the continuing game of "musical presidents," requested Admiral Dewey to go to Santo Domingo and investigate the situation as the President's personal envoy.[44] The conclusions of the navy are presented in a confidential statement forwarded to the State Department in mid-summer of 1903: "The information indicates that the country is bankrupt, and the only means it now has of obtaining money is by borrowing from merchants at high interest and allowing the merchants to bring their goods in free of duties. Consequently the whole

---

[39] Hill, *Roosevelt and the Caribbean*, p. 141.

[40] Samuel Flagg Bemis, *The Latin American Policy of the United States: An Historical Interpretation* (New York: Harcourt, Brace and Company, 1943), p. 147.

[41] Munro, *Intervention and Dollar Diplomacy*, pp. 87–111, offers a complete account of the American attempt to rationalize Dominican finances.

[42] Challenger, IV: 193.

[43] Munro, *Intervention and Dollar Diplomacy*, p. 86.

[44] Challenger, IV: 203.

country is running behind more and more and it is predicted that very soon the government will not be able to raise any money at all with which to pay its foreign debts."[45]

On February 22, 1904, with Dominican affairs still worsening, the Hague Court handed down its decision in the case of the Venezuelan payments. It was a unanimous judgment in favor of the claims of the blockading powers. According to the Court, Venezuela had recognized the preferential claims of the blockading powers, but not those of neutral claimants.[46] The effect of the decision was to enhance the value of armed intervention for the collection of debts. By April 1904 Roosevelt was already receiving reports that Italy was planning to intervene in the Dominican Republic to secure the interests of her nationals and that she would base her action upon the decision of the Hague Court.[47] By the end of the year, two or three European powers had notified Roosevelt that they intended to seize Dominican seaports.[48] It was under this shadow of European intervention that Roosevelt pushed through plans for the United States customs receivership in the Dominican Republic. In presenting one of the needed protocols to the Senate, he proclaimed the policy which was to be known as the "Roosevelt Corollary":

An aggrieved nation can without interfering with the Monroe Doctrine take what action it sees fit in the adjustment of its disputes with American States, provided that action does not take the shape of interference with their form of government or of the despoilment of their territory under any disguise. But, short of this, when the question is one of a money claim, the only way which remains, finally, to collect it is a blockade, or bombardment, or the seizure of the customhouses, and this means what is in effect a possession, even though only a temporary possession, of territory. The United States then becomes a party in interest, because under the Monroe doctrine it can not see any European power seize and permanently occupy the territory of one of these republics; and yet such seizure of territory, disguised or undisguised, may eventually offer the only way in which the power in question can collect any debts, unless there is interference on the part of the United States.[49]

Thoughtful scholars since Roosevelt have produced a multiplicity of critiques of the assertion of the President that, if the United States would not allow foreign powers to intervene in the Caribbean to protect their

[45] *Ibid.*, IV: 199–200.
[46] A text of the Hague Court decisions can be found in 58th Cong., 3rd sess., Senate Document 119.
[47] Bemis, *Latin American Policy*, p. 154.
[48] Roosevelt, *Autobiography*, p. 507.
[49] *Foreign Relations, 1905*, pp. 334–35.

interests, then the United States would have to assume the role of international policeman of the Caribbean. In general, these criticisms fall into three broad categories. Critics, such as J. Fred Rippy,[50] have suggested that the United States proclaimed an unnecessary unilateral right of intervention, when it could have allowed the other foreign powers to shift for themselves and continued to pursue its policy of nonintervention for pecuniary claims. Other writers, best represented by Arthur P. Whitaker,[51] have lamented the choice of the unilateral intervention policy over the multilateral approach proposed by Luis Maria Drago in December 1902.[52] The Drago Doctrine was proposed as a multilateral policy statement to the effect "that the public debt cannot occasion armed intervention nor even the actual occupation of the territory of American nations by a European Power."[53] A third and final related criticism questions the relationship between the intervention policy and the Monroe Doctrine.[54] For example, Bemis maintains that "the Monroe Doctrine did not give to, nor did it withhold from the United States a right or policy of intervention"[55] and he laments the confusion which the President's association of the two policies has caused.

As we have attempted to illustrate, the prevailing military strategy in 1905, with its emphasis upon the necessity of controlling the Windward Passage, placed Santo Domingo in a key position for the maintenance of U.S. security. Control of the island by an enemy power would have been tantamount to control of the Windward Passage—in so far as the strategists were concerned. Next to the Panama Canal, the General Board considered the Dominican island to be the "most important strategic point in the Caribbean."[56] Consequently, if the strategic analysis of the General Board is accepted, the prevention of enemy lodgment (in this case, of German lodgment) in the island was a matter of self-defense. To this extent, the intervention policy shared a common basis with the Monroe Doctrine. It might well be justified in the same terms with which Elihu Root was to explain the Monroe Doctrine:

> The doctrine is not international law but it rests upon the right of self-protection and that right is recognized by international law. . . . It is well understood that the exercise of the right of self-protection may and frequently

[50] J. Fred Rippy, "The Initiation of the Customs Receivership in the Dominican Republic," *Hispanic American Historical Review* 17 (November 1937): 419–57.

[51] Arthur Preston Whitaker, *The Western Hemisphere Idea: Its Rise and Decline* (New York: Cornell University Press, 1954), pp. 86–89.

[52] *Foreign Relations 1903*, p. 3.

[53] *Ibid.*

[54] Bemis, *Latin American Policy*, p. 157.

[55] *Ibid.*

[56] Challenger, IV: 193.

does extend in its effects beyond the limits of the territorial jurisdiction of the state exercising it. . . . The most common exercise of the right of self-protection outside of a state's own territory and in time of peace is the interposition of objection to the occupation of territory, of points of strategic military or maritime advantage, or to indirect accomplishment of this effect by dynastic arrangement.[57]

The same strategic elements that made the Dominican Republic of central importance to American security, made it impossible for the United States to take the chance of gaining general acceptance for its policy of nonintervention for pecuniary claims unless the same restraint was exercised by the European naval powers. By standing aside in the Venezuelan crisis the United States had run the risk of European lodgment. The subsequent resort to arbitration had resulted in the Hague Court's putting its stamp of approval on the use of force for the collection of debts. There was no reason to believe that standing aside from the Dominican situation would have had different results; yet the strategic stakes, as perceived by American strategists, were much higher. It is notable in this regard that the United States did not abandon the attempt to gain international acceptance for the nonintervention-for-pecuniary-claims policy. On the contrary, it supported a proposal at the Hague Peace Conference in 1907 which would have barred intervention for the collection of contract debts so long as the defaulting nation would accept arbitration and the arbitral award.[58] This proposal was codified in Convention II of the Hague Conventions of 1907; but the convention was not ratified by the South American republics, who resented the violation of national sovereignty that the commitment to arbitration implied.[59] However, for the first two decades of the twentieth century, no general acceptance of the principle of nonintervention could be hoped for. One theoretical alternative would have been for the United States to espouse the Drago Doctrine—thereby denying the right of any non-American power to intervene for the collection of pecuniary claims in any American nation. But what the theory would have meant in practice is that the United States, as the only modern military power in the Western Hemisphere, would have been required to enforce the Doctrine upon the European powers. This might have been militarily possible against either Britain or Germany if they acted alone. But because U.S. military hegemony in the Caribbean rested in large part

[57] Elihu Root, "The Real Monroe Doctrine" (Presidential address at the Eighth Annual Meeting of the American Society of International Law—Washington, April 22, 1914); *Addresses on International Subjects*, Robert Bacon and James Brown Scott (eds.) (Cambridge: Harvard University Press, 1916), p. 111.

[58] Mecham, *Inter-American Security*, p. 68.

[59] Bemis, *Latin American Policy*, p. 237.

upon the mutual hostility of those two European powers, it is doubtful that the United States could have effectively enforced the Drago Doctrine against a coalition of those powers such as was formed for the Venezuelan venture.

Thus in the early stages of the intervention policy international law played but a negative role. The general acceptance of forceful collection of debts, approved by the Hague Court, gave an air of legality to actual and potential European claims to intervene in the Caribbean area. And the American recognition of the strategic importance of the area made it imperative that such interventions not take place. Given the prospect of extra-hemispheric intervention, the political and financial stability of the Caribbean republics was prerequisite to American security. And given the failure of these republics to obtain anything resembling stability, U.S. intervention was prerequisite to the continued pacification of the area.

## Elihu Root: Attempts at Inter-American Cooperation

Just as the personal character of Theodore Roosevelt dominated U.S. policies in Latin America in the first years of his administration, from the middle of 1905 until 1909, Latin American policy bore the unmistakable imprint of Roosevelt's new secretary of state, Elihu Root. According to Roosevelt's own admission, Root was overseer of the bulk of the work in Latin American policy during his term as secretary.[60] Essentially, Root's ideas as to the strategic importance of the Canal and the Caribbean area differed little from those of Roosevelt. As secretary of war, Root was the originator and active advocate of a general staff, designed upon the blueprint of the German general staff.[61] Even before the assassination of McKinley and Roosevelt's accession to the presidency, Root had been responsible for the founding of the War College, which for many years afterward combined the functions of military education with strategy planning at the staff level.[62] In short, Root was no newcomer to the dictates of military strategy in the formulation of foreign policy. In January 1905 Root wrote to a friend: "The inevitable effect of our building the Canal must be to require us to police the surrounding premises. In the nature of things, trade and control, and the obligation to keep order which go with them, must come our way."[63]

Yet Root differed from Roosevelt in one important aspect; he emphasized cooperation rather than coercion as offering the greatest possi-

---

[60] Munro, *Intervention and Dollar Diplomacy*, p. 112.
[61] Philip L. Semch, "Elihu Root and the General Staff," *Military Affairs* 27 (Spring 1963): 16–27.
[62] *Ibid.*
[63] Philip C. Jessup, *Elihu Root*, 2 vols. (New York: Dodd, 1938), I: 471.

bility for hemispheric security. He exhibited an absolute repugnance for the use of force except in cases of absolute necessity. Yet he was to live to see his best efforts at inter-American cooperation collapse under the impact of intra-Latin American nationalistic jealousy.

One concomitant of the changed strategic configuration which resulted from the prospect of the isthmian canal was the increased importance of the Central American region to U.S. security. Under the old order of sea power there had been little possibility that European nations which had not acquired bases in the Caribbean would intervene in Central America as a first move toward lodgment in the Caribbean, and Britain had been barred from doing so both by her commitments under the Clayton–Bulwer Treaty and by the exposed position of Canada.[64] But as the hypothetical canal moved ever closer to a reality, American concern with Central American politics increased.

There was a good deal of cause for concern. Central America's brand of political chaos differed in kind as well as degree from that of other Caribbean countries. The idea of an economically and politically integrated Central America, represented today by the Central American Common Market, in the early 1900's took the form of desired domination of all Central America by each of her component states. The political divisions of the area were a heritage of the defunct confederation of Central American states; consequently, political hostilities showed no respect for national boundaries. All five Central American states at different times intervened quite actively in the internal politics of their neighbors—with the result that interstate conflicts were not infrequent.

For most of the nineteenth century the isolation of these countries, which was a heritage of their Spanish colonial past, meant that their general turmoil passed unnoticed by the rest of the world. But by 1900, thanks to British and American investment, they began to play a part in the international politics of the day. Playing a part, in this case, meant defaulting on their foreign debts and thereby raising the specter of European lodgment within cruising distance of the canal.

American concern with the Central American area had risen during the period of preliminary negotiations with Nicaragua for a canal route, but promptly subsided with the final election of the Panamanian route. Consequently, early in 1903 the United States had offered her good offices for the settlement of a dispute between Guatemala and two neighboring countries; but in 1907 Root had only two chiefs of mission in all of Central America.[65] In the summer of 1906 it most certainly appeared that two ministers could not possibly be enough.

[64] Bemis, *Latin American Policy*, p. 159.
[65] Munro, *Intervention and Dollar Diplomacy*, p. 143.

Guatemala under the oppressive dictatorship of Manuel Estrade Cabrera had found its national purpose in overthrowing governments in neighboring Honduras and El Salvador. By June 1906 tensions between the Guatemalan government and the government of El Salvador were rising to a war fever, and Honduras had joined in on the side of El Salvador. These countries exchanged several rounds of mutual "revolutionary" invasions in the early part of the year; and war finally erupted when the war minister of El Salvador went on a drunken spree, attempted to destroy the presidential palace in El Salvador, and then led an army into Guatemala.[66] To the everlasting gratitude of Marxist historians, for whom this episode would have to prove indigestible, the Salvadoran war minister was killed in the invasion attempt.

To the U.S. government the Central American conflict presented a thorny problem. In Cuba and in Panama there was at least a minimum justification for intervention in existing treaties. But in the Central American area no such justification was available. This consideration undoubtedly played a large role in the mind of the secretary of state, who had always shown a "concern for the proprieties of international behavior and for the effect of his action on opinion in other countries."[67] In any case, Root succeeded in convincing Roosevelt to attempt to unite the Central American republics into a regional organization that would provide for peaceful settlement of their multiple disputes.[68] The first step in this multilateral solution was to engage the participation of the government of Mexico in an attempt at arbitration. The Diaz government agreed, and the warring countries accepted the joint offer of mediation. So successful was the mediation attempt that the Third International Conference of American States, which was at that time meeting in Rio de Janeiro, adopted a resolution expressing the gratitude of the American states for the successful arbitration by the American and Mexican presidents.[69] Roosevelt was also pleased; and when hostilities again broke out in January 1907 between Nicaragua and Honduras, he again resorted to joint mediation with Mexico.[70] This second mediation attempt was likewise successful, and the prospects looked favorable for Root's larger plan to construct a regional peace-keeping organization for Central America.

On November 14 the Central American republics met at the Bureau of American Republics in Washington. The harmonious tenor of the meeting was set when El Salvador announced that it had no claims to present to the

---

[66] *Ibid.*, p. 145.
[67] *Ibid.*, p. 113.
[68] Jessup, *Elihu Root*, pp. 500–14.
[69] Hill, *Roosevelt and the Caribbean*, p. 130.
[70] *Ibid.*, p. 184.

other Central Americans. The final result of the Washington conference was a series of treaties designed to provide a ready-made structure for a Central American League of Nations. The most important of these treaties was the General Treaty of Peace and Amity.[71] Article I of this instrument bound the signatories to "decide every difference or difficulty that may arise amongst them, of whatsoever nature it may be, by means of the Central American Court of Justice" which was to be established by a second convention.[72] Article III declared the neutrality of Honduras and bound the signatory states never to violate Honduran territory. The central location of Honduras had in the past made it the theater of most Central American conflicts. By neutralizing the country it was hoped that the larger Central American powers—namely, Nicaragua and Guatemala—would be unable to get at each other. Root had hoped that the Central Americans would request the United States and Mexico to guarantee Honduran neutrality, but since they did not, the treaty-neutralization was to prove almost meaningless.[73] It was simply a case of an idealistic treaty commitment being unsupported by either intentions or power.

By an additional convention to the general treaty, the Central Americans attempted to reduce the incentive for revolutions and intermeddling. Article I of the additional convention declared that the contracting parties would "not recognize any other Government which may come into power in any of the five Republics as a consequence of a *coup d'état*, or of a revolution against the recognized Government, so long as the freely elected representatives of the people thereof have not constitutionally reorganized the country." Article II prohibited the intervention of one state in the affairs of another during a civil war.[74]

Another convention signed at the Washington conference actually established the Central American Court of Justice and reiterated the pledge to submit all controversies, without exception, to the Court's jurisdiction.[75] The Court's constitution provided for five justices, one being appointed by each republic. It was expressly stipulated that the justices were not to bar themselves from consideration of cases involving their nation of origin. This was in deference to the rather dubious assertion that the Court represented the "national conscience of Central America." This proviso did not, as some writers have suggested, reflect "the feeling that Central America was a political community whose members were bound to one another by special ties."[76] It is more probable that the stipu-

[71] *Foreign Relations, 1907*, II: 692–95.
[72] *Ibid.*, p. 693.
[73] Munro, *Intervention and Dollar Diplomacy*, p. 154.
[74] *Foreign Relations, 1907*, II: 696.
[75] *Ibid.*, pp. 697–791.
[76] Munro, *Intervention and Dollar Diplomacy*, p. 153.

lation simply continued a long Central American tradition of political justice. Such a judgment is borne out by the partisan bias exhibited in the first case brought before the Court.[77] And in 1911 a justice of the Court was even replaced for political reasons, in open violation of the Treaty of 1907.[78] The debilitating effect of the politicization of the Court requires further comment, since it seems to have been somewhat neglected by most historians. Quite unlike the present Hague Court, the Central American tribunal was completely uninsulated from the partisan politics of the countries over whom the Court claimed jurisdiction. The five justices of the Court became little more than permanently located representatives of their respective governments. In practice, this meant that the Court decisions were direct reflections of the balance of power which might exist at the time. Such a system might only have worked if the neutrality of Honduras could have been assured. The Honduran vote might then have served as a "swing vote" on the Court and the Honduran military as the balancing force in the political arena. Thus, the two issues of partisanship on the Court and the neutrality of Honduras were not as easily separated as the delegates to the Washington conference seemed to think.

A second problem of the entire regional security system was that it rested upon an imaginary picture of the configuration of regional politics. Mecham points out without comment that "these security measures were the result of, and were designed to meet, problems characteristic of Central America. They did not confront threats from any non-Central American source."[79] But this is only partly true. The system was designed to meet Central American problems, but its formulation was the result of increasing U.S. involvement in the Central American area. The system might have worked in isolation, but by 1907 its success depended upon American support. That support would be forthcoming only if the system could insure the preservation of minimum U.S. security interests. As we shall see in the following section, the final collapse of the system resulted from its failure to assure just those interests.

Both the necessity of a balance of political power and the necessity of U.S. involvement were illustrated by the Central American Court's only real success, in its first case in 1908. The case resulted from the continuing intrigues of the Nicaraguan dictator, José Santos Zelaya, and his Guatemalan counterpart and avowed enemy, Estrada Cabrera. Both dictators were apparently aiding their respective lackeys in Honduras, the "neutralized state." Zelaya was also hard at work in El Salvador, which

[77] Mecham, *Inter-American Security*, p. 69.
[78] *Ibid.*
[79] *Ibid.*

fact forced the unholy alliance of El Salvador and Guatemala.[80] The Honduran president, Davila, was surely no friend of Zelaya, but his fully reciprocated hatred of Cabrera was sufficient to force him into the Nicaraguan camp. In July 1908 El Salvador and Guatemala launched invasions of Honduras as a first step to reaching Nicaragua.

Fortunately Costa Rica managed to stay out of the fray and requested the Central American Court to intervene in the matter. In other words, Costa Rica not Honduras acted as the swing state in the affair. Honduras and Nicaragua, who were militarily in the more precarious position due to the internal upheaval in Honduras, formally charged El Salvador and Guatemala with violation of the Central American treaties, and the Court assumed jurisdiction. As a prerequisite to arbitration the Court demanded that both sides withdraw their troops from the frontiers. The compliance of both sides with this demand—not the Court's subsequent decision in the case—forms the basis for the oft-repeated refrain that at least the Court "proved its usefulness as an instrument to prevent a general Central American war."[81]

But enthusiasm for the Court's success needs to be tempered with the realization that the system worked in this case because of the support of countries that were not even included in that arrangement. Both the United States and Mexico backed up the Court's demand for withdrawal with strong diplomatic representations and were even exploring the possibility of backing up the Court with military force.[82] It should also be noted that Mexico's support of the Court in this case was as important as U.S. support. Because of their military inferiority, Nicaragua and Honduras were more than happy with mutual compliance with the withdrawal demand. The question was really whether or not El Salvador and Guatemala would agree. At the time of the conflict, as noted earlier, El Salvador was experiencing extreme difficulty in suppressing internal insurgency; and Salvadoran revolutionists were known to be organizing in Mexican territory.[83] Consequently the viability of the Salvadoran government depended

---

[80] There is no little disagreement among historians as to the actual conspiracies that were taking place in Central America at this time. (See, for example, conflicting accounts in Hill, *Roosevelt and the Caribbean;* Munro, *Intervention and Dollar Diplomacy;* Bemis, *Latin American Policy;* and Dexter Perkins, *A History of the Monroe Doctrine* [Little, Brown & Company, 1955].) There is a consensus that Zelaya was the villain; but so little real evidence is offered for the uniqueness of his wickedness that this author is inclined to suspect that interpretation has been clouded by subsequent relations between Zelaya and the United States. The account which follows is a synthesis of evidence from all of the authors mentioned.

[81] Munro, *Intervention and Dollar Diplomacy,* p. 158.

[82] *Ibid.,* p. 157.

[83] *Ibid.,* p. 156; and Bemis, *Latin American Policy,* p. 161.

upon the willingness of Mexico to prevent revolutionary invasion from her own territory. This configuration of pressures was a fortunate one for the success of the Court in this one case, but it was doubtful that it would be repeated in subsequent confrontations. As we shall see, the absence of U.S. support for one of the Court's decisions was the factor that finally brought about the collapse of the entire Central American structure, but not before U.S. attempts to enforce compliance with the system had resulted in a full-scale armed intervention in Nicaragua.

But whatever the faults of the Central American system—and they finally proved to be fatal faults—they arose from the application of an outmoded idea to an impossible situation. The system was based upon a community of interests shared by the Central American states, and it would be difficult to argue that it could never have been expanded to include the United States, or even Mexico. The expansion of U.S. influence into the southern part of the hemisphere was already beginning to engender the strident anti-American sentiment that was to become such a characteristic aspect of U.S.–Latin American relations. That feeling was given free expression both by Mexico and the delegates to the Rio Conference of American States, where Latin Americans such as Drago were pressing hard to circumscribe U.S. intervention by legalistic means. Mexico under the *Porfirato* was likewise suspected of expansionist tendencies, and during this entire period she carried on a controversy with Guatemala over the placement of their common boundary.

Root made every effort to create an alternative to Roosevelt's interventionism, but he did so with full realization that intervention might ultimately be necessary to protect the security of the canal. He doubtless spoke his own convictions when he told the delegates to the Rio conference: "We wish for no victories but those of peace; for no territory except our own; for no sovereignty except the sovereignty over ourselves."[84] He even went so far in the last two years of his term of office as to negotiate bipartite treaties of obligatory arbitration with six Latin American countries.[85] But during all the efforts at peace-making, he was careful to maintain sufficient naval power in the Central American area.[86] And even the arbitration treaties excepted from arbitration disputes which affected "the vital interests, independence, or honor of the contracting parties," as well as disputes involving third parties.[87] In other words, they barred U.S. intervention for pecuniary claims, so long as the matter was not complicated

[84] Third International Conference of American States, *Minutes, Resolutions, and Documents* (Rio de Janeiro, 1907), pp. 131–32.

[85] Mecham, *Inter-American Security*, p. 71. The countries with whom treaties were signed were Mexico, Peru, El Salvador, Costa Rica, Ecuador, and Haiti.

[86] Challenger, III: 182.

[87] Mecham, *Inter-American Security*, p. 71.

by the danger of extrahemispheric involvement. And in 1909 Root still emphasized the protection of the canal as the irreducible goal of American policy. Shortly before leaving office he wrote to his friend Dr. Lyman Abbott, "In that region (the Caribbean) the United States must exercise a dominant influence. It is there that the true justification and necessity for the Monroe doctrine (sic) is found. We must control the route to the Panama Canal."[88]

### Rooseveltian Policy without Roosevelt

The Taft administration, which replaced the imagination of Elihu Root with the intellectual desolation of Philander C. Knox, is usually distinguished by its adherence to a policy somewhat loosely labeled "dollar diplomacy." It is not intended here to carry on a step-by-step analysis of the multiplicity of mistakes that led to limited interventions in the Dominican Republic and Nicaragua, but only to indicate the changing strategic context and the failure of cooperative peace-keeping methods which lend to those interventions an aura of inevitability.

Just as the combination of political feasibility and technological capability drastically altered military thinking and strategic concepts at the turn of the century, so strategic thought continued to alter American perceptions of where her vital interests lay as the first decade of the century came to a close. As has been noted, the enthusiastic demand of the navalists for overseas bases rested in large part upon the problems of fuel supply and maintenance for the coal-consuming capital ships. The strategists had usually followed Mahan in the belief that the fleet needed fixed land bases where supplies of coal could be stored. One of the less heralded effects of the voyage of the White Fleet around the world was to call this necessity of fixed bases into question. In the judgment of the Joint Board, the world cruise demonstrated that the American fleet had a much greater power of self-maintenance than had been previously anticipated.[89] In 1909 estimates of cruising radius and coal endurance were apparently revised upwards.[90] And as early as 1907 it had begun to be argued that refueling at sea by the use of specially designed colliers might be an alternative to fixed land

[88] Root Papers, Library of Congress, Box 304. Quoted in Munro, *Intervention and Dollar Diplomacy*, p. 113.

[89] Challenger, I: 44.

[90] According to Challenger's notes, in 1909 the General Board reduced the estimated time required for mounting a Far Eastern campaign from four months to seventy-five days. The revision was based upon a somewhat belated analysis of the world cruise of the White Fleet. Since there had been no change in ship design and the canal had not yet been opened, the only possible conclusion is that the Board had decided that a ship going from the Atlantic to the Pacific would have to make fewer stops.

bases.[91] Finally the formation of the Joint Board and the National Coastal Defense Board diluted the naval monopoly upon strategy formulation with the army's point of view. One product of this admixture was a series of recommendations that the Panama Canal could be defended by fortifying the termini.[92] Quite naturally this new strategy led to a reduction of base requirements in the immediate vicinity of the canal.

It is impossible to tell, however, just how much of the navy's decreased interest in naval bases was simply a reflection of political feasibility. The Taft administration had to contend with a growing Progressive bloc in the Congress that was not noted for the enthusiasm with which it received naval bills; and after 1910 the Democratic party even controlled the House. Nevertheless, Taft attempted to carry on the naval policies of his predecessor. The new president's policy of naval expansion was based upon the vague notion that it was necessary to keep pace with the Anglo–German naval race, then going full-steam across the Atlantic.[93] The President's justification for this rivalry was that the European navies constituted a threat to the continental United States and the Panama Canal. Indeed, the approaching completion of the canal was a compelling argument for developing an adequate system of naval bases in the West Indies; and the secretary of the navy, George von Lengerke Meyer, strove mightily— though to little avail—for just that purpose.[94] "By 1909, it was decided that the best site was Guantanamo Bay on the southeast coast of Cuba. With a well equipped station at Guantanamo, the American fleet could command all the passages into the Caribbean and the Gulf of Mexico."[95] The failure of the Congress to vote sufficient funds for the development of Guantanamo resulted in an attempt to transfer some of the existing equipment from Gulf coast bases at Pensacola and New Orleans. The result was a congressional reaction by Gulf state representatives that effectively wrecked plans for building up Guantanamo.[96]

At the same time, the prospective opening of the canal increased fears of European intervention. Admiral Dewey was particularly concerned that the opening of the canal would stimulate a German attempt to gain a foothold in the Caribbean.[97] The Germans had been particularly active in Haiti, where they were beginning to play a large role in the commercial and financial affairs of the country.[98] This presented a twofold threat to American security. In the first place, the perennial defaults of the Haitian govern-

[91] Challenger, I: 43.
[92] Ibid., I: 42.
[93] Sprout, American Naval Power, pp. 288–89.
[94] Ibid., pp. 293–99.
[95] Ibid., p. 229.
[96] Ibid.
[97] Challenger, I: 46.
[98] Munro, Intervention and Dollar Diplomacy, pp. 245–58.

ment could lead to German intervention; and, more importantly, coaling stations established for commercial ships could, in time of war, be converted to military purposes.

The navy's answer to the problem was to devise an economy program that seemed to offer the best of all possible worlds. They developed the so-called "advanced base" concept or, quite simply, the idea that the navy should be prepared to seize advanced operational bases at the opening stages of any war. The most important of these plans for the defense of the eastern seaboard and, particularly, of the Caribbean area was the plan for seizure of the island of Hispaniola or the Haiti–Santo Domingo Plan.[99] The "Hi–Sd" plan was premised upon the same assumption as earlier color plans: that Germany would be the enemy and that she would move first against the Caribbean. In order to forestall a German seizure of key bases in Hispaniola, the first move of the navy in the event of hostilities would be a preemptory seizure of those points. A fully equipped striking force of marines was stationed at League Island in Philadelphia with a standing three-month supply of rations. Through the instrumentality of the Joint Board, the Hi–Sd plan was coordinated with proposed army operations. It was agreed that the navy would be responsible for the initial seizure, but that within thirty days the army would provide the permanent occupation forces.[100]

What is notable about the Hi–Sd plan is that it completely ignored U.S. obligations under international law. The discussion by the General Staff of this point and the possibility that such an unlawful invasion of Hispaniola might engender active hostility on the part of the islanders elicited the candid position of the General Board that the necessity of an advanced base in the event of hostilities overrode all other considerations.[101] Second, the navy's later enthusiastic support of the negotiations for the Dutch West Indies indicates that the advanced base concept was no more than a stop-gap measure in recognition of the domestic political barriers to preferable alternatives. The great irony of this new strategical development is that the "peaceful" inclinations of the Progressive bloc had forced the navy into its most belligerent position to date. Indeed, the Hi–Sd plan is rivaled in its disregard for legal norms of international behavior only by the German Schlieffen Plan, which has been so-much decried for its disregard of Belgian neutrality.

But what did these new strategic concepts mean for the sensitivity of various Caribbean countries? In the first place, the plan was a form of

[99] Challenger, loose notes on naval war plans.
[100] Challenger, I: 48.
[101] *Ibid.*

"perimeter defense" which could not help but increase the importance of Haiti, the Dominican Republic, and Le Mole St. Nicolas. Control of the Bahia de Guantanamo, even with an underdeveloped base, could give the United States domination of the Windward Passage so long as there was no European lodgment in Hispaniola. In the absence of such lodgment the only immediate danger was British installations in Jamaica and in Andros Island. But by 1909 Anglo–American relations had so improved that this aspect was apparently not even considered by the strategists. The other area of increased sensitivity was, of course, Central America. The decision for terminal fortifications was premised upon naval control of the Caribbean by defense at the Windward Passage entrance. Enemy lodgment in Central America would outflank that defense and render it meaningless.

Any discussion of the approach of the Taft administration to the problems of protecting American security interests in Central America and the Caribbean must be prefaced by a common understanding of what the policy of "dollar diplomacy" really was. In recent years too little attention has been given to what alternatives were available to Taft and Knox when they initiated State Department support of American financiers in the Caribbean. To look first at Central America, it is necessary to remember the distinction between the two kinds of problems that were faced in that area. *Intra*regional security took first priority. As long as the major Central American governments were intent upon crushing or subverting each other, political and economic stability in the region was unattainable. Root's plans for regional organization of the Central American states were directed toward the solution of this first problem. But the whole structure that revolved around the Central American Court was in no way competent to "confront threats from any non-Central American source."[102] And the perennial financial difficulties of the individual states and the threat of foreign intervention which those difficulties created remained untouched by Root. In other words, intraregional security was necessary to, but not sufficient for, the protection of U.S. security interests.

To shore up governments in financial straits, Taft had two logical courses of action: (1) he could support them with direct capital transfers or (2) he could attempt to stimulate private capital to enter the area. The first alternative was no more politically possible for Taft than it would be for Wilson and Bryan a few years later. The second alternative was in itself no small job, since the attractiveness of domestic investment precluded the necessary profit incentives for Wall Street financiers. The high risks involved in Latin American investment naturally inclined companies, such as J. P. Morgan and Company, to seek interest rates which were high enough

---

[102] Mecham, *Inter-American Security*, p. 69.

to allow quicker amortization, whereas State Department participation meant that a more lenient attitude would have to be taken toward the borrowing governments.[103] Some State Department representatives have even gone so far as to say that an appeal to "patriotic duty" was usually necessary to secure the loans.[104] In any case, loans and customs receiverships—which had resulted in apparent success in the Dominican Republic —were the only choice that the Taft administration had, except the third alternative of armed intervention and occupation. And "to Taft, using dollars instead of bullets seemed humane and practical."[105]

Nor did Taft's dollar diplomacy have a great deal to do with the eventual collapse of the Central American Court. As we have pointed out in the previous chapter, the inadequacies of the system were so great that only the informal participation of the United States and Mexico had made it workable in the beginning. In March 1909 American and Mexican warships were still stationed off the coast of Nicaragua to preserve the enforced peace.[106] Realizing that the informal system was apt to breakdown, Secretary Knox was anxious to formalize Mexican–American participation in the Central American system. On March 26 he proposed to the Mexican ambassador a new treaty that would not only guarantee Mexican–American support of Honduran neutrality but the participation of both countries in the Central American Court.[107] Second, he sounded out Mexico concerning a plan of mutual financing that would have been equivalent to joint dollar diplomacy.[108] Mexico, however, would have no part of such an arrangement. In the following year the *Porfirato* in Mexico was eliminated by the beginnings of the civil war which was to convulse the country until World War I, and the United States was left as the sole sponsor of the Central American arrangement. The main competition in the area came from the Nicaraguan dictator Zelaya, who seemed as determined as ever to dominate all of Central America. "Nor did reports of Zelaya's plans to make secret advances to Japan for a canal treaty ingratiate the dictator with the United States Government."[109]

In 1909, however, Zelaya was overthrown by a revolution at Bluefields. During the actual fighting U.S. troops intervened to protect American life and property, and there can be little doubt that the intervention favored

---

[103] Munro, *Intervention and Dollar Diplomacy*, p. 164.

[104] *Ibid.*

[105] *Ibid.*, p. 163.

[106] *Ibid.*, p. 166.

[107] *Ibid.*

[108] *Ibid.* That Knox should make such a proposal argues very strongly against the position that dollar diplomacy was designed to benefit American bankers—a point which Munro apparently overlooks.

[109] Bemis, *Latin American Policy*, p. 162.

the anti-Zelaya faction.[110] But there is little evidence that the United States had anything to do with the outbreak of hostilities.[111] After the usual game of "musical presidents," Adolfo Diaz, a former employee of the United States–Nicaragua Concession, emerged victorious and was recognized by the United States. A treaty (the Knox–Castrillo Convention), similar in most respects to the 1907 treaty which established the Dominican customs receivership, was quickly negotiated.[112] An arrangement was made with New York bankers to refund the Nicaraguan debt—most of which was in the hands of English and French syndicates. But further revolution finally brought a request for intervention from Diaz, and the American marines came in 2,700 strong.[113] It is difficult to see how the United States could have acted otherwise. The New York bankers had begun their operations at the express request of the State Department, and the only alternatives to Diaz were followers of Zelaya. The intervention, however, solved very little; it was "barely adequate to maintain elected governments in power and thus keep the pledged finances in order."[114]

The problem of adequate finances still remained; and with the government of Nicaragua almost in default, it was hardly a propitious time to go begging to Wall Street. At the same time, there were rumors of German and Japanese interests in a Nicaraguan waterway.[115] Knox attempted to kill two birds with one stone and negotiated a treaty for $3,000,000 that would have given the United States exclusive rights to any waterway, a naval base on the Gulf of Fronseca, and a lease on the Great Corn and Little Corn Islands. This was a stop-gap measure, at best; and it could not even be negotiated quickly enough to be considered by the Senate. But it was to be revived by Wilson and to become known as the Bryan–Chamorro Treaty.

With varying success, the Taft formula for financial reorganization was repeated in Honduras, the Dominican Republic, and Haiti. But it was really successful nowhere. From its initiation it was never anything more than a second-best alternative to intervention. Strategy determined the location of American security interests, and a due regard for the integrity of national sovereignty placed untenable restrictions upon the protection of those security interests. Taft and Knox, like Root, had sought limited intervention through the control of Latin American finances, because the financial difficulties of the Latin American governments were the most

---

[110] *Ibid.*
[111] Munro, *Intervention and Dollar Diplomacy*, pp. 174–75.
[112] *Foreign Relations, 1912*, pp. 1074–75.
[113] Bemis, *Latin American Policy*, pp. 163–64.
[114] *Ibid.*, p. 164.
[115] *Ibid.*, and Munro, *Intervention and Dollar Diplomacy*, p. 214.

probable stimulus for foreign intervention. The most striking fact about American intervention of any degree was that it was limited to those areas in which strategy dictated that U.S. security interests were to be found. The Monroe Doctrine was invoked with respect to South America in only three cases in the first decade of the 1900's: in Venezuela, when Anglo–German occupation was threatened; in Colombia, with an eye toward the Isthmus of Panama; and in Ecuador, when transfer of the Galapagos Islands was feared.[116] "In general it was assumed either that the countries of southern South America were not exposed to European intervention or conquest, or that they were capable of taking care of themselves. The Monroe Doctrine was still a defense device limited mainly to the Caribbean danger zone."[117] The administration of Woodrow Wilson was to demonstrate just how compelling the maintenance of the "defense device" could be.

### "Liberal" Intervention: Roosevelt Policy a la Wilson

It was reasonable for Latin American observers in 1913 to expect that the arrival of this "new kind of President" on the American scene presaged radical alterations in the Latin American policy of the United States. Although Woodrow Wilson had been relatively silent on the subject, his secretary of state, William Jennings Bryan, had loudly condemned the dollar diplomacy and military intervention of the Taft administration.[118] As early as March 1913 the new President had announced to the press his intention of revising U.S. policy in Latin America: "The United States has nothing to seek in Central and South America except the lasting interests of the people of the two continents, the security of governments, intended for the people, and for no special group or interest, and the development of personal and trade relationships between the two continents, which shall redound to the profit and advantage of both and interfere with the rights and liberties of neither."[119] A new approach to Latin American relations was evident almost immediately. One of the early acts of the new administration was to open negotiations with the Colombian government for settlement of differences deriving from the Panamanian separation.[120] An indemnity of $25,000,000 was settled upon, and the American government expressed its "sincere regret" to Colombia over the

---

[116] J. Fred Rippy, South America and Hemisphere Defense (Baton Rouge: Louisiana State University Press, 1941), p. 8.
[117] Ibid., p. 9.
[118] Arthur S. Link, Wilson: The New Freedom (Princeton: Princeton University Press, 1956), p. 319.
[119] New York Times, March 12, 1913. Quoted in Link, Wilson: New Freedom, p. 320.
[120] Link, Wilson: New Freedom, p. 321.

incident.[121] This was the administration that was to propose a new Pan-American pact which anticipated the Organization of American States. Yet this was also the administration that was to carry the Roosevelt policy of intervention farther than it had ever been carried before. In many ways the interventionist result of the Wilson policies derived from the excessive zeal of the Democratic Progressives for demonstrating to the "southern brethren" the multiple benefits of democracy and efficient self-government. But beneath this concern for "moral politics" was a continuation by other means of the defense strategy of the United States. As we have attempted to demonstrate, the political expression of these strategic interests was the Monroe Doctrine and its Roosevelt Corollary. And in reality Wilson and Bryan never intended the repudiation of these policies; "rather they strove to strengthen influence and control in these regions (in the Caribbean) in order to remove further than ever justification for any European intervention."[122]

The Wilson administration intervened in Haiti, the Dominican Republic, Nicaragua, and Mexico. But the stories of those interventions are remarkably similar. The recurring tale has been described by Arthur Link as: "one of men with noble motives being lured on by their own good intentions and sometimes by foolish or interested advisers, being influenced by subtle pressures and subconscious motivations that they did not recognize, and finally being trapped by events that they could not control. In short, it is a tale of what happened when evangels of democracy set out to teach other peoples how to elect good leaders and govern themselves well."[123] Also, the intensification of American intervention in Caribbean political life represented no change in the strategic context which Wilson inherited from Taft, though the increased perception of the German threat brought on by the outbreak of war in Europe seems to have weighed heavily in the Dominican case[124] and to have, in fact, triggered the armed interventions in Haiti.[125] The strategic importance of Mexico has not been previously discussed, but the fact of its contiguity to the United States makes such a discussion unnecessary.[126] In this chapter we will focus

[121] *Foreign Relations, 1914*, p. 163.

[122] Bemis, *Latin American Policy*, p. 185.

[123] Arthur S. Link, *Wilson: The Struggle for Neutrality, 1914–1915* (Princeton: Princeton University Press, 1960), p. 496.

[124] See Link, *Wilson: Struggle for Neutrality*, pp. 496–516; and Munro, *Intervention and Dollar Diplomacy*, pp. 269–325.

[125] Link, *Wilson: Struggle for Neutrality*, pp. 516–38; and Munro, *Intervention and Dollar Diplomacy*, pp. 326–87.

[126] The works cited by Arthur Link contain discussions of Wilson's policies in Mexico from Wilson's point of view. For a more balanced account which is also less favorable to Wilson, see Howard F. Cline, *The United States and Mexico* (rev. ed.; New York: Atheneum, 1965), pp. 135–88.

instead upon the failure and ultimate collapse of the two main alternatives to the intervention policy: the Pan-American Pact and the Central American Court.

## PAN AMERICAN PACT—Revised Draft

### ARTICLE I

That the high contracting parties to this solemn covenant and agreement hereby join one another in a common and mutual guaranty of territorial integrity and of political independence under republican forms of government.

### ARTICLE II

To give definitive application to the guaranty set forth in Article I, the high contracting parties severally covenant to endeavor forthwith to reach a settlement of all disputes as to boundaries or territory now pending between them by amicable aggreement or by means of international arbitration.

### ARTICLE III

That the high contracting parties further agree, First, that all questions, of whatever character, arising between any two or more of them which cannot be settled by the ordinary means of diplomatic correspondence shall, before any declaration of war or beginning of hostilities, be first submitted to a permanent international commission for investigation, one year allowed for such investigation; and, Second, that if the dispute is not settled by investigation, to submit the same to arbitration, provided the question in dispute does not affect the honor, independence, or vital interests of the nations concerned or the interests of third parties.

### ARTICLE IV

To the end that domestic tranquility may prevail within their territories, the high contracting parties further severally covenant and agree that they will not permit the departure from their respective jurisdictions of any military or naval expedition hostile to the established government of any of the high contracting parties, and that they will prevent the exportation from their respective jurisdictions of arms, ammunition, or other munitions of war destined to or for the use of any person or persons notified to be in insurrection or revolt against the established government of any of the high contracting parties.

*Source:* Charles Seymour, *The Intimate Papers of Colonel House*, 4 vols. (New York: Houghton Mifflin Company, 1926), I: 233–34.

The Pan-American Pact, which is reproduced above in its final form, began as a plan to multilateralize the Monroe Doctrine. It was, at first, an attempt to replace U.S.–Mexican cooperation with the hemispherewide

cooperation of the ABC powers (Argentina, Brazil, and Chile.)[127] But
the Pact eventually evolved into a plan designed to include all of the nations
of Latin America. Bryan did not enter the negotiations until Colonel House,
the apparent originator of the plan, had left for Europe in January 1915;
but Article III of the final draft evidences concern with extending the
principle of the Bryan "cooling off" treaties to intra-Latin American relations.[128] Largely on the grounds of its comprehensive scope, the proposed
pact has been proclaimed by some writers as "the final proof that the
Wilson administration meant to abandon the Roosevelt–Taft policies of
intervention through force and 'dollar diplomacy.' "[129] But the correspondence between Wilson and Colonel House clearly indicates the
motivation of the negotiations from which the Pact derived as being a
desire to establish multinational machinery for intervention in Mexico.
Colonel House was given a free hand by Wilson in the original negotiations
with the ABC powers. In mid-January 1915 he reported to the President
on the progress of those negotiations. House's diary entry for that date
gives a clear view of the purpose of the Pact: " I suggested (to Wilson) that
the Mexican problem could best be solved now by calling in the A.B.C.
Powers and ourselves. The President thought this an excellent idea and
that it was merely a question of when to put it in operation. I offered to see
the Ambassadors to-morrow if he thought well of it. He believed this
would be too soon, for conditions were not quite ready in Mexico for such
a move, and he was afraid the A.B.C. Ambassadors would not want to
move so quickly."[130]

Essentially this new approach to insuring stability in the security-sensi-
tive areas of Latin America was a consequence of the added flexibility that
was possible for American policy so long as the European powers were
engaged in war. House indicated this consideration in a letter written to
Wilson from Paris in March.[131] He encouraged Wilson to push ahead the
plans with the ABC powers as quickly as possible so that order might be
restored in Mexico. This, he said, should be done before the war ends,
because afterwards "the belligerent Governments will become insistent
that order be restored there."[132]

[127] Charles Seymour, *The Intimate Papers of Colonel House*, 4 vols. (New York:
Houghton Mifflin Company, 1926), I: 203.

[128] Mecham, *Inter-American Security*, p. 74. By 1914 the United States had entered
into such treaties with eleven Latin American nations. Yet, the failure of the Latin
American countries to ratify the Treaty for Arbitration of Pecuniary Claims and the
continuing Central American conflicts indicated that the real necessity was for treaties of
compulsory arbitration between the Latin American states themselves.

[129] Link, *Wilson: New Freedom* p. 324.

[130] Seymour, *Colonel House*, p. 219.

[131] *Ibid.*, p. 220.

[132] *Ibid.*

The main opposition in this first stage of the negotiations came from Chile, who, because of boundary disputes with Peru, was unwilling to assure "territorial integrity" or arbitration. This had been the Chilean position during the International Conferences of American States prior to World War I.[133] The enlargement of the Pact to include the smaller states came as the result of an attempt to defeat Chilean opposition. House was again responsible for the tactic. He decided that if Chile continued to obstruct the attempt the United States should "go ahead without her." "The smaller republics would agree and, with Argentina and Brazil, it made but little difference whether Chile came in or remained out."[134] In the end, however, the Chilean delay proved fatal. On March 8, 1916, Pancho Villa, Mexico's "liberal patriot"—who also happened to be in revolt against Carranza—crossed the American border and murdered seventeen American citizens. A punitive expedition under Pershing crossed into Mexico in pursuit, and before many days had passed the two nations were verging on war. Needless to say, the American intervention did not promote the cause of inter-American solidarity. The pact was retired for a few months, only to be abandoned entirely with America's entry into the war.

There is always some hesitancy to belittle such idealistic attempts at alternatives to the intervention policy, but there may be good reason to be thankful that the Pan-American Pact never saw the official light of day. It was more a statement of intentions than a system of regional security, and it is doubtful that internal political conditions in the Caribbean and Central American countries would have been dramatically altered by good intentions. Even if the multilateral support of the ABC powers could have been mustered for interventions in Mexico, Haiti, the Dominican Republic, and Nicaragua, the commitment to preserve territorial integrity could probably not have been maintained. Revolutions— and the financial difficulties which accompanied them—were not the result of the unilateral use of American military power; they were part of the internal politics of the countries involved. At the Second Pan-American Scientific Conference, where Wilson publicly unveiled the proposed pact, there were some who recognized the necessity for intervention. Speaking the day before Wilson, John Foster Dulles proposed the establishment of a system of multilateral intervention.[135] His idea was to exclude non-American states from involvement in Caribbean problems by setting up a "quasi-trustee" arrangement on a multilateral basis. His proposal was no more acceptable then than it was in the 1960's, when a very similar proposal by the United States was rejected by the Latin American members of the Organization of American

---

[133] Mecham, *Inter-American Security*, pp. 48–76.
[134] Seymour, *Colonel House*, p. 222.
[135] Whitaker, *Western Hemisphere Idea*, p. 4.

States. The simple fact—then and now—is that Nicaraguan, Haitian, or Dominican nationalists find an occupation force of multilateral composition no more acceptable than one made up of American marines.

The basic weakness of the Pan-American Pact was its failure to recognize that where the vital interests of the United States were perceived to be involved, there was no substitute for the protection of those interests with military power. And, as we have pointed out several times, the protection of vital American security interests in the first two decades of the twentieth century was perceived to require American supremacy in the Western Hemisphere. The conflict involved in Wilson's espousal of the Pan-American ideal was probably best articulated by Secretary of State Lansing in a memorandum written in June 1914:

> The Monroe Doctrine should not be confused with Pan-Americanism. It is purely a national policy of the United States, while Pan-Americanism is the joint policy of the American group of nations. . . . In its advocacy of the Monroe Doctrine the United States considers its own interests. The integrity of other American nations is an incident, not an end. . . . The primacy of one nation, though possessing the superior physical might to maintain it, is out of harmony with the principle of the equality of nations which underlies Pan-Americanism, however just or altruistic the primate may be. . . . (When) therefore, the Monroe Doctrine and Pan-Americanism may come into conflict, the Monroe Doctrine will in case of conflict prevail so long as the United States maintains the Doctrine and is the dominant power among the American nations. The equality of American republics and, in a measure, their independence are legal rather than actual.[136]

But Wilson and Bryan "never thought of choosing between perpetuating or ending American supremacy in the approaches to the Panama Canal. They thought only of choosing the most effective methods and instruments to maintain the basic American foreign policy."[137]

It was American intervention in Mexico—without benefit of an internationalist framework—that finally signaled the death of the Pan-American Pact; and no consideration of Wilsonian policy would be complete without some discussion of the proverbial topic of "Wilson and Mexico." In general, the mountains of literature generated by American intervention in Mexico has served mostly to obscure the issue. But most major authorities seem to agree that the Wilsonian venture into the question of constitutional legitimacy as a test for recognition resulted primarily from a personalized moral quirk of a man who tried to do too much with a

---

[136] Robert Lansing, "Memorandum by the Counselor for the Department of State," dated June 11, 1914. Quoted in Link, *Wilson: New Freedom*, p. 328.
[137] Link, *Wilson: New Freedom*, p. 329.

portable typewriter.[138] The concept of nonrecognition of "unconstitutional" governments was not an original Wilson creation. It had already been tried without notable success in the Central American treaties. What Wilson added to the formula was a sort of subjectivistic moralism—which is another way of saying expedient manipulation. For the warring Mexican factions, after 1911, U.S. recognition meant quite simply the availability of arms. Hence, the "legitimate" government in Mexico could very nearly be decided in Washington. Wilson mercilessly attempted to use this lever to depose the de facto regime of Victoriano Huerta and later to exact favorable concessions from the successor regime of Venustiano Carranza. This the President did over the loud protestations of his advisers—most notably Ambassador Henry Lane Wilson—whom the President considered pawns of perfidious Wall Street. The patent failure of Wilson's efforts finally returned the selective recognition policy to its appropriate idealogical pigeonhole, and the whole episode is most easily understood as an unfortunate display of overzealous populism.

The military excursions into Mexican territory are somewhat more complex and deserve further consideration. As already noted, the Pershing expedition of 1916 was a direct reaction to the invasion of American territory by the bandit Villa. Mexico at this time was in a state of utter chaos, there was no Mexican constabulary capable or remotely willing to attempt to control such invasions, and the Pershing expedition was the only available method of protecting American citizens living in New Mexico. The 1914 landing of American marines at Veracruz, however, was directly related to an American attempt to prevent German arms from reaching Huerta.[139] The port of Tampico was a major oil refining center, important to both sides of the civil war then raging in Mexico. It was no less important to the British and other Europeans who owned the great majority of the facilities. When a large-scale battle seemed imminent in April 1914, "British, French, German, and even Spanish war vessels converged to protect the threatened interests of their nationals."[140] Wilson, in turn, "had the Navy outnumber and outgun the combined European units there."[141] With the atmosphere tense, several American sailors and one officer were arrested by Huerta's men in the port. They were soon released; but a strong American demand for amends, designed primarily to embarrass Huerta, followed. The give and take over the American demands for redress soon reached the cabinet level, but before action could

---

[138] For example, see discussion of Wilsonian Latin American policy in Cline, *United States and Mexico*, pp. 135–87.
[139] Hubert Herring, *A History of Latin America* (2nd ed. rev.; New York: Alfred A. Knopf, 1961), p. 358.
[140] Cline, *United States and Mexico*, p. 155.
[141] *Ibid.*

be taken, word reached Washington that a large shipment of German arms was on its way to Veracruz. The occupation of Veracruz, therefore, became the logical way to enforce demands for redress by the authorities at Tampico.[142] Veracruz was then taken on April 21, with the loss of 19 American lives and over 300 Mexican lives.

Within three days after the occupation of Veracruz the ABC powers (Argentina, Chile, and Brazil) finally offered to mediate the problems outstanding between the United States and Mexico. The United States accepted the offer of mediation; but Wilson, in effect, merely reactivated the old idea behind the Pan-American Pact—to use a multilateral organ as a cover for his own attempt to control Mexican politics. He continually delayed the beginning of the Niagara Mediation Conference, while aiding Carranza.[143] In August 1914 Wilson's policies seemingly paid off—Carranza's Constitutionalists took Mexico City, and Huerta left for exile in France.

The entire history of U.S. relations with Mexico during the Wilson administration seems to reflect the idiosyncrasies of the man. But even here the standard preoccupation with hemispheric security was not absent. "One sinister aspect of the Mexican problem was the German effort to take advantage of the civil wars to make trouble for the United States."[144] It was a shipment of German arms to Huerta that touched off the occupation of Veracruz, and as late as 1915 the Germans were still trying to help Huerta organize an invasion of Mexico from American territory. Finally in 1917 German efforts culminated in the Zimmermann telegram.[145] Wilson's antipathy for Huerta is no doubt best explained by the well-known streak of self-righteousness that was to continue to dominate Wilson's political style, but, notably, even the professionals in the War Department and the Department of State did not oppose him. Opposition to Huerta was a point upon which everyone seemed to agree. The simple fact was that the United States—quite apart from the peculiarity of its President's moral predispositions—could not tolerate an unfriendly government in Mexico with war clouds gathering in Europe.

After the abortive Niagara Conference, Wilson's test of "constitutional legitimacy" was left far behind, and the more basic strategic considerations became ever more apparent in U.S.–Mexican relations. During the period leading to and during World War I, the United States walked a thin policy line between the necessity for neutralizing German and anti-American activity in Mexico and the impossibility of committing a large number of

[142] *Ibid.*, p. 160.
[143] *Ibid.*, p. 161.
[144] Munro, *Intervention and Dollar Diplomacy*, p. 290.
[145] *Ibid.*

troops there so long as the German threat loomed to the east. The main demand that the United States had to make of Mexico was stability, and it mattered little whether stability came from Carranza, Obregon, or any other leader who could gain and maintain control. When the Carranza–Obregon alliance settled this question once and for all, U.S. efforts were reduced to withdrawing the troops as quietly and as quickly as possible. When war came, Mexico was certainly no friend of the United States. Carranza exploited the situation fully to obtain a number of concessions from both the U.S. government and from U.S. companies operating in Mexico, who suddenly found themselves without diplomatic support against a tax-hungry government. But if the Mexicans were not friends they were not enemies either, and that was the minimum goal of American policy. Once fully commited to the European war the United States was unable to do more than simply pay Carranza off and hope to maintain the Mexican situation in relative tranquillity.

But the Pan-American Pact and the "legitimacy" policy by no means exhausted the inventiveness of the new administration. Bryan, the new secretary of state, remained particularly creative. With an eye toward Nicaragua, Bryan came up with a plan for jettisoning the dollar diplomacy and eliminating foreign creditors from the Caribbean at the same time. With a characteristically biblical flair Bryan suggested that the United States should be a "modern Good Samaritan" and cure the Latin American financial ills with the potent medicine of direct transfers.[146] The United States could raise money by selling its own bonds at 3 percent and lend to the Latin Americans at 4½ percent. The profit from this transaction would go into the sinking fund that would help pay the debt of the borrowing countries. In this way the Latin Americans would be relieved of plaguing foreign debt. But the real advantage of this method, according to Bryan, was that "the plan would give our country such an increased influence . . . that we could prevent revolutions, promote education, and advance stable and just government."[147] In other words, even Bryan was interested in keeping a firm hand on Latin American affairs.

But the government loan plan did not quite satisfy Bryan's newly acquired imperialistic tastes. In conjunction with the Good Samaritan policy Bryan proposed an extension of the Monroe Doctrine. In 1913 Bryan urged President Wilson to promulgate a new corollary to the Doctrine which would "give the United States the power to pass upon the actions of foreign residents and corporations in Latin America."[148] With a

---

[146] Bemis, *Latin American Policy*, p. 186.
[147] *Ibid.*
[148] Selig Adler, "Bryan and Wilsonian Caribbean Penetration," *Hispanic American Historical Review* 20 (May 1940): 211.

realistic eye toward the domestic political situation, Wilson vetoed both ideas, saying that he feared that it would "strike the whole country . . . as a novel and radical proposal."[149] "I think for the present," he continued, "there are enough difficult questions on the carpet, particularly with regard to our foreign relations."[150]

Wilson's rejection of Bryan's loan plan marked the last attempt to reconcile the dictates of American defense strategy with "progressive" principles. Bryan resorted to backing a revised version of the Knox–Castrillo convention that would have given an option on a Nicaraguan canal route and naval bases on the Great Corn and Little Corn Islands and on the Gulf of Fronseca. "Revised," however, meant two new articles that would have given the United States an almost total domination of Nicaraguan affairs. Article IV of the new treaty stipulated that Nicaragua should never conclude "any treaty or other compact with any foreign power or powers which will impair or tend to impair the independence of Nicaragua, nor in any manner authorize or permit any foreign power or powers to obtain by colonization or for military or naval purposes, or otherwise, lodgment in or control over any portion of said Republic."[151] Article VI was a direct descendant of the Platt Amendment and read as follows: "The Government of Nicaragua consents that the United States may exercise the right to intervene for the preservation of Nicaraguan independence, the maintenance of a government adequate for the protection of life, property, and individual liberty and for discharging any obligations which it may assume or contract in accordance with the provisions of Article IV above."[152] This was the treaty which was described by one of Bryan's fellow Nebraskans in the Senate as making dollar diplomacy look "like the proverbial 30 cents."[153]

Before continuing the story of the negotiations with Nicaragua, it is legitimate to confront the question of the reasons for Bryan's seeming conversion to an "imperialist" position, in order to ascertain just how important a role security considerations played. In the first place, Bryan, even in the heyday of progressivism in Nebraska, "had made coaling stations and naval bases an exception to his anti-expansionist philosophy."[154] Once he arrived at the State Department it was inevitable that his endemic patriotism should be reinforced by the members of the Depart-

---

[149] Wilson to Bryan, March 20, 1914. Quoted in Adler, "Bryan," p. 218.
[150] *Ibid.*
[151] Draft of a Nicaraguan treaty, sent to Bryan on June 11, 1913, by C. A. Douglas, MS. in the State Department Papers, Quoted in Link, *Wilson: New Freedom*, p. 333.
[152] *Ibid.*
[153] George W. Norris in the New York *World*, August 3, 1913. Quoted in Link, *Wilson: New Freedom*, p. 337.
[154] Adler, "Bryan," p. 204.

ment who had worked with the difficult problems of Caribbean politics for many years. Bryan's lack of experience in foreign affairs forced him to rely heavily upon the Division of Latin American Affairs of the State Department, which was staffed by ex-naval officers and hardened career diplomats. Four years experience under the Taft administration had produced in this group an attitude which was "traditional, realistic, and devoted to the well-established precedent of government protection of American capital abroad."[155] The growing crisis in Europe undoubtedly played its role in convincing Bryan that European aggression was threatening the Monroe Doctrine in the Caribbean.[156]

But whatever the background of his concern with American security in the Caribbean, it is unquestionable that security considerations were paramount in Bryan's mind when he presented his proposed treaty to the Senate. In July 1914, while the Foreign Relations Committee was considering the treaty, Bryan forwarded a memorandum for the Committee's perusal: "As long as the canal route is upon the market for sale, we shall be continually disturbed by the reports, even if they be without foundation, that other governments are trying to secure the right to build a canal along the Nicaraguan route. We have recently learned of (German) efforts being made to dissuade the Nicaraguan Government from selling to the United States, on the ground that the option would bring a higher price in Europe than we have offered to pay."[157] Bryan also submitted testimony by Admiral Dewey and the General Boards to the effect that the planned naval base on Fronseca Bay would greatly add to the defense of the Panama Canal.[158] Finally, in discussing with Wilson the manner in which the $3,000,000 to be paid for the canal option should be spent, Bryan admitted, "As I am more interested in the securing of the option and the naval base than I am in the manner in which the money is spent, I would not regard the change (in the manner of expenditure) as vital."[159]

The Democratic Congress that had come into office with Wilson and Bryan balked at the Platt Amendment clauses in the new treaty, and for a time it appeared as if the whole project might be dropped. Bryan, realizing that the financial benefits of the canal treaty might come too late for the Diaz government in Nicaragua, resorted to the hated methods of his predecessors and went, hat in hand, to Wall Street. A new contract was negotiated between Nicaragua and Brown Brothers and Seligman and

---

[155] *Ibid.*, p. 203.
[156] *Ibid.*
[157] W. J. Bryan to W. J. Stone, July 2, 1914, enclosing "Memorandum. Presented by Mr. Bryan before the Foreign Relations Committee of the Senate," State Department Papers. Quoted in Link, *Wilson: New Freedom*, p. 335.
[158] *Ibid.*
[159] Quoted in Link, *Wilson: New Freedom*, p. 334.

Company, and the Nicaraguans were again saved from default. But in May 1914 a report arrived that the German charge d'affaires in Managua had proposed to Diaz to pay more than $3,000,000 for the option on the canal route.[160] This report immediately stirred Bryan and Wilson to action. Opposition to the Platt Amendment clauses proved so great that Bryan was forced to negotiate another treaty with the Nicaraguan minister in Washington, Emiliano Chamorro.[161] The Bryan–Chamorro Treaty was essentially a rewrite of the Knox–Castrillo convention. Nevertheless, it still proved too much for the Congress until February 1916, when the threat of war with Germany over the submarine issue hung heavily over the congressional heads. At that time fear of German activities in the Caribbean and Central American areas and new rumors of German attempts to purchase the Nicaraguan canal route combined with the expressed desire of the General Board for the Fronseca naval base to force passage of the treaty.[162]

"The strategic objectives of the United States were obligingly incorporated by the Diaz government in the Bryan–Chamorro Treaty of 1916."[163] The United States got the canal option, ninety-nine year leases on the Great and Little Corn Islands, and a naval base in the Gulf of Fronseca; the Nicaraguans got their somewhat belated $3,000,000. But if Nicaraguans were happy about the outcome of the treaty negotiations, almost no one else in Central America was. Based upon a multiplicity of grounds, protests came from Costa Rica, El Salvador, and even Colombia, who maintained a claim to the Great and Little Corn Islands.[164] Bryan made some attempt to placate Costa Rica and El Salvador, but held tenaciously to the naval base in the Gulf of Fronseca.[165] It was the specific claim of El Salvador that a base so close to one of her major ports threatened her autonomy. Bryan was successful in settling practically none of these claims, but it would seem that there was no way to meet El Salvador's objections. Finally in March and August 1916 Costa Rica and El Salvador appealed to the tottering Central American Court of Justice to declare the Bryan–Chamorro Treaty null and void. The Court's decisions, handed down in September 1916 and March 1917, did not declare the treaty null and void, but it did declare that Nicaragua had violated the rights of Costa Rica and El Salvador.[166] The Nicaraguan government had refused to appear at the

---

[160] *Ibid.*, p. 338.
[161] *Foreign Relations, 1916*, pp. 849–51.
[162] Link, *Wilson: New Freedom*, p. 340.
[163] Edwin Lieuwen, *U.S. Policy in Latin America: A Short History* (New York: Frederick A. Praeger, 1965), p. 45.
[164] *Foreign Relations, 1913*, pp. 1022, 1027, 1031–34.
[165] Munro, *Intervention and Dollar Diplomacy*, pp. 397–401.
[166] *Ibid.*, p. 403.

proceedings, arguing that the Court lacked jurisdiction; and when the Court handed down its ruling favorable to Costa Rica, Nicaragua withdrew its member from the Court in protest.[167] When the Court decided in favor of El Salvador a few months later, Nicaragua denounced the treaty under which the Court had been established. Shortly thereafter the regional peace structure disintegrated.[168]

Why Wilson and Lansing (Bryan resigned in July 1915 over European issues) pushed for the ratification of the Nicaraguan treaty, in spite of the intense opposition of the Central American republics, is not entirely clear. It may have been that "it seemed the only way to save Nicaragua from financial collapse and political chaos."[169] But the urgency of that salvation undoubtedly had a great deal to do with the intensification of German–American hostility in the closing months of 1915. Lansing had already made his views quite clear as to the priority of American security interests in the Caribbean and Central America,[170] and it is probable that he accepted the viewpoint that he had elicited from the General Board in November 1915. In reply to an inquiry from Lansing the General Board had indicated that a naval base in the Gulf of Fronseca would be useful. But in any case it was necessary to forestall any European attempt to establish a foothold in the vicinity of the Panama Canal.[171]

Nicaragua was by no means the only area in which the Wilson administration faced the necessity of choosing between American security interests and the territorial integrity of the Caribbean states. In Haiti and the Dominican Republic political and financial chaos combined with the threat of increased foreign influence to force ultimate armed intervention. But in these areas too the story was the same: strategy won over the best intentions. In the first months of office, Bryan "came to realize the strategic importance of Hispaniola, which lay between the two great trade routes linking the Atlantic side of the canal with important European and American ports."[172] He was particularly concerned lest the French or Germans acquire Le Mole St. Nicolas. In June 1913 he proposed to Wilson the American purchase of a twenty-mile-wide strip of land around the Mole "so as to give us not only the harbor but enough land around it to safeguard the harbor from land attack."[173] Bryan was unable to secure the desired strip of land, but he did secure a promise from the Haitian

---

[167] Link, *Wilson: New Freedom*, p. 345.
[168] Munro, *Intervention and Dollar Diplomacy*, pp. 397–401.
[169] *Ibid.*, p. 404.
[170] See above.
[171] *Ibid.*
[172] Adler, "Bryan," p. 221.
[173] Bryan to Wilson, June 20, 1913. Quoted in Adler, "Bryan," p. 221.

government that no territory would be alienated to a European power.[174] So far as the General Board of the Navy was concerned this was all that was necessary, since under the advanced base strategy the United States had no need of a stationary base on the Mole. This opinion was reiterated to Lansing in August 1915, when negotiations were under way for the Haitian Treaty of 1915.[175] The 1915 treaty, besides establishing a virtual semiprotectorate status for Haiti, contained a clause preventing territorial alienation to non-American powers.

*     *     *     *

By the time the United States severed relations with Germany on February 4, 1917, she was the possessor of five de facto protectorates in the Caribbean and Central American areas. Cuba and Haiti were under U.S. control by treaty arrangements, and the Canal Treaty implicitly placed Panama in the same position. Nicaragua and the Dominican Republic were actually under U.S. military occupation and could certainly not be said to have any autonomy in their foreign relations. Eight Latin American nations —Brazil, Cuba, Costa Rica, Guatemala, Haiti, Honduras, Nicaragua, and Panama—eventually declared war on Germany.[176] U.S. control of the Dominican Republic was so complete as to make belligerency status as much a de facto certainty as a formal declaration would have been a de jure absurdity. Costa Rica, Guatemala, and Honduras were not immune to U.S. diplomatic pressure and had a great deal to gain by taking this opportunity for seizure of German holdings in their territories. Brazil's declaration of war may have been a sign of continental solidarity,[177] but German investment in that country was undoubtedly an attractive compensation. Furthermore, favorable relations with the United States dating back to the mediation of the ABC powers in Mexico probably played an important role in the Brazilian decision. In general, however, it cannot be said that there were any serious attempts to establish a system of regional defense. The only real cooperation was between Brazil and the United States in the effort to control sporadic German attempts to initiate submarine warfare in the Caribbean.[178] "At that time, the concept of hemi-

[174] *Foreign Relations, 1914*, p. 340.
[175] The final text of the treaty will be found in *Foreign Relations of the United States, 1915*, pp. 449–51. The story of the negotiations for the treaty, including the role of the General Board, can be found in Munro, *Intervention and Dollar Diplomacy*, pp. 356–65.
[176] Mecham, *Inter-American Security*, p. 80.
[177] *Ibid.*, p. 82.
[178] *Ibid.*

sphere defense did not even exist, let alone the machinery to implement it."[179]

Just as American defense strategy had largely dictated her activities before the war, wartime strategy made no provision for any hemispheric cooperation in the war effort. The success of the British Admiralty in bottling up the German capital fleet in the North Sea meant that German naval strategy would be largely defensive. Even after America entered the war in 1917 there was never any danger of a German offensive in the Western Hemisphere. Germany's main effort was directed toward disruption of Allied shipping in the Atlantic by means of submarine warfare. This effort was countered by means of the convoy system and effective antisubmarine weaponry.[180] Even the unreasonable fear of German attacks in the Caribbean, which did exist in the days immediately following American entry into the war, did not dictate hemispheric cooperation. The Latin American countries simply did not have anything to contribute in the area of naval warfare; and with the huge land operations going on in Europe, naval threats were about all the Germans had to offer. Consequently, however much the war may have stimulated a psychological awareness of the common interests of the American states, it presented no strategic motivations for a change from the Roosevelt policy of unilateral domination of the hemisphere. Hence the policy remained unchanged. Whatever leeway states such as Mexico gained in their relations with the United States resulted from the impossibility of any sizable troop commitments by the United States. Second, as Wilson's attention was increasingly turned toward more important problems in Europe the management of Latin American relations was returned to the hands of the professionals—the career diplomats. Howard Cline's description of Wilson's Mexican policy for this period could well be applied to all of Latin America: "no use of force under any circumstances or provocation. Threats, yes; force, no."[181]

In summary, from 1900 through World War I American policy in Latin America—a policy of unilateral intervention—had been severely conditioned by the same principle that underlay the Monroe Doctrine—that of self-defense. Caribbean security was viewed as essential to the protection and defense of American coasts and later of the Panama Canal. The Canal itself was an essential element in the American defense posture, in that it

[179] Edwin Lieuwen, *Arms and Politics in Latin America* (rev. ed.; New York: Frederick A. Praeger, 1961), p. 188. For a somewhat contrary view see Mecham, *Inter-American Security*, pp. 84–87. Mecham fails to recognize that what he calls evidence for the sentiment of continental solidarity was more often the result of the exigencies of domestic politics in the various Latin American countries.

[180] For the story of the successful Allied naval effort and American participation in it, see Sprout, *American Naval Power*, pp. 347–77.

[181] Cline, *United States and Mexico*, p. 185.

cut the U.S. fleet requirement almost in half and made possible American military and commercial operations in Asia. The most important strategic factor was the fear of European encroachment. The Caribbean islands and ports were potential staging bases for naval operations against the United States. Since the usual chaos of Caribbean political and economic affairs offered the greatest danger of European lodgment—especially after the Hague Court decision on the Anglo–German intervention in Venezuela— American policing of those affairs came as a natural corollary to the American defense strategy. The one possible alternative to regional systems for the stabilization of the domestic situation in the Caribbean states was tried, but the attempts to launch such systems never really got off the ground. In this context it is quite probable that "the problem of naval strategy in the Caribbean would have been quite as important and led to very similar actions on the part of the United States government if there had never been any Monroe Doctrine."[182] This was the real reason that the intervention policy could never be a partisan matter in American domestic politics. It was in fact Bryan, whose newspaper *The Commoner* had once been a bulwark of anti-imperialism, who negotiated a treaty with Nicaragua that was so tainted with American imperialism as to be unacceptable to the U.S. Senate.

American naval strategy in the Caribbean had both positive and negative aspects in the first two decades of the twentieth century.[183] The negative aspect consisted of prohibiting the acquisition of naval bases by non-American powers. This was the expressed purpose of Article I of the Platt Amendment, the Lodge Resolution of 1912, and the Haitian Treaty of 1915. The positive or aggressive aspect was demonstrated in the multiple attempts of the U.S. government to acquire naval bases for itself—i.e., the leasing of Guantanamo and the site in the Gulf of Fronseca and the purchase of the Danish West Indies in 1916. But both the positive and negative aspects were no more than the reflections of the dominant strategic ideas at the time. At no point was American policy, regardless of the ideological leanings of civilian political leaders, able to stray outside of the bounds determined by the dictates of strategy. As Bemis puts it: "Not until the menace of European intervention had temporarily disappeared as a result of the First World War could a President of the United States safely

---

[182] Norton, "United States in the Caribbean," in Jones, Norton, and Moon (eds.), *The United States and the Caribbean*, p. 88.

[183] The idea of this positive-negative dichotomy originally comes from Thomas Parker Moon, " 'Self-Defense' and 'Unselfish Service' in the Caribbean," in Jones, Norton, and Moon (eds.), *The United States and the Caribbean*.

think of liquidating the protective imperialism that had been established in the vital Caribbean area at the beginning of the century; not until then could there be a reasonable expectation, during the period between two great wars, that the non-American powers would refrain from intervention in the New World to secure justice denied to their nationals.[184]

[184] Bemis, *Latin American Policy*, p. 158.

# V.

# Nonintervention in Law and Practice

IN THE YEARS between World Wars I and II the United States initiated radical changes in its Latin American foreign policy. From 1922 to 1933 American diplomats laid the groundwork for the second Roosevelt's good neighbor policy by beginning the liquidation of the system of American protectorates in the Caribbean, and by 1933 it was possible for an American president to dedicate the nation to the "policy of the good neighbor" and be believed south of the Rio Grande. The international political flexibility that made this new turn of American policy possible resulted, of course, from the unquestioned dominance of American military power in the Western Hemisphere. "In 1922 the two oceans were safe. No danger of non-American intervention was in sight in the Caribbean and Central America."[1] At the same time, the Latin American attempt at legalistic restriction of American intervention reached its culmination.

This new condition of isolated security made it possible for the American statesmen to indulge the juridic tastes of their Latin American counterparts for territorial integrity. In its well-intentioned desire to improve the tenor of Latin American relations, the administration of Franklin Roosevelt committed the nation to a policy of almost total nonintervention. Yet the necessity of defending the entire hemisphere as a sine qua non of the defense of the continental United States did not disappear and, in fact, emerged with increased acuity when the Axis threat again put the hemisphere under siege in the late 1930's.

[1] Samuel Flagg Bemis, *The Latin American Policy of the United States: An Historical Interpretation* (New York: Harcourt, Brace and Company, 1943), p. 202.

96

But one of the problems of hemispheric defense was not to reappear. As a result both of League of Nations commitments and of internal political factors, the legitimacy of armed intervention for the collection of defaulted debts was called into serious question during the years immediately following World War I. More importantly, the basic incentive for non-American intervention in the Western Hemisphere—default on the public debt—no longer played such a decisive role in European–Latin American relations. This development was the result of the shift of the main source of Latin American credit from London and Paris to New York. Until World War I there had been very little activity in foreign bonds on the American market.[2] But between 1920 and 1930 "nearly two billion dollars worth of Latin American securities were sold on the American market."[3] When the international depression of the 1930's resulted in default of all but $400,000 of the Latin American issues outstanding, it was American, rather than European, creditors who were hard hit.[4] Only British investment even closely approximated that of the United States, and British investment was highly concentrated in Argentina—one of the most stable nations in Latin America at that time and one of the few countries that did not default on its external debt during the depression.[5] Latin Americans in the 1930's might—and did—worry about the possibility of American intervention for the protection of investments, but for the Europeans it would scarcely have been worth the trip across the Atlantic.

European influence in Latin America was also reduced in the area of foreign trade. In the Caribbean the United States finally realized Jefferson's dream and consolidated its position as the "first supplier and the best customer" of the Latin Americans.[6] In South America the results were not so spectacular, but gains were evident. In 1929 the United States still took only 25.44 percent of total South American exports and supplied but 31.3 percent of their total imports. But these figures were almost double the percentages for 1913.[7] Notably, it was in South America where the Nazi trade drive was most successful and where the danger of Axis lodgment was to prove greatest during World War II.[8]

[2] Dexter Perkins, *The United States and Latin America* (Baton Rouge: Louisiana State University Press, 1960), p. 109.

[3] *Ibid.*, p. 110.

[4] *Ibid.*, p. 111.

[5] Arthur Preston Whitaker, *The Western Hemisphere Idea: Its Rise and Decline* (New York: Cornell University Press, 1954), p. 113.

[6] Perkins, *United States and Latin America*, pp. 90–91.

[7] J. Fred Rippy, *South America and Hemisphere Defense* (Baton Rouge: Louisiana State University Press, 1941), p. 49.

[8] *Ibid.*, pp. 49–53.

For the United States the veritable elimination of a perceived threat to the hemisphere—and in particular to the Caribbean—meant that the foundations were cut away from the Roosevelt Corollary. American interventions in Latin America had always been of a preemptory nature, and after 1922 there was simply no one to preempt. On the other hand, nonintervention seemed to be the order of the day both internationally and in Latin America. Continued refusal to recognize the demands of Latin American jurists and politicians seemed a needless aggravation of inter-American relations. The United States, therefore, gave in to Latin American demands for a commitment to nonintervention in the hemisphere.

When, in the late 1930's, the danger of foreign encroachment again reared its head in Latin America, the policy of nonintervention was severely threatened. But two factors enabled the embryonic system of regional security to perform the security functions that had previously been assigned to the American navy and the marine corps: (1) The expected military threat never actually materialized; and (2) more subtle methods of controlling the Latin American nations had been developed. In time the apparent success of the regional security system led to a great deal of enthusiasm over the potential of a multilateral approach to national security as an alternative to the methods of intervention of prewar administrations in the United States. In recent years the failure of that approach to provide for the minimum security requirements of the dominant country of the hemisphere has turned that enthusiasm into pessimistic disillusionment.

In this chapter, therefore, we will attempt to analyze the special factors and international environment that made possible the original acceptance of nonintervention and its continued practice in the face of apparent crisis. We will then turn to a study of the intensive juridical and diplomatic campaign waged by both Latin Americans and Americans in favor of the principle of nonintervention. In the following chapter we will attempt to illustrate how the partial success of the regional system rested upon the limited strategic requirements that the system had to fulfill and how, even then, the system was in danger of a complete collapse.

## The Strategic Context

Two commonplace assumptions about the general configuration of the international system between the two world wars will be opposed in this section. The first is that the destruction of German naval power in World War I eliminated, in the American view, any threat to the Western Hemisphere. As we will attempt to demonstrate, it was not until the agreements for the limitation of naval armaments of 1922 assured unchallenged American dominance in the hemisphere that American strategists and diplomats could feel that the danger of European encroachment in Latin America was over.[9] In the overall history of U.S.–Latin American relations the point to be made is extraordinarily minor, but it goes a long way toward explaining the apparent hesitancy with which American policymakers approached the nonintervention commitment from 1919 to 1933. It also helps explain the American insistence upon the provision of Article 21 of the Covenant of the League of Nations to the effect that "Nothing in this Covenant shall be deemed to affect the validity of international engagements, such as treaties of arbitration or regional understandings like the Monroe Doctrine, for securing the maintenance of peace." Our second argument is much more basic. It is against the oft-heard contention that technological developments between the wars significantly altered the strategic position of the United States with regard to the Western Hemisphere.[10] We will argue that this contention amounts to a fallacy of composition; that because the tools of warfare change, strategic configurations of warfare do not necessarily change. In short, in spite of radical innovations in war machinery—namely, the development of aircraft as a basic tool of warfare—the importance of the Caribbean as a possible and necessary stepping-stone for directly threatening the continental United States remained undiminished, and the strategic importance of South America was in fact enhanced. Aircraft extended the potential "danger zone" to the United States, but that zone still remained well within the Western Hemisphere.

The defeat of Germany in World War I did not destroy a dangerous competitor in the Caribbean area so much as it released one. As some strategists had recognized from the beginning of the century, the naval competition between Germany and Britain had chained both to the eastern Atlantic.[11] With the destruction of the German fleet, Great Britain could be expected to attempt to resume her Caribbean expansion. The exigencies of the war had urged the United States into a massive program of naval construction, and, to a large extent, the American fleet was capable by 1919

[9] See, for example, Bemis, *Latin American Policy, passim,* and Herbert L. Matthews, *The United States and Latin America* (2nd ed.; Englewood Cliffs: Prentice–Hall, 1964), p. 132.

[10] See, for example, Eugene M. Emme, "Technical Change and Western Military Thought—1914–1915," *Military Affairs* 24 (Spring 1960): 6–19. See also, articles in Emme's *The Impact of Air Power* (Princeton: D. Van Nostrand Company, 1959).

[11] As we have pointed out several times in the context of the prewar foreign threat, Germany had not been so much a real competitor in the Caribbean as an imagined one. Mahan, himself, recognized and applauded the fact that the technical limitations of the German fleet alone sufficed to render her an ineffective opponent, so long as she was unable to acquire bases in the Caribbean area. See, for example, Sprout, *Toward a New Order of Sea Power: American Naval Policy and the World Scene, 1918–1922* (Princeton: Princeton University Press, 1946), p. 24.

of maintaining the balance of power with Britain that Germany had provided free of cost.[12] But "the British Admiralty was, understandably, reluctant to accept the logic of a situation which seemed in some of its major outlines so painfully like the one that Britain had just fought a successful war to liquidate."[13] The Anglo–Japanese accord in the Pacific further intensified the problem, for it presaged a situation in which the United States would be forced to compete in naval armaments with not one but two potential naval competitors.

Naval strategists immediately recognized the possibility of future Anglo–American competition and attempted to shape American policy at the Paris Peace Conference accordingly. In March 1919 the naval advisory staff that accompanied Wilson to Paris began to warn the President of the potential danger presented by British naval power. The first memorandum prepared by the staff argued strongly for the destruction rather than the distribution of captured German and Austrian capital ships.[14] The staff argued that (1) Article VIII of the proposed covenant of the League recognized the need of arms reduction and (2) the United States needed a navy as large as that of Great Britain, if the League was to be able to restrain its strongest member. But the staff's main argument rested upon the anticipation of Anglo–American competition. According to the navalists:

> There are in the world but two great Powers whose existence depends on naval strength. These are Great Britain and Japan. In the past Great Britain built with the exclusive idea of keeping a safe superiority over the German Fleet. In the future her sole naval rival will be the United States, and every ship built or acquired by Great Britain can have in mind only the American fleet.
>
> Japan has no rival in the Pacific except America. Every ship built or acquired by Japan can have in mind only opposition to American naval strength in the Pacific.[15]

Since any distribution of the Austrian and German vessels would probably be beneficial either to Britain or one of her potential allies, argued the staff, America must remember "the necessity of national safety" and must, therefore, oppose the distribution of the enemy ships.[16]

---

[12] Whitaker, *Western Hemisphere Idea*, pp. 111–12.
[13] *Ibid.*
[14] Memorandum, dated March 13, 1919, of the United States Naval Advisory Staff on "Disposition of German and Austrian Vessels of War," Ray Stannard Baker, *Woodrow Wilson and World Settlement*, 3 vols. (New York: Doubleday, Page and Company, 1922), III, Doc. 22: 197–205.
[15] *Ibid.*, pp. 220–1.
[16] *Ibid.*, p. 201.

As the Paris Conference went on, the navalists began to clarify their ideas with regard to the British threat. Subsequent memorandums to the President tended to de-emphasize the necessity of Anglo–American naval equality to the viability of the proposed League and to rely more upon the possibility of Anglo–American conflict.[17] In April the staff presented the President with an analysis of international power politics that was worthy of Hans Morgenthau.[18] They reminded the President that the "principle of exchange" between nations, as envisioned by the League, rested upon equality of power. "When questions of great national importance are at issue, expediency rather than principle governs."[19] For example: "If England cannot get by the mild terms of diplomatic notes the decisions she desires regarding equal rights in the use of the Panama Canal, she presents a note that uncovers the idea of a military superiority sufficient to enforce what she considers a just decision."[20] In the international world of 1919 naval power was the index of one nation's ability to exert pressure on another nation. Britain's advantage in the area of naval power was enhanced, vis-à-vis the United States, by the possibility of an alliance with Japan against U.S. power in the Pacific. And above all, according to the advisers, the United States must not forget that *every great commercial rival of the British Empire has eventually found itself at war with Great Britain—and has been defeated*" (italics in the original.)[21]

The problem of incipient Anglo–American naval competition—with Japan on the side of the British—proved impervious to solution at the Paris Peace Conference. For more than two years the danger of an international naval armaments race hung over the heads of American diplomats. The final solution to the problem was not reached until the Washington Conference on the Limitation of Armament that lasted from November 12, 1921, to February 6, 1922. There is not space here to enter into a detailed discussion of the progress and machinations of the Washington Conference,[22] but a general outline of the agreements reached will suffice for our purposes.[23] The United States, Great Britain, and Japan agreed upon a limitation ratio of 5:5:3, with a limitation on total tonnage of 525,000 tons and 315,000 tons. A further limitation of 135,000 tons and

---

[17] Memorandum, dated April 7, 1919, of the United States Naval Advisory Staff on "United States Naval Policy," Baker, *Woodrow Wilson*, III, Doc. 23: 206–17.

[18] *Ibid.*

[19] *Ibid.*, p. 208.

[20] *Ibid.*, p. 209.

[21] *Ibid.*, p. 211.

[22] A detailed treatment of the Washington Conference and the events leading to it will be found in Sprout, *Toward a New Order of Sea Power, passim.*

[23] Official reprints of the treaties, as well as detailed material on the Conference proceedings, can be found in *Foreign Relations of the United States, 1922*, pp. 1–384.

81,000 tons was placed upon the total tonnage that might be allotted to aircraft carriers. The Armament Limitations Treaty provided for the maintenance of the status quo with regard to fortification and naval bases in the territories and possessions of the contracting powers. This article specifically meant that the United States was barred from further fortifying the Panama Canal and from obtaining additional naval bases in the Caribbean area. What the limitations agreements effected in fact was the regional distribution of naval dominance. As Whitaker interprets the results of the agreements: "(Britain) was still mistress of the seas in the eastern Atlantic, the North Sea, and other areas; but Japan was now accorded this role in the Western Pacific, and the United States in the Western Hemisphere. As a result, so far as sea power was concerned, the position of the United States in the Western Hemisphere had never been stronger."[24] Battle fleet parity with Great Britain meant that the United States navy could certainly keep any combination of future enemies from the continental United States and the Panama Canal; but the United States would not be able to challenge foreign naval dominance in the eastern Atlantic or the western Pacific.[25] Consequently, so long as the treaty commitments were observed both the United States and Great Britain could feel relatively secure in their proper spheres. It was this security—not that achieved by the elimination of Germany—that permitted the so-called "liquidation of imperialism" in the Western Hemisphere.

But even while the ink was drying on the Washington treaties the irresistible movement of modern technology was rendering the goals of the statesmen at the Conference inaccessible. The Armament Limitations Treaty failed to deal adequately with the two weapons that were ultimately to change the nature of modern warfare—the airplane and the submarine. Both these weapons ultimately produced great problems for the international rules of warfare, and both contributed heavily to the phenomenon of "total war," or the blurring of the traditional distinction between combatant and noncombatant in international warfare. In fact, the approach of the delegates to the Washington Conference to the problem of restricting the use of the submarine was one which relied upon traditional distinctions in the rules of warfare. The unratified Treaty Relating to the Use of Submarines and Noxious Gases in Warfare[26] attempted to impose unrealistic restrictions upon the use of submarine craft in commerce and,

---

[24] Whitaker, *Western Hemisphere Idea*, p. 112.
[25] Sprout, *Toward a New Order of Sea Power*, p. 288.
[26] *Foreign Relations, 1922*, pp. 267–70.

in consequence, was notably unsuccessful.[27] Apart from the restrictions upon the production of aircraft carriers, the Washington Conference scarcely dealt with the problem of air power. In the first place, the revolutionary nature of air power was not generally recognized in 1921; and, second, it was felt that any attempt to limit the air components of navies would restrict the development of commercial aviation.[28]

But the question to which we must address ourselves here is that of whether or not the development of the submarine and airplane substantially altered the strategic requirements for the defense of the United States in the minds of U.S. strategists. One result of World War I was, indeed, the growth of a strategic school of thought that held that the advent of the submarine and the airplane meant that the battleship was obsolete.[29] Had this doctrine been accepted, the assumed security of the Western Hemisphere would have been called into serious question. But however popular the idea of battleship obsolescence may have become among some members of the American Congress, it was completely rejected by the U.S. Navy Department and the army.[30]

In the case of the submarine, it was a simple matter to belittle its importance. The success of the convoy, the development of undersea explosives, and the introduction of sonar detection lent a great deal of credibility to the contention that the technology of antisubmarine warfare was keeping pace with the new weapon. It was usually pointed out that the control that the British fleet had exercised over the North Sea had both prevented the Germans from utilizing their capital fleet for transport protection and invasion and had allowed the British and Americans to undertake successful antisubmarine operations.[31] In short, control of the subsurface was still contingent upon control of the surface, "and events had shown that the battleship was still the decisive factor in exercising a surface command of the sea."[32]

[27] For a full discussion of the problems relating to the legal regulation of the use of the submarine in warfare, see Myres McDougal and Florentino Feliciano, *Law and Minimum World Public Order* (New Haven: Yale University Press, 1961), pp. 626–32. For a discussion of the role of the submarine in contemporary strategic doctrine, see Leland C. Allen, "The Role of Undersea Warfare in U.S. Strategic Doctrine," *Military Affairs* 23 (Fall 1959), pp. 153–57.

[28] Sprout, *Toward a New Order of Sea Power*, pp. 218–19.

[29] See, for example, L. O. Battle, "The Battleship and the Junk Heap," *Scientific American 124* (April 16, 1921).

[30] Harold and Margaret Sprout, *The Rise of American Naval Power, 1776–1918* (Princeton: Princeton University Press, 1946), pp. 372–73.

[31] *Ibid.*, pp. 373–74.

[32] *Ibid.*

Aircraft posed a somewhat stickier problem. In the summer of 1921 bombing tests conducted off the Virginia coast had resulted in the destruction by aerial bombardment of submarines, destroyers, and a light cruiser.[33] The climax came in July 1921, when the German dreadnought *Ostfriesland* was sent to the bottom by a bomb delivered alongside of her midships. This was the ship that was supposedly "unsinkable." Brigadier General Billy Mitchell, the greatest American proponent of air power, lost little time in "leaking" his report on the Virginia tests to the press. "Air forces," he reported,

> with the type of aircraft now in existence or in development, acting from shore bases, can find and destroy all classes of seacraft under war conditions with a negligible loss to the aircraft.
>
> The problem of destruction of seacraft by air forces has been solved and is finished. . . .
>
> There are no conditions in which seacraft can operate efficiently in which aircraft cannot operate efficiently.[34]

The assault upon traditional military doctrines also found less spectacular forms in 1921. In that year an Italian brigadier general named Giulio Douhet published his first book on the strategy of aerial warfare—*The Command of the Air*.[35] Although Douhet's work was not translated into English for several years his thinking was thoroughly familiar to American strategists by 1920.[36] Douhet's strategy, simply stated, envisioned a war in which infantry and naval forces would merely fight a holding action until command of the air could be established by the aerial branch. "To have command of the air means to be in a position to prevent the enemy from flying while retaining the ability to fly oneself."[37] To deny the enemy the ability to fly, one must strike hard and strike first. The enemy's air forces must be destroyed on the ground before he has a chance to counterattack. The bomber force is, therefore, essential to Douhet's strategy. There is simply no possibility for defense in Douhet's thought, except an effective offense. "Viewed in its true light, aerial warfare admits of no defense, only offense. *We must therefore resign ourselves to the offensives the enemy inflicts upon us, while striving to put all our resources to work to inflict even*

---

[33] Harry H. Ransom, "The Battleship Meets the Airplane," *Military Affairs* 23 (Spring 1959): 21–27.

[34] *Ibid.*, pp. 22–23.

[35] Giulio Douhet, *The Command of the Air*, trans. Dino Ferrari (New York: Coward–McCann, 1942).

[36] The devious but effective route by which Douhet's strategic thought came to America is brilliantly recounted in Bernard Brodie, *Strategy in the Missile Age* (Princeton: Princeton University Press, 1959), pp. 71–77.

[37] Douhet, *Command of the Air*, p. 24.

*heavier ones upon him*"[38] (italics in the original). Once the command of the air was established, the air force could then proceed to the leisurely annihilation of the enemy's resource base and morale by massive bombing.

There is, of course, no way to measure the extent of Douhet's influence over the American air strategists, such as Billy Mitchell. But there can be little doubt that some of the extraordinary claims made for the efficacy of air power were inspired by the Italian general.[39] The obvious problem with Douhet's thesis was that it was totally unsuited to the American situation. Unlike the nations of the continent, the United States was separated from its nearest potential enemy by several thousand miles of ocean; and until the development of long-range aircraft a war such as envisioned by Douhet between the United States and any other power was impossible. At the end of World War I the range of America's DH-4 was about 350 miles, that of the Fokker D-7 was even more limited.[40] Even the B-29 used in World War II had a range of only 4,000 miles.[41] These short-range aircraft could threaten U.S. defenses only if they were brought into range by an aircraft carrier; and in order to operate aircraft carriers within range of the continental United States the enemy would have to control the sea lanes. In short, the United States could suffer air attack only from bases in the Western Hemisphere, and the development of bases required prior lodgment. In this respect the situation was identical to that of the Wilson period. The only difference was that as the operating range of ships and aircraft was extended the area of American strategic interests would be expanded beyond the Caribbean.

In spite of the glamour with which popular history and Hollywood have veiled the early proponents of air power, the rejection of major doctrinal alterations by the ranking military planners of the period was undoubtedly well-advised. Shortly after Mitchell's headline-making "leak" of the results of the Virginia bombing tests the Joint Board—in a rare moment of agreement between its army and navy constituents—issued its own interpretation of the results of the confrontation between battleship and airplane.[42] The report admitted the need of redesigning naval vessels to withstand aerial attack, but the Board was sure that "means of defense develop rapidly to meet the developments of offensive weapons."[43] For example,

---

[38] *Ibid.*, p. 55.

[39] Brodie claims great influence for Douhet over Mitchell himself and further states that the subsequent influence of Douhet on the American air force has been greater than that of Mitchell (*Strategy*, p. 77).

[40] Emme, *Impact of Air Power*, p. 17.

[41] *Ibid.*

[42] Report of the Joint Board on the Results of Aviation and Ordnance Tests Held During June and July, 1921 (quoted in Ransom, "Battleship Meets Airplane," pp. 22–23).

[43] *Ibid.*

antiaircraft defenses could be improved. But the general outlines of naval doctrine remained unaffected.

> The battleship is still the backbone of the fleet and the bulwark of the nation's sea defense, and will so remain so long as the safe navigation of the sea for purposes of trade or transportation is vital to success in war.
> The airplane, like the submarine, destroyer, and mine, has added to the dangers to which the battleship are exposed, but has not made the battleship obsolete. The battleship still remains the greatest factor of naval strength.
> The development of aircraft, instead of furnishing an economical instrument of war leading to the abolition of the battleship has but added to the complexity of naval warfare.[44]

In the years that followed before the outbreak of World War II the strategists of the navy and army continued to reject the doctrine of the supremacy of air power. But more and more they began to adopt the concept of air power as an adjunct of land and sea operations. Especially the navy became "air minded in a big way."[45] "They even went out of their way to find new means of using aircraft in naval operations."[46] In 1924 and 1925 the Eberle Board, headed by the chief of naval operations, and the President's Aircraft Board, headed by Dwight Morrow, conducted inquiries into the proper role of air power and came to similar conclusions.[47] Both reports stressed the limitations of the airplane as an independent instrument of war and pointed to the area its "legitimate" use as being found "only in operations closely connected with the defeat of the enemy forces."[48] In short, the army and navy viewed the airplane as requiring major changes in tactics but not in strategy.

The resistance of the strategy boards to the innovating assaults of the "air radicals" was one case in which institutional conservatism was to pay off. The great aeronautic inventions that were foretold by the proponents of air power, such as Mitchell and Alexander Seversky, did not emerge from the realm of science fiction until World War II was well under way.[49] And even in that war, "it was in tactical employment that success was most spectacular and that the air forces won the unqualified respect and admiration of the older services. By contrast, the purely strategic successes, how-

---

[44] *Ibid.*

[45] General H. H. Arnold, quoted in Ransom, "Battleship Meets Airplane," p. 24.

[46] *Ibid.*

[47] The results of both studies are condensed in Ransom, "Battleship Meets Airplane" pp. 24–27.

[48] *Ibid.*, p. 27.

[49] For a cataloguing of the predictions of the "air radicals," see Edward Warner, "Douhet, Mitchell, Seversky: Theories of Air Warfare," in Edward Mead Earle (ed.), *Makers of Modern Strategy* (Princeton: Princeton University Press, 1941), pp. 485–503.

ever far-reaching in particular instances, were never completely convincing to uncommitted observers."[50]

Thus, during the period between the wars the requirements for continental defense were essentially unchanged. The airplane, like the battleship, could threaten American domination of the Caribbean only from bases within the Western Hemisphere. But after 1922 there was no European nation capable of challenging American power in that hemisphere. If trouble came it would most probably come from the Japanese in the Pacific: "Thus, U.S. strategic thought in the years from 1919 to 1938 was largely concentrated on the problems presented by a conflict arising out of Japanese aggression against American interests or territory in the Far East."[51]

With the reorganization of the Joint Board in 1919, war planning became the province of the Joint Planning Committee, which combined the planning functions of each of the services. From 1919 until 1938 this group continued the elaboration of the Orange Plan originally formulated by the General Board of the Navy in the early 1900's to deal with the contingency of possible Japanese aggression. It will be remembered that the original Orange Plan had called for a holding action in the Pacific until sufficient naval forces could be mustered to seek out and destroy the Japanese fleet. This emphasis upon the naval offensive against the Japanese fleet was not changed by the Planning Committee during the 1920's and early 1930's.[52] The Orange Plan envisioned war with Japan alone and consequently did not foresee possible Japanese occupation of positions in the Western Hemisphere. As Louis Morton describes the assumptions underlying the Orange Plan: "A war with Japan would be primarily a naval war fought in the Pacific. So far as anyone could foresee, there would be no requirement for large ground armies. There was a possibility, of course, that Japan would attack the Panama Canal, Hawaii, and even the West Coast of the United States, but no real danger that Japan could seize and occupy any of these places."[53] Although other plans were prepared from time to time as a theoretical exercise, the Orange Plan was the only operative plan which had been approved by the Joint Board up to the late 1930's.[54] There was simply nothing in the international situation to give cause for alarm. From the standpoint of the military planners, the period

---

[50] Brodie, *Strategy*, p. 107.
[51] Louis Morton, "Germany First: The Basic Concept of Allied Strategy in World War II," in Kent Roberts Greenfield (ed.), *Command Decisions* (New York: Harcourt, Brace and Company, 1959), p. 4.
[52] *Ibid.*, pp. 7–11.
[53] *Ibid.*, p. 7.
[54] *Ibid.*

from the Washington Conference to the late 1930's was one of almost absolute security for the Western Hemisphere.

## Nonintervention in the Inter-American System

Finding themselves suddenly alone in the hemisphere, the Republicans who followed Wilson began the process of U.S. withdrawal from interference in the internal affairs of Latin American states—a process that was to culminate in the 1930's in an airtight legal commitment to nonintervention. The story of the "liquidation of imperialism" and the subsequent commitment to nonintervention has been told in detail elsewhere.[55] Here we will deal with those events in only the briefest outline and concentrate, instead, upon those instances in which the process seemed in danger of being reversed. In this way, it may be possible to illustrate that American infatuation with the policy of nonintervention never got in the way of the national love affair with strategic security.

The first moves toward the elimination of the American protectorate system in the Caribbean were made under Secretary of State Charles Evans Hughes. In 1922, Hughes began working out a plan for the withdrawal of American troops from the Dominican Republic, and in 1924 that policy came to fruition. Second, Hughes turned to the problem of the Central American states. By 1922 Honduras, El Salvador, and Nicaragua were again on the verge of war. Since the American rejection of the League of Nations and the stipulation of Article 21 had by this time rendered League mediation in the Western Hemisphere virtually impossible,[56] Hughes sought to re-establish the defunct Central American system that Root had so laboriously created in 1907. The Second Conference on Central American Affairs, which met in Washington from December 4, 1922 to February 7, 1923, established an International Central American Tribunal and an International Commission of Inquiry; but the regional system that was organized in 1923 was much more restricted in scope than its predecessor. The tribunal's jurisdiction was not compulsory, and questions involving sovereignty, independence, honor, and vital interests were specifically excluded. But the delegates to the conference avoided one of the most serious omissions of the previous system—this time, the United States signed

---

[55] Good accounts of this period can be found in Bemis, *Latin American Policy*, pp. 202–96; J. Lloyd Mecham, *The United States and Inter-American Security, 1889–1960* (Austin: University of Texas Press, 1961), pp. 77–148; and Ann Van Wynen and A. J. Thomas, *Nonintervention* (Dallas: Southern Methodist University Press, 1956), pp. 55–64. The running account which follows is based on these sources.

[56] The League, itself, contributed to its ineffectiveness in the Western Hemisphere by refusing participation in the Tacna–Arica controversy between Chile and Peru and in the boundary dispute between Costa Rica and Panama (Mecham, *Inter-American Security*, pp. 93–94).

the arbitration conventions. By special protocol the United States agreed to cooperate with the Central American states for the realization of the purposes of the Convention.[57]

The United States was forced to make good this promise even before the treaties were ratified. A defeated presidential candidate in Honduras threw the country into revolution, in disregard of the stipulation of Article II of the General Treaty of Peace and Amity that the Central Americans would not recognize "any other Government which may come into power in any of the five Republics through a coup d'état or a revolution against a recognized Government, so long as the freely elected representatives of the people thereof have not constitutionally reorganized the country."[58] U.S. troops intervened to stop the fighting between factions; but instead of occupying the country, the United States and the other four Central American countries selected a provisional government to serve, pending free elections.[59] The successful conclusion of this venture in regional security led Hughes to view the prospect of a "Central America for Central Americans" somewhat more favorably. In November of 1923 Nicaragua was given notice that the remaining American troops would be withdrawn after the Nicaraguan election of January 1925; and, in spite of the requests of the newly elected president that the American troops remain, they were withdrawn in August of the year.

It was in Nicaragua that the new American policy met its most serious reversal. Shortly after the American troops were withdrawn the fears of the Nicaraguan President Solorzano were realized. He was ousted from office by a coup d'état led by General Chamorro. Again the Central American states joined with the United States in refusing to recognize the General. Again U.S. troops intervened to stop the fighting. But this time the troops did not promptly withdraw, and were not withdrawn again until 1933. Two major factors affecting the security of the canal intervened to prevent the State Department from leaving Nicaragua on its own. First, the Chamorro faction, which continued its revolutionary activities even after American intervention, was heavily supplied and partially controlled by aid from Mexico. Whether rightly or not, Coolidge's Secretary of State Kellogg suspected that Nicaragua was in danger of falling into the hands of Bolshevists operating from Mexico.[60] Consequently, it was thought necessary for the United States marines to attempt to establish and train a new Nicaraguan constabulary to deal with a potential internal threat. But

---

[57] Texts of the Convention and the Protocol are printed in *Foreign Relations of the United States, 1923*, I: 320–27.
[58] *Ibid.*
[59] Bemis, *Latin American Policy*, p. 209.
[60] *Ibid.*, p. 212.

it may certainly be argued that this goal had been accomplished by the end of 1928. And indeed, the terms of the original truce negotiated between the contending factions by Colonel Henry L. Stimson would have allowed the withdrawal of American troops after the Nicaraguan elections of 1928.[61] But even after the successful accomplishment of free elections, the Coolidge administration granted the request of the Diaz government to extend the American occupation of the country.[62] This was an obvious reversal of the policy of withdrawal initiated by Hughes.

What led to this temporary return to the earlier interventionist policy was a renewed interest, in late 1928 and early 1929, in the Nicaraguan canal route.[63] The late 1928 naval exercises in the Caribbean had indicated the vulnerability of the Panama Canal to attack by carrier-transported aircraft. In accordance with the still functional "color" plans, an enemy "Black Fleet" hypothetically destroyed the canal by aerial bombing.[64] Combined with occasional reports that the Panama Canal would soon not be able to carry the total load of the growing trans-isthmian traffic, this event proved sufficient to stimulate congressional interest in a second trans-isthmian canal.[65] Senator Walter E. Edge led the Senate movement for a secondary waterway, and he rested his case heavily upon the results of the naval exercises. Edge argued that: "Under present conditions, the blocking of the Panama Canal by bombs dropped from aircraft could effectually separate the Atlantic and Pacific fleets and place the United States in wartimes in a position similar to that of 1898, when the battleship *Oregon* made her historic voyage down the west coast of South America, through the Strait of Magellan, and up the east coast to the Caribbean."[66] As the movement gained momentum, William Randolph Hearst threw his influence and that of his newspapers behind the drive for a second canal; and a majority of military and naval experts were convinced by the defense arguments.[67] Although there was congressional opposition, a survey of the Nicaraguan route was authorized by the Congress on March 1, 1929; and

---

[61] *Ibid.*

[62] It should be noted, however, that the Coolidge administration rejected a request of the Nicaraguan government to negotiate a treaty of alliance which would have given the U.S. Platt Amendment rights of intervention, in order to protect its proprietary rights in in the Nicaraguan canal route (*ibid.*, p. 211).

[63] For a detailed account of American interest in the Nicaraguan route, see Thomas A. Bailey, "Interest in a Nicaragua Canal, 1903–1931," *Hispanic American Historical Review* 16 (February 1936): 2–28.

[64] *New York Times*, January 1, 1929.

[65] Bailey, "Nicaragua Canal," *passim*.

[66] Walter E. Edge, "The Nicaragua Trade Route," *Saturday Evening Post* (May 11, 1929).

[67] Bailey, "Nicaragua Canal," pp. 17, 25. Bailey's assertion that a majority of military experts favored the second canal is based upon an unpublished study by Professor Ralph H. Lutz.

shortly thereafter the Interoceanic Canal Board was established—notably, under the auspices of the secretary of war.[68] Unfortunately the results of the survey were not made available to the Congress until 1931, by which time the congressmen were far too concerned with the country's economic depression to give serious consideration to any large allocation of money for a second waterway.[69]

In assessing the effects of this renewed interest in the Nicaraguan route, it is first necessary to determine how important was the role of the defense argument for the second waterway. As we have already indicated, the leading proponent of the second canal, Senator Edge, definitely based his position, in large part, upon the defense argument. Second, during the occupation of Nicaragua both President Coolidge and his personal representative in Nicaragua, Colonel Stimson, made repeated reference to the necessity of protecting our proprietary rights in the Nicaraguan route.[70] Third, there is no doubt that members of the State Department in the late 1920's were dominated by Stimson's idea that "it is of vital importance to this country not only that the canal shall be open to our fleet in case of war, but that it shall be closed to the fleet of our enemy."[71] Finally it should be pointed out that the only other major argument for the second route—namely, that the Panama Canal could not support the growing trans-isthmian traffic—could not have been a major consideration, because it was simply untrue—a point which opponents of the Nicaragua route in Congress were never loath to indicate.[72] The truth was that in 1929 the Panama Canal was utilizing only one-half of its 60,000,000 tons capacity.[73] It is impossible to prove with certainty that President Hoover's decision to continue the occupation of Nicaragua was based upon the military desirability of a second route, but the defense arguments were undoubtedly available to him through his military advisers. And it is notable that when the Congress set aside the plans for a second waterway in 1931, Hoover began the withdrawal of the occupying forces.[74]

But even while U.S. diplomats were in the process of liquidating the Caribbean protectorate system, other forces in the inter-American system

[68] Thomas Parker Moon, " 'Self-Defense' and 'Inselfish Service' in the Caribbean," Jones, Norton and Moon (eds.), *The United States and the Caribbean* (Chicago: University of Chicago Press, 1929), p. 170.

[69] Bailey, "Nicaragua Canal," p. 20.

[70] See examples in Bemis, *Latin American Policy*, pp. 211–13.

[71] Stimson, quoted in Moon, "Self-Defense," in Jones, Norton, and Moon (eds.), *The United States and the Caribbean*, p. 167.

[72] Bailey, "Nicaragua Canal," *passim*.

[73] Moon, "Self-Defense," in Jones, Norton, and Moon (eds.), *The United States and the Caribbean*, p. 170.

[74] Bemis, *Latin American Policy*, p. 221.

were acting to give that liquidation permanence by committing the United States to a comprehensive policy of nonintervention. We have said little thus far of the impact of American policy upon Latin Americans; and perhaps little need be said. Yankeephobia was the inevitable Latin American answer to the years of U.S. intervention and economic expansion in the Western Hemisphere. In the 1920's and 1930's, what had been a mild detestation took on the larger proportions of a hysterical nationalistic hatred.[75] Particularly after 1930, when the spreading international depression resulted in a series of Latin American revolutions directed toward complete social and economic restructuring, nationalism in Latin America became almost synonymous with anti-Americanism. Even in 1922 Latin Americans were concerned with the problem of controlling the "colossus of the North." In that year the distinguished Argentine sociologist and literary critic, Jose Ingenieros, was heard to say: "We are not, we do not want to be any longer, we could not be Pan Americanists. The United States is to be feared because it is great, rich, and enterprising. What concerns us is to find out whether there is a possibility of balancing its power to the extent necessary to save our political independence and the sovereignty of our countries."[76]

The attempt to balance the power of the United States in the Western Hemisphere was evident in the attitudes of the Latin American nations towards the League of Nations. There is little doubt that "one of the motives which animated a considerable number of Latin American nations in joining the League was the belief that it would act as a counterpoise to the United States."[77] As we have pointed out, the failure of the United States to join the League and the freedom accorded U.S. policy in the Western Hemisphere by Article 21 of the League Covenant dashed any hopes of circumscribing American policy through the League; and, accordingly, Latin American interests in the world organization declined quickly.[78] By 1926 five Latin American nations had either withdrawn from the League or were abstaining from participation in it; the attendance of Latin American delegates was irregular at best; and the Latin American countries showed a "woeful indisposition to ratify the international agreements negotiated under League auspices."[79]

In light of the inefficacy of the League in the Western Hemisphere, Latin Americans increasingly turned toward the still adolescent inter-

---

[75] For a comprehensive survey of the growth of nationalism in various Latin American countries, see, Arthur P. Whitaker and David C. Jordan, *Nationalism in Contemporary Latin America* (New York: The Free Press, 1966).

[76] Quoted in Whitaker, *Western Hemisphere Idea*, p. 129.

[77] Henry Duggan, quoted in Mecham, *Inter-American Security*, p. 89.

[78] Mecham, *Inter-American Security*, pp. 92–93.

[79] *Ibid.*

American system in the search for tools with which to control the United States. In that area several important juridical tools were already available. In 1902 Louis Drago, foreign minister of Argentina, had sent a note to the American State Department declaring that "the public debt of an American State can not occasion armed intervention, nor even the actual occupation of the territory of American nations by an European power."[80] With reference limited to European powers, the United States had essentially agreed. Drago had based his case, in part, upon the writings of Carlos Calvo, an Argentine diplomat. In his *Le droit international théorique et pratique*, published in 1896, Calvo had outlined the doctrine that was to bear his name: no external protection of resident aliens or their property should be permitted, so long as equal treatment is given to nationals and aliens alike.

As early as 1898 attempts were made to include variations of the "Calvo Clause" in treaties between Latin American countries and Europe.[81] But the attempt at treaty stipulation had never been successful, due to the countertendency to include qualifications to the effect that a clear denial of justice was cause for protective measures. Likewise, Calvo Clauses have been included in Latin American constitutions and legislative acts, but with little or no effect upon third party states.[82] Finally, Calvo Clauses have long been included in transnational contracts between private entities and Latin American governments. Only here did the clauses meet with limited success. In 1926 the American Mexican Claims Commission dismissed claims against Mexico for alleged violations of a dredging contract with North American Dredging Company.[83] But even in this case the Commissioners did not deny the right of a state to protect its nationals; it found instead that the relevant contractual clause required exhaustion of local remedies prior to diplomatic recourse and that local remedies had not been exhausted.[84]

In light of this failure in bilateral negotiations the Latin Americans began to turn toward multilateral arrangements to guard themselves against the interventions of the "colossus of the North." During the Fifth International Conference of American States that met in Santiago, Chile, in March 1923, methods for controlling American intervention in the hemisphere were paramount in Latin American minds. Uruguay presented a proposal for an American League of Nations that would have multilateralized the Monroe Doctrine, while Costa Rica proposed a Pan-

---

[80] *Foreign Relations, 1903*, pp. 1–5.
[81] See, for example, the Peruvian–Spanish Treaty of 1898.
[82] See, for example, present Colombian Constitution and monetary regulations.
[83] *United States* (North American Dredging Company Claim) *vs. United Mexican States*, United States–Mexico General Claims Commission, 1926.
[84] *Ibid.* Opinions of Commissioners (1927), p. 21.

American Court of Justice that would have had jurisdiction over all hemispheric disputes.[85] The United States quietly rejected both proposals. At the same time, however, the United States supported the so-called Gondra Treaty, which, inspired by the previous Bryan "cooling off" treaties, provided for investigation of controversies between signatory states.[86] United States willingness to restrict itself even to this limited degree hardly accords with an interpretation of malicious intent on the part of the United States. The contradictory unwillingness of the United States to enter into an American League in all probability was simply an expression of the American isolationism that followed World War I. With the threat of European encroachment eliminated from the hemisphere there was little need to "entangle" the nation in a mutual security arrangement, "Therefore, believing that there was no need for a regional defensive arrangement, the Republican administrations of the 1920's felt that Pan Americanism approached the ideal of regional association in ratio to the elimination of security considerations."[87]

A second important accomplishment of the Santiago Conference was the revival of the movement for codification of inter-American law that had begun in 1912 with the first meeting of the Inter-American Commission of Jurists.[88] Ironically, the resuscitation of the failing Commission was largely the work of Secretary Charles Evans Hughes, who was a staunch advocate of organs of juridical codification.[89] Hughes believed, as he instructed the American delegation to the Santiago Conference, that: "The government of the United States should take a leading part in the effort to develop a *true body* of international law, and to this end to provide appropriate means for the authoritative statement of accepted principles of rules and for the harmonizing of differences."[90] The Santiago Conference re-established the Commission of Jurists with two delegates from each republic. The result, of course, was to give a heavily Latin American flavor to all

[85] Edwin Lieuwen, *U.S. Policy in Latin America: A Short History* (New York: Frederick A. Praeger, 1965), p. 57.

[86] Charles G. Fenwick, *The Organization of American States: The Inter-American Regional System* (Washington: Kaufmann Printing, Inc., 1963), p. 53.

[87] Mecham, *Inter-American Security*, p. 100.

[88] The movement for a codification of inter-American law, as opposed to general international law, actually began much earlier than 1912. It was largely the result of Latin American dissatisfaction with the Hague Conventions of 1907 (notably Convention II). For a detailed history of the inter-American codification movement see Bemis, *Latin American Policy*, pp. 226–55; and Wynen and Thomas, *Nonintervention*, pp. 56–61.

[89] Bemis, *Latin American Policy*, p. 243.

[90] *Ibid.*

future formulations of the Commission.[91] Thereafter, the recommended codifications of the Commission evidenced the juridical fixation of the Latin Americans with the doctrine of total nonintervention.[92]

The Sixth International Conference of American States, which met in Havana in 1928, was doubly notable: it marked the most direct assault to date upon the American intervention policy and the Conference made important organizational changes in the Pan-American Union that were later to have a strong influence upon the structure of the Organization of American States.[93] But the most important debate of the Havana Conference centered around the proposed Convention on the Rights and Duties of States presented to the Conference by the Commission of Jurists. The central article of the proposed convention was quite naturally the nonintervention article which read: "No state has a right to interfere in the internal affairs of another."[94] The debate in both the plenary sessions and the committees was tantamount to a juridical civil war.[95] The United States, with limited interventions still in progress in the Caribbean and Central America, was hardly in a position to accept what looked like a total renunciation of intervention; and there is some indication that the

[91] For a brief survey of the views of Latin American jurists on intervention, see Isidro Fabela, *Intervencion* (Mexico: Escuela Nacional de Ciencias Politicas y Sociales, 1959), pp. 131–76. In general, Latin American juridical thought is characterized by a temporal division with regard to the question of intervention. Before Luis Maria Drago, writers followed European lines of thought and justified intervention under general international law for limited protection of life and property of nationals. But, notably, there was early discussion of the possibility of collective intervention, such as the Tovar (Tobar) Doctrine. But after the turn of the century, there was an uninterrupted movement among Latin American jurists toward the doctrine of absolute nonintervention. The doctrine of collective intervention enjoyed a brief revival in the works of Jose Maria Yepes, in the late 1920's, but, in general, the idea of absolute nonintervention has prevailed down to the present. For example, Lleras Camargo, like Yepes, a Colombian, informed the Counsel of the O.A.S. in his final year as secretary general: "The attempt to establish a distinction between collective and unilateral intervention, in order to justify the former and maintain the condemnation of the latter, constituted a dangerous threat for the principle of nonintervention. The fact that a majority of nations within a given group comes together in order to intervene in the internal affairs of a state in no way assures the benevolence or rectitude of their intentions. No settled norm of individual or collective interests of the states would be applicable in such an emergency" (Fabela, *Intervencion*, p. 168. Translation my own).

[92] For examples, see Bemis, *Latin American Policy*, pp. 242–55.

[93] See Mecham, *Inter-American Security*, pp. 100–6, for a full account of the Havana Conference.

[94] Wynen and Thomas, *Nonintervention*, p. 59.

[95] For the high points of the debate at the Havana Conference, see Fabela, *Intervencion*, pp. 205–15.

nonintervention proposal took the American delegation by surprise.[96] Nevertheless, Hughes, head of the American delegation, took the occasion to deliver a classic defense of American policy. What was most notable about Hughes's statement to the Conference, however, is that his defense of American intervention was grounded in general international law, instead of the security requirements of the United States. As Hughes told the delegates:

> We want no aggression. . . . We desire to respect the rights of every country and to have the rights of our country equally respected. We do not wish the territory of any American Republic. We do not wish to govern any American Republic. We do not wish to intervene in the affairs of any American Republic. We simply wish peace and order and stability and recognition of honest rights properly acquired so that this hemisphere may not only be the hemisphere of peace but the hemisphere of international justice. . . . Now what is the real difficulty? Let us face the facts. The difficulty, if there is any, in any one of the American Republics, is not of any external aggression. It is an internal difficulty, if it exists at all. From time to time there arises a situation most deplorable and regrettable in which sovereignty is not at work, in which for a time in certain areas there is no government at all—in which for a time and within a limited sphere there is no possibility of performing the functions of sovereignty and independence. Those are the conditions that create the difficulty with which at times we find ourselves confronted. What are we to do when government breaks down and American citizens are in danger of their lives? Are we to stand by and see them killed because a government in circumstances which it cannot control and for which it may not be responsible can no longer afford reasonable protection? . . . Now it is the principle of international law that in such a case a government is fully justified in taking action—I would call it interposition of a temporary character—for the purpose of protecting the lives and property of its nationals. I could say that that is not intervention. . . . Of course the United States cannot forgo its right to protect its citizens. International law cannot be changed by the resolutions of this conference.[97]

[96] The nonintervention article, though considerably modified, was apparently accepted by the Commission of Jurists in 1927 (Wynen and Thomas, *Nonintervention*, p. 59). But the spokesman for the Commission, Victor Maurtua of Peru, did not include the nonintervention article in his presentation of the Commission's work on February 4 (Fabela, *Intervencion*, pp. 206–8). He was immediately challenged by the delegate from El Salvador, who forced the nonintervention proposition to the floor. The later coalition between the United States and Peru, in support of a more limited project, might be taken to indicate some form of prior agreement on which proposal was to be supported. The problem in discovering what really took place both at the prior meeting of the Commission of Jurists and the Havana Conference is virtually insoluble, for official accounts differ from the unofficial ones and the Commission's supposed acceptance of the nonintervention principle was not in accordance with their own rules of procedure (Fabela, *ibid*).

[97] *New York Times*, February 19, 1928. Quoted in Mecham, *Inter-American Security*, p. 104.

Hughes's defense of American policy solely upon the grounds of what he perceived to be the accepted norms of international law brings into serious question the oft-heard contention that the nonintervention resolution would have passed the Havana Conference had it not been for the opposition of the United States.[98] As we shall soon see, the ultimate acceptance of the principle of nonintervention by the United States was made with the reservation that Washington's policy of nonintervention would continue to be based upon the principles of international law. In essence, the import of Hughes's statement is that the United States would retain the right to intervene within the bounds of international law; he avoided basing his argument upon the Roosevelt Corollary or the Monroe Doctrine. Had some of the Latin American states been willing to accept a less comprehensive restriction of intervention, the American case for opposition to the principle of nonintervention would have been demolished. The absolute terms in which the restriction was formulated—"No state has a right to interfere in the internal affairs of another"—superficially, would have declared American intervention in Cuba, Nicaragua, and Haiti illicit, in spite of treaty rights or compliance with the request of the incumbent government. Such a position quite naturally lost the support not only of the United States but also of the states in which the United States was intervening in favor of the incumbent government. For example, Doctor Orestes Ferrara, president of the Cuban delegation, supported the principle of intervention in terms which must have brought a blush even to American faces:

> The word "Intervention," which for a momentary political impulse is placed on the "Index" in this meeting, has everywhere a glorious past. How much nobility and grandeur there has been in some interventions! If Gladstone, that illustrious English statesman, might live again, he would hardly follow us in a generic repudiation of the word which to him always represented the saving of human lives, the renovation of institutions and the freeing of people from tyranny. The splendid phrases which he pronounced on many occasions, pleading for a civilizing movement against the barbarian, would provide the discourse in reply to the opinions expressed here this afternoon. . . .
>
> These words, then, which today we condemn without distinction, were the longing, the hope and the last recourse for large persecuted groups of humanity. . . .
>
> (If we declare) in absolute terms that intervention is under no circumstances possible, we will be sanctioning all the inhuman acts committed within determined frontiers and, what is worse, we will not be avoiding that which is in the hearts of all to avoid, the onslaught upon the people's rights of

[98] Mecham, *Inter-American Security*, p. 105; and Wynen and Thomas, *Nonintervention*, p. 60.

sovereignty and independence, which cynical force can always trample upon.[99]

In short, whatever the extent of agreement among Latin American jurists upon the doctrine of absolute nonintervention, politically the Latin Americans were divided among themselves. And it must never be forgotten that regardless of the jurisprudential tone of the rhetoric at the Havana Conference the Latin American delegates as well as those from the United States were representing very political governments. Among those governments were some that considered the doctrine of nonintervention as a possible shield for their questionable domestic politics and others that depended upon the support of the United States for their very existence. In the end the proponents of the nonintervention doctrine withdrew from the field, not because the United States alone could have defeated the measure, but because the support of the United States would have been insufficient to pass it.[100] And, as the distinguished jurist Barcia Trelles points out, the failure of the Conference to condemn interventionism would have been tantamount to an admission to, and implicit acceptance of, the "evil of America"—namely, the complete absence of Hispanic solidarity in the power politics of the hemisphere.[101]

But in spite of the disunity of the Havana Conference, the course of United States policy was moving steadily toward a commitment to nonintervention. Limitation of intervention was implicit in the Kellogg–Briand Pact, signed in Paris on August 27, 1928. The Pact bound the signatory nations to renounce war as an instrument of policy and to seek the solution or settlement of all disputes and conflicts arising between them only by pacific means. The intention of the Pact was "to render wholly illegal all resort to war otherwise than in self-defence or as a sanction for the violation of the Pact."[102] In his presentation of the Pact to the Senate Committee on Foreign Relations, Secretary Frank Billings Kellogg gave indication that he believed that the Pact of Paris would circumscribe American intervention in Latin America, but he emphasized that that intervention would no longer be necessary in light of the apparent security of the hemisphere. "Even without this treaty," queried the Secretary, "does anybody believe that the present governments of Europe are in any position

[99] Quoted in C. Neale Ronning, *Law and Politics in Inter-American Diplomacy* (New York: John Wiley and Sons, 1963), pp. 65–66.

[100] Camilo Barcia Trelles, *Doctrina de Monroe y Cooperación Internacional* (Madrid: Compania Ibero-Americana de Publicaciones, 1931), pp. 737–38.

[101] *Ibid.*

[102] J. L. Brierly, *The Law of Nations: An Introduction to the International Law of Peace* (6th ed.; New York: Oxford University Press, 1963), p. 410.

to attack any one of the South American countries and impose upon them their form of government?"[103]

Since the Monroe Doctrine had often been characterized as a "doctrine of self-defense," U.S. commitment to the Pact of Paris naturally raised the question of whether or not the United States continued to view the Roosevelt Corollary as a logical sequitur of the Monroe Doctrine. That the Roosevelt Corollary had been jettisoned was the obvious implication of both Hughes's statements at the Havana Conference and the fact that the United States did not append any reservations to the Pact of Paris, after the fashion of Great Britain who had declared "certain regions of the world" to constitute such a vital interest for her peace and security that she would have to defend them from any attack. The problem was settled in favor of the Hughes interpretation by a State Department memorandum, prepared at the request of Secretary Kellogg by Undersecretary of State J. Reuben Clark.[104]

The famous Clark memorandum cleanly severed the Roosevelt Corollary from its traditional roots in the Monroe Doctrine. To carry the analogy further, it might be said that during the operation the plant died. Clark indicated that the Monroe Doctrine was nothing more than an expression of the recognized right of self-defense, with specific regard to the danger of European attack upon the nations of the Western Hemisphere. The Doctrine, said Clark, "does not apply to purely inter-American relations. Nor does the declaration purport to lay down any principles that are to govern the inter-relationship of the states of this Western Hemisphere as among themselves. The Doctrine states a case of United States vs. Europe, not of United States vs. Latin America."[105] The Roosevelt Corollary, according to Clark, was also based upon the right of self-defense, in as much as it stipulates "that in case of financial or other difficulties" in the Latin American countries, the United States "should attempt an adjustment thereof lest European governments should intervene, and intervening should occupy territory." Consequently, the Corollary is not justified by the Monroe Doctrine, "however much it may be justified by the application of the doctrine of self-preservation."[106]

Since the League was effectively barred from participation in the settlement of inter-American disputes by U.S. nonmembership and Article 21 of the Covenant, the assent of the American states to the Pact of Paris might

[103] *General Pact for the Renunciation of War*, Hearings before the Senate Committee on Foreign Relations, U.S. Senate, 70th Cong., 2nd sess., December 7, 11, 1928.

[104] U.S., State Department, *Memorandum on the Monroe Doctrine*, prepared by J. Reuben Clark (Washington: GPO, 1930).

[105] *Ibid.*, p. 19.

[106] *Ibid.*, pp. 23–24.

have been a meaningless gesture, so long as adequate machinery for pacific settlement of disputes was nonexistent in the Western Hemisphere. "The original Gondra treaty was little more than an agreement to consider submission to an investigation."[107] The problem was partially solved at the International Conference of American States on Conciliation and Arbitration, held in Washington in December 1928 and January 1929. This conference produced a general treaty of arbitration and a convention on conciliation.[108] "These two instruments became the central part of the inter-American system of pacific settlement of international disputes."[109]

The preambles to both instruments "condemn war as an instrument of national policy and adopt obligatory arbitration as the means for the settlement of their international differences of a juridical character."[110] The conciliation instrument made no exception to the nature of the disputes that should be submitted to conciliation procedures, and the arbitration convention exempted only domestic questions and questions concerning third states not a party to the treaty.[111] The latter instrument was subsequently weakened by reservations—especially, the reservation of six nations that exempted disputes arising out of acts prior to the treaty. But the special Protocol of Progressive Arbitration provided a procedure for subsequent abandonment of reservations to the treaty.[112] In general, it cannot be said that the inter-American peace treaties had any immediate success.[113] Most of the major inter-American controversies in the period immediately following the ratification of the treaties resulted from long-standing disputes between Latin American nations and were, therefore, exempted from the Washington agreements of 1929. But the long-range effect of the Washington treaties was to provide a solid alternative to the intervention policy.

The administration of Herbert Hoover, who took office in 1929, continued the general movement toward nonintervention. Hoover completed the repudiation of the Roosevelt Corollary by making public the hitherto secret Clark Memorandum in 1930, and he repeated the position of previous presidents that "it has never been and ought not to be the policy of the United States to intervene by force to secure or maintain contracts between

---

[107] Mecham, *Inter-American Security*, p. 99.
[108] Texts of these two documents, including a protocol on progressive arbitration, can be found in *Foreign Relations, 1929*, I: 653–69.
[109] Mecham, *Inter-American Security*, p. 106.
[110] *Foreign Relations, 1929*, I: 653, 660.
[111] *Ibid.*, pp. 655, 662.
[112] *Ibid.*, p. 668.
[113] Mecham, *Inter-American Security*, pp. 109–11, gives a brief account of the successes and failures of the treaties.

our citizens and foreign states or their citizens."[114] He made his statement good by informing American investors in some Latin American countries that they would have to exhaust local remedies before applying to the State Department for diplomatic help, and Secretary of State Stimson backed him up by not allowing the State Department to back American claims in Latin American countries.[115] Finally, outside of the Central American area, where the United States had treaty commitments with regard to recognition, Hoover abandoned the Wilsonian *de jure* recognition policy in favor of de facto recognition.[116]

When Franklin Roosevelt came to power in 1933, there existed a solid foundation for "the policy of the good neighbor," which the new president announced in his inaugural address. First and foremost, the hemisphere was still apparently safe from the danger of non-American encroachment. The withdrawal of American troops from Nicaragua was complete, a similar withdrawal from Haiti was well under way, and a nonintervention article had been accepted for discussion at the up-coming conference of American states at Montevideo.[117] While the new inter-American peace machinery established at Washington in 1929 was not yet working effectively, attempts at peaceful settlement of inter-American disputes had been brought to successful conclusions through the mediation of the United States and even the League of Nations.[118] One of the first pronouncements of the new administration was Roosevelt's proposal: "that all the nations of the world enter into a solemn and definite pact of non-aggression: that they shall solemnly reaffirm the obligation they have assumed to limit and reduce their armaments, and, provided these obligations are faithfully executed by all signatory powers, individually agree that they will send no armed force of whatsoever nature across their frontiers."[119] And against this background of universal denial of the right of armed violation of national sovereignty, maintaining the right of intervention in one area of the world would have seemed illogical, if not hypocritical.

On the other hand, there were good reasons to seek improvement in the badly deteriorated relations with the Latin American countries. The expanded Latin American market might offer some alleviation for the American economic crisis, but that market was bounded by tariff walls erected,

[114] Address at the Gridiron Club, Washington, April 13, 1929. Quoted in Bemis, *Latin American Policy*, p. 222.

[115] Mecham, *Inter-American Security*, p. 113.

[116] *Ibid.*

[117] Bemis, *Latin American Policy*, pp. 221, 269.

[118] *Ibid.*, pp. 268–69; and *Foreign Relations of the United States, 1929*, I: 720–817. The latter reference relates to the successful arbitration of the long-standing Tacna–Arica dispute between Chile and Peru.

[119] Quoted in Bemis, *Latin American Policy*, p. 260.

like the Smoot–Hawley Tariff of 1930, in reaction to the world depression. Also, American influence in the Pan-American movement was under serious challenge by Argentina.[120] An army revolt in 1930 had temporarily reversed the progressive political atmosphere of that country and returned power to the willing hands of a conservative oligarchy.[121] This group looked quite naturally to Europe in the political and economic relations of Argentina. The positive aspect of this development was Argentina's resumption of active membership in the League of Nations and her expansion of economic relations with Great Britain. The negative side took the form of active opposition to American influence in the Western Hemisphere.[122] The Argentine desire to displace the United States as leader of the Pan-American movement resulted, shortly before the Montevideo Conference, in Saavedra Lamas's proposed Anti-War Treaty of Non-Aggression and Conciliation, which was designed to provide an alternative to U.S. mediation in the on-going Chaco War between Paraguay and Bolivia.[123] The Anti-War Treaty contained a prohibition of intervention, "either diplomatic or armed." "Diplomatic intervention," it may be noted, was exactly the label that Dr. Lamas had earlier attached to the efforts of a Commission of Neutrals, created under the auspices of the Washington Treaties of 1929 to mediate in the Chaco conflict.[124] The Argentine Anti-War Treaty marked such an unmistakable change of heart for the nation that had earlier refused to ratify any of the inter-American peace instruments or the Kellogg–Briand Pact and had withdrawn its representatives from the League, that it is difficult to believe that Dr. Lamas was motivated solely by an altruistic love of universal peace. His proposal was, however, an effective challenge to U.S. policy, and upon this basis alone he perhaps deserved his Nobel Peace Prize.

In December 1933 these elements coalesced at the Seventh Pan American Conference at Montevideo. The American delegation, headed by Cordell Hull, arrived with instructions "to remove obstacles standing in the way of harmony and friendly relations with Latin America."[125] Dr. Lamas arrived with his Anti-War Treaty. The result was what Arthur Whitaker has called "a horse trade."[126] "In return for Hull's partial abandonment of intervention and his support of a universalist Peace Pact

[120] The various Argentine attempts to gain a dominant position in the Pan-American movement are recounted in Arthur P. Whitaker, *The United States and Argentina* (Cambridge: Harvard University Press, 1954).

[121] *Ibid.*, pp. 60–66.

[122] *Ibid.*, pp. 104–6.

[123] Fenwick, *Organization of American States*, pp. 179–81.

[124] Bemis, *Latin American Policy*, p. 264.

[125] Wynen and Thomas, *Nonintervention*, p. 62.

[126] Whitaker, *United States and Argentina*, p. 105.

fathered by Saavedra Lamas, the latter supported the declaration in favor of lowering trade barriers proposed by Hull. As a result, in sharp contrast to Havana, Montevideo turned into a love-feast, with Hull and Saavedra Lamas playing Daman and Pythias."[127] In addition, Lamas apparently committed himself to securing the missing Latin American signatures to previous peace treaties. He began by pledging the signature of his own government to the Gondra Treaty of 1923, to the Kellogg–Briand Pact of 1928, and to the Washington Treaties of 1929.[128] The Argentine pledge set off "a rivalry of eloquent good will" as other nonsigners competed to pledge their governments' signatures to the forementioned treaties.[129]

It can be said that as a "horse-trader" Dr. Lamas was Hull's inferior. Except for the nonintervention clause, the Anti-War Treaty was a more limited commitment than the United States had already made by accepting the Kellogg–Briand Pact.[130] On the other hand, the treaty committed Argentina to procedures of peaceful settlement that the nation had previously been unwilling to accept. Also, Lamas's acceptance of Hull's reciprocity principle in tariff reductions was not only to prove a hindrance to Argentine attempts to develop special trade relationships with Europe but also to provide a valuable tool for establishing a U.S. monopoly on Latin American raw materials during World War II.[131] Finally, the Argentine Minister's elation over his newly acquired U.S. commitment to nonintervention was to prove short-lived, for the final diplomatic performance at the Montevideo Conference belonged to Cordell Hull.

One of the items on the agenda of the Montevideo Conference was a proposed Convention on the Rights and Duties of States.[132] The document was largely a replay of its predecessor at the Havana Conference—a veritable digest of Latin American jurisprudence. But the key article was Article VIII, which quite simply stated: "No State has the right to intervene in the internal or external affairs of another." The addition of "external affairs" to the prohibition of intervention was an Argentine extension of the original principle of nonintervention.[133] This prohibition would seem to severely circumscribe the Monroe Doctrine which had in the past been used to prevent the secession of hemispheric territory to non-American powers. Also, it might legitimately be contended that the prohibition would

---

[127] *Ibid.*

[128] Bemis, *Latin American Policy*, p. 271.

[129] *Ibid.* The Argentine government later reneged on its Minister's promise.

[130] Mecham, *Inter-American Security*, p. 119, describes the treaty as "quite innocuous."

[131] For an account of Hull's use of the reciprocity principle in the years immediately preceding the war, see Percy W. Bidwell, "Latin America, Germany, and the Hull Program," *Foreign Affairs* 17 (January 1939): 374–90.

[132] *Foreign Relations, 1933.*

[133] Bemis, *Latin American Policy*, p. 272.

prevent a signatory state from interfering with the establishment of a hostile "fifth column" in another signatory state. But in 1933 the danger of fifth-column activity was scarcely recognized, and the Monroe Doctrine and the no-transfer principle were considered to be firmly based in the right of self-defense. Moreover, as Bemis points out:

> It is doubtful whether the statesmen at Montevideo, including Saavedra Lamas, grasped the full significance of this now expanded dogma. It meant not only a prohibition of such interventions as had characterized the protective imperialism of the United States in the first third of the twentieth century, and were now being liquidated in a supposedly safer age. It could mean further, what doubtless no one really intended it to mean: that if one of the sovereign and equal American republics should negotiate away its independence, no third state could step in to stop it, no matter how much the process might endanger the security of the third state.[134]

However, to point to the expansion of the Doctrine with such fear and trepidation is to raise a straw man. When Hull, much to the joy of the Latin Americans, accepted the Convention for the United States he appended a long reservation that preserved for the United States all of its rights "by the law of nations as generally recognized."[135] While this reservation was largely motivated by hesitancy over the definition of terms,[136] it should not be forgotten that one of the rights "by the law of nations" was the right of self-defense—upon which the Monroe Doctrine was solidly founded. Any further suspicion of the reservation was most certainly allayed by President Roosevelt's public interpretation of the nonintervention clause on December 28, 1933:

> The definite policy of the United States from now on is one opposed to armed intervention. The maintenance of constitutional government in other nations is not, after all, a sacred obligation devolving upon the United States alone. The maintenance of law and the orderly processes of government in this hemisphere is the concern of each individual nation within its borders first of all. It is only if and when the failure of orderly processes affects the other nations of the continent that it becomes their concern, and the point to stress is that in such an event it becomes the joint concern of the whole continent in which we are all neighbors.[137]

The sincerity of the U.S. commitment to nonintervention is a matter of subsequent history. In 1934 the remaining U.S. troops were withdrawn from Haiti; and in 1941 the treaty by which the United States maintained

---

[134] *Ibid.*, p. 272.
[135] Mecham, *Inter-American Security*, p. 116.
[136] Fenwick, *Organization of American States*, pp. 57–58.
[137] *New York Times*, December 29, 1933.

legal control of Haitian finances was allowed to lapse.[138] Later in 1934 the United States abrogated the Platt Amendment and, thereby, its treaty-right to intervene in Cuba.[139] In 1941 the United States undertook to abrogate—four years in advance of expiration—the treaty under which she collected and administered the customs receipts of the Dominican Republic.[140] Only Panama presented any problem to the new policy. In 1936 the State Department negotiated a new treaty with Panama which replaced the right of the United States to unilateral intervention with a pledge for mutual consultation in case of danger to the security of the canal.[141] Article X provided for necessary "measures for prevention and defense," but indicated that such measures would be "the subject of consultation between the two Governments." The Senate refused to ratify this new treaty until 1939, when an exchange of notes assured the United States that in case of emergency U.S. military action could be taken without prior consultation.[142]

By the middle 1930's the United States seemed firmly committed to the path of nonintervention. In 1936 the Roosevelt administration even went one step further in this commitment by superseding even the Hull reservations. But, as we shall soon see, what some have termed the "triumph of absolute nonintervention" was a phenomenon contemporary to the rise of the greatest threat to the doctrine of nonintervention—the necessity of defending the hemisphere once again.

[138] Wynen and Thomas, *Nonintervention*, pp. 36–39.
[139] *Ibid.*, pp. 21–28.
[140] *Ibid.*, p. 36.
[141] *Foreign Relations, 1936.*
[142] Wynen and Thomas, *Nonintervention*, p. 32.

# VI.

# Nonintervention vs. National Security

EVEN AS THE DELEGATES at the Montevideo Conference competed with one another in their expressions of good will and benign intent, events in Europe and in Latin America were already foretelling the twilight period of national and hemispheric isolation. Once again it was to be necessary to prepare the nation and its Latin American neighbors for defense against foreign encroachment. It is impossible to exaggerate the threat that this new national necessity posed for the principle of nonintervention. Isolation was the outstanding characteristic of the hemispheric strategic configuration from 1922 until the mid-1930's. Isolation was the condition that had placed military considerations in the background of the formulation of American policy in Latin America for the entire period of the Republican restoration. And "viewed in the context of the early years of the Roosevelt Administration, even the Good Neighbor Policy was only an expression of a modified isolationism."[1] Therefore, it was inevitable that the "end of isolation" might mean a short life for the principle of nonintervention, if intervention was ever considered necessary for the defense of vital national security interests.

As we have already pointed out, American strategists had long been convinced that the defense of the hemisphere was essential to the defense of the North American continent. Particularly vital were those areas related to the Panama Canal, and this consideration had caused some difficulty for the good neighbor policy even in 1936. But the advent of the airplane had expanded the "radius of security" to the entire hemisphere.

[1] Langer, "Political Problems of a Coalition," *Foreign Affairs* 26 (October 1947): 75.

126

With the approach of hostilities, it was only natural that diplomatic and strategic thinking should again develop striking similarities. In 1940 Henry L. Stimson (then secretary of war) was again invoking the Monroe Doctrine, but this time he was arguing that enforcement of that doctrine necessitated the extension of the American line of defense "far out into the Atlantic Ocean."[2] In May of that year President Roosevelt was terrorizing the Congress with the prospect of an air attack against the continental United States from bases in the Western Hemisphere.[3] Two Gallup polls taken in February and April 1941 indicate the extent to which hemispheric defense had become associated with continental defense in the public mind. The April poll indicated that four-fifths of the American people were still opposed to immediate entry into the war.[4] But in spite of the impermeability of American isolationism the February poll revealed that 86 percent of the people in the United States were in favor of defending all of Latin America against Axis aggression.[5]

The problem of hemispheric defense naturally raised the question of "Who is going to defend?". The inter-American system as it stood at the close of the history-making Montevideo Conference was admirably structured to facilitate *inter-American* relations and to mediate in *inter-American* disputes. But it made no provisions for defense against an external aggressor, whether that aggression might come by direct military action or by subversive activities within the hemisphere. Also, the changing nature of international warfare "ruled out the possibility that any nation in Latin America might make a major military contribution."[6] What the United States needed from Latin America was military bases, internal political stability, access to strategic raw materials, and political support. In short, good neighborism and nonintervention was no longer a strategic possibility for the United States unless the Latin Americans reciprocated by cooperating extensively in the defense of the hemisphere.[7]

---

[2] Quoted in Arthur P. Whitaker, *The Western Hemisphere Idea: Its Rise and Decline* (New York: Cornell University Press, 1954), p. 159.

[3] Franklin D. Roosevelt, "Fifty Thousand Airplanes," speech delivered before joint session of Congress, May 16, 1940. Reprinted in Eugene M. Emme, *The Impact of Air Power* (Princeton: D. Van Nostrand Company, 1959), pp. 69–72.

[4] Whitaker, *Western Hemisphere Idea*, pp. 158–59.

[5] J. Fred Rippy, *South America and Hemisphere Defense* (Baton Rouge: Louisiana State University Press, 1941), p. 9.

[6] Edwin Lieuwen, *Arms and Politics in Latin America* (rev. ed.; New York: Frederick A. Praeger, 1961), p. 189.

[7] Jerome Norman Slater, "The Role of the Organization of American States in United States Foreign Policy, 1947–1963, Ph.D. dissertation (Dept. of Politics, Princeton University), pp. 14–15.

That a system of multilateral security was developed during the war and that American military intervention was to prove unnecessary is usually taken to evidence the success of the good neighbor policy and viability of the inter-American system.[8] However, a closer look reveals a less enticing picture. The security of the hemisphere was never assured by any multilateral security system. Defense cooperation was largely achieved through bilateral arrangements with individual Latin American governments.[9] Internal stability in most cases was achieved at the cost of strengthening the hold of the Latin American armed forces upon the reins of government power in their respective countries. Where friendly political regimes could not be assured in this fashion, the nonintervention commitment was ignored. In some cases intervention took the limited form of political pressure and economic sanctions; but in other cases it took on all of the familiar aspects of the threat and actual use of armed force. "Nonintervention, in the face of an outside threat to hemispheric stability, was no longer compatible with United States interests."[10]

It is difficult to pinpoint exactly when Washington came to the conclusion that preparations for hemispheric defense, including measures to deal with Axis subversion, were a matter of *vital*—as opposed to cautionary—importance. From the outbreak of the first European hostilities, areas such as the Panama Canal were apparently considered highly sensitive,[11] but it is difficult to ascertain how much of this concern with the security of the canal had become essentially Pavlovian among American defense planners and diplomats. President Roosevelt complicated the question to some extent by waving the flag of hemispheric defense as a means of getting armaments appropriations passed by an isolationist Congress.[12] It is probable, however, that it was not until June 1940 that the necessity of hemispheric defense moved from the planning boards to the Cabinet meetings. Up to that time, according to Stull Holt, writing in 1941: "There were no serious doubts of the ultimate victory of the Allies and no serious fears for the safety of the two American continents. During this period there was relatively little joint action, for hemispheric organization has varied directly with Hitler's fortunes in Europe, and the dominant desire was to preserve neutrality and avoid incidents."[13] But by the summer of

---

[8] Mecham, *Inter-American Security*, p. 181.

[9] Eventually arrangements were concluded with all Latin American countries, except Argentina.

[10] Slater, "Role of the O.A.S.," p. 15.

[11] Lieuwen, *Arms and Politics*, p. 118.

[12] Langer and Everett Gleason, *The Challenge to Isolation*, 2 vols. (New York: Harper and Row, 1952), I: 39–40.

[13] W. Stull Holt, "The United States and the Defense of the Western Hemisphere, 1815–1940," *Pacific Historical Review*, 10 (March 1941): 36.

1940 the collapse of France and the imperiled position of the British navy raised the specter of a Germany freed for action outside of the eastern Atlantic.

The problem of timing is important for two reasons: (1) it helps explain American flexibility in light of initial resistance in Latin America to a multilateral approach to hemispheric security, and (2) it provides a key to understanding the apparent transfer of the formulation of American foreign policy in Latin America to the military. Since both of these points are contentious, they will require analysis. Taking the summer of 1940 as a pivotal point, we will first examine developing trends in American policy from the Montevideo Conference to June 1940. Next we will examine how patterns established in this first period conditioned the American approach to hemispheric security in the period from mid-1940 to 1945.

### Atavisms and Neutralisms

As previously mentioned, some American policies in Latin America were continuations from earlier periods and remained relatively untouched by the advent of good neighborism. Such was particularly the case with regard to the security of the Panama Canal. We have already seen that the Senate was hesitant to abrogate U.S. rights to intervene for the protection of the canal even in 1939. But another aspect of American policy in the Central American area—dating back to the Hoover administration— provided an interesting precedent for the late 1930's. In spite of their commitment to the nonsupport of American investment in Latin America, Hoover and Kellogg made one exception to this policy. In July 1929 the State Department had instituted a campaign of full support for American airline companies desiring to operate in the area of the Panama Canal.[14] Initially this policy of diplomatic support was to apply to any American company desiring to establish operations in the area, but soon it became a definite diplomatic effort to secure a monopoly for Pan-American Airways. The reasons for the program of investment support were quite simply stated in a departmental memorandum written by Assistant Secretary of State White, the originator of the support policy.[15] White gave due recognition to the fact that support of a single company would constitute an

---

[14] The State Department documents relating to this episode are reprinted in *Foreign Relations of the United States, 1929*, I: 542–652. A highly critical account of the Pan-American episode can be found in Carleton Beals, *The Coming Struggle for Latin America* (2nd ed. rev.; New York: J. B. Lippincott Company, 1939), pp. 275–80. However, it should be noted that Beals often fails to distinguish the businessmen from the diplomats—an omission rendered doubly pernicious by the almost total absence of documentation in the book.

[15] *Foreign Relations, 1929*, I: 542–45.

important change of policy, but he noted: "It is important that American mails be carried in American planes by American companies. The strategic importance of having most of the flying in the Caribbean area and especially near the Panama Canal Zone in the hands of Americans is obvious. . . . it is certainly desirable and perhaps essential that the United States should, in so far as possible, control aviation in the Caribbean region."[16] The problem, according to White, was that the French and German companies in the area were fully subsidized and were, therefore, in a strong competitive position *vis-a-vis* interested American companies. To support all of the American companies that might desire to enter the competition would be self-defeating; it would only intensify the competition. It was necessary to pick one strong American company and back it with diplomatic support and a subsidy from the U.S. Post Office. Although such a policy was certain to be attacked, it was "one of those cases where vital national interests have to be considered and given preference over the particular interests of individual companies."[17]

By 1930 Pan-American Airways was already operating over one hundred planes and had eighty-nine airports in thirty-one countries.[18] Its operations were heavily concentrated in Central America and northern South America. However, by 1938 Panagra, a Pan-Am subsidiary jointly owned with the Grace Company, was extending its services from Panama to Buenos Aires.[19] Panair, another subsidiary, bought into the German operated *Scadta*, based in Colombia. With the help of an important mail contract, Panair was able to gain control of more than 80 percent of the *Scadta* stock by January 1939.[20] Whatever may be said of the ruthless tactics of the Pam-Am owners in utilizing the support of the American State Department to gain a virtual monopoly over air transport in Central and northern South America, the support of the American monopoly was to prove one of the most foresighted moves the Department ever made. As we shall see, when America went to war in 1941, one of the biggest dangers to the hemispheric war effort was the large network of German airlines in South America. But with the exception of a few remaining German personnel in *Scadta*, the airways within single-flight striking distance of the Panama Canal were filled with American fliers. Pan-Am landing fields, radio service, and meteorological reports were to provide substitutes for the airbases that good neighborism would not permit the United States to obtain and build.

[16] *Ibid.*, pp. 542–43.
[17] *Ibid.*, p. 544.
[18] Beals, *Coming Struggle*, p. 277.
[19] *Ibid.*
[20] Langer and Gleason, *Challenge to Isolation*, I: 274.

A second "atavism" that survived the advent of the new U.S. image for Latin America was the military mission system. Limited use of the military mission system was initiated in Latin America during World War I. The emergency mission sent to Brazil in 1918 was made permanent by congressional legislation in 1922, and under that same legislation a naval training mission in Peru was also given permanent status.[21] In addition, the U.S. army maintained a bewildering array of representatives and one-man missions in Guatemala, Cuba, Brazil, and Panama; but their activity before 1937 was intermittent.[22] An act of May 19, 1926, authorized the U.S. army to send further missions to Latin America, but little seems to have been done toward implementing the authorization.[23] Two factors contributed to this neglect: (1) there was the general political policy of avoiding relations that might be construed as intrusion in Latin America, and (2) in the previous military planning the role of the army was limited in most cases to continental defense.[24] The military mission system was not to be significantly expanded until 1937 and 1938, but the limited existing arrangements were to prove valuable both as precedents and as a training ground in the fine art of dealing with the Latin American military. And in Brazil the twenty-plus-year-old relations between American and Brazilian military men were to prove pivotal in the choice between cooperation and intervention.

Although the U.S. military mission system provided the United States with little more than a foothold of influence over the Latin American military, the military leaders of Italy and Germany were far more appreciative of the potentialities of good relations with the Latin Americans in uniform.[25] German and Italian military missions throughout Latin America spent the period of the 1920's and early 1930's liberally distributing advice, arms, and political indoctrination. Even by 1934 the implications of this European monopoly on military missions were only vaguely recognized. There were, however, a few voices in the wilderness. In September 1934 A. J. Miranda, a Mexican businessman, attempted to convince members of the Senate munitions investigation committee of the danger of allowing South America to remain a European military pre-

---

[21] Lieuwen, *Arms and Politics*, p. 188.
[22] Stetson Conn and Byron Fairchild, *The Framework of Hemisphere Defense* (Washington: Department of the Army, 1960), pp. 172–73.
[23] Lieuwen, *Arms and Politics*, p. 188.
[24] Conn and Fairchild, *Hemisphere Defense*, p. 173.
[25] By far, the best account of the extent and influence of the European military missions in Latin America is: Fritz T. Epstein, "European Military Influences in Latin America" (manuscript in the Library of Congress, Manuscript Division, 1941). Unfortunately, copies of Epstein's work are not readily available. An extremely short review of some of Epstein's material will be found in Lieuwen, *Arms and Politics*, pp. 189–91.

serve. He gave an exhaustive discussion of the profound effects, cultural and political, of the European military training of the Latin Americans.[26] He advocated a program of American munitions exports, designed to underbid the European armaments producers and to mitigate Latin American dependence upon the Germans and Italians for an adequate supply of arms. By this plan he hoped to facilitate the reorientation of the Latin American military away from the Axis powers. As Miranda put it: "It is not only furnishing the material, but along with it will come the American training methods, American instructors, and that is what is going to help the American idea into the mind of the South American people."[27]

The Miranda plan was ultimately important because it finally became the most salient program in the whole complex of U.S.–Latin American military relations. But in 1934 the Senate Committee was more interested in discrediting such non-pacifist practices as the sale of munitions. Senator Bone stated the thought that seems to have been the Munitions Investigation's only conclusion from Miranda's painstaking presentation: "The presence of these military and naval missions in South America, sent there by European Governments, has had a tendency to greatly stimulate the interest of people in the preparation for war and the expansion of their military and naval machinery."[28]

The importance of the late American entry into the military mission business is probably best illustrated by a single general statistic: "By 1936 half of Latin America was ruled by governments predominantly military in character."[29] For a multiplicity of reasons which the limitations of space prevent us from discussing, in the 1930's militarism in Latin America surged back upon the political scene after almost twenty years of relative decline.[30] But by the 1930's the average Latin American military corps was no longer representative of particular classes or oligarchies in Latin American society. It was an interest group of its own, it was highly profes-

---

[26] Epstein, "Military Influences," pp. 11–13.

[27] Ibid., p. 12.

[28] Ibid., p. 13.

[29] Edwin Lieuwen, "Militarism and Politics in Latin America," in John J. Johnson (ed.), The Role of the Military in Underdeveloped Countries (Princeton: Princeton University Press, 1962), p. 131.

[30] Broad generalizations about the Latin American military must always fall prey to the extreme individuality exhibited by the national military institutions of the twenty republics. With this qualification in mind, it is possible to say that during the 1920s and 1930s the typical Latin American military leader ceased to be the caudillo and became the administrator. Governments that were once overthrown by men on horseback, in the 1930s were overthrown by military juntas. The professionalization of the Latin American military, after World War I, made it the only truly national institution in most Latin American countries. Specialized training made the military the national repository

sionalized; and in most cases it was the decisive factor in internal politics.[31] To control the military of most Latin American countries was to control the reins of the national government. It was this conclusion that the Axis powers could derive from their own experience, and it was this conclusion that ultimately provided the Americans with a viable alternative to intervention.

But the military mission policy and the State Department's support of Pan-American Airways were minor dark spots upon the immaculate record of the good neighbor policy. In the United States and Latin America these remnants of the past went virtually unnoticed. Good neighborism rapidly became the automatic diplomatic response in U.S.-Latin American relations. The attention of the American State Department was rapidly directed elsewhere. In Europe the growth of Nazi Germany and the Italo–Ethiopian conflict reminded American observers that their relations within the hemisphere were not the only relations that needed improvement.

The American reaction to the first appearance of the European war clouds was to buy an umbrella. The Neutrality Act of 1935 and the neutrality legislation of 1936 and 1937 gave dramatic expression to American isolationism. Somewhat as a secondary thought, it was remembered that American neutrality would be impossible to maintain unless the neutrality of the entire hemisphere could be assured. To this end, the extraordinary Peace Conference of 1936 was called by President Roosevelt at Buenos Aires.[32]

The course of the Buenos Aires Conference simply does not support the contention that the purpose and effect of the Conference was to "multilateralize the Monroe Doctrine."[33] The United States and its southern neighbors sought to multilateralize neutrality and nothing else. This much is clear from Roosevelt's letter inviting the Latin American countries to Buenos Aires. In proposing the extraordinary conference, the President suggested that steps to be taken might "supplement and reinforce the efforts of the League . . . in seeking to prevent war."[34] And Hull backed

---

of the methods of modernization; and the democratization of the officer corps ultimately provided military leaders whose vested interest in national modernization outweighed its allegiance to the traditional, landed oligarchy. When the depression of the 1930's raised a cry for reform, it was the Latin American military that responded. For full discussions of the changing nature and role of the Latin American military, see: John J. Johnson, *The Military and Society in Latin America* (Stanford: Stanford University Press, 1964); and articles in Johnson (ed.), *Role of the Military*.

[31] Epstein, "Military Influences," p. 4.

[32] J. Lloyd Mecham, *The United States and Inter-American Security, 1889–1960* (Austin: University of Texas Press, 1961), p. 122.

[33] Langer and Gleason, *Challenge to Isolation*, I: 40.

[34] Mecham, *Inter-American Security*, p. 122.

up the neutrality idea by making the Pan-Americanization of the U.S. neutrality legislation one of the official American proposals at the Buenos Aires Conference.[35]

Part and parcel of the hemispheric neutrality proposed by the United States at Buenos Aires was the U.S. plan for a reciprocal assistance commitment in the event of attack by a non-American power.[36] But this idea proved too much for the Latin Americans and in particular for Argentina. Argentina, of course, had the most to lose from neutrality or from a commitment to reciprocal defense. That country was highly dependent upon her trade with European countries, and her relations with the Axis powers were friendly. She had nothing to gain from being pulled into a war "on the coat-tails of the United States." Accordingly, to get even its minimum proposals for mutual consultation through the Conference the United States again had to bargain with Argentina.

Whether through experience or fate, Savedra Lamas proved the better trader in his second round with Hull. The U.S.–Argentine compromise on intergovernmental consultation simply provided that the American governments would consult in the event of internal conflict or external attack. But the Conference set up no standing organ of consultation, nor did it significantly improve the machinery for the settlement of hemispheric conflicts.[37] The only result of the entire Conference that could reasonably be called a move toward the creation of a collective security system was the recognition that "every act susceptible to disturbing the peace of America affects each and every American State."[38] In return, the United States had to agree to an even stronger statement of the nonintervention commitment that it had made at Montevideo. The Buenos Aires resolution prohibited the "intervention of any (American state) . . . directly or indirectly, and for whatever reason, in the internal or external affairs of any other of the Parties."[39] This time the United States made no reservations to its acceptance of the principle of nonintervention.

The remaining conferences that took place before the summer of 1940 were distinguished only by their consistency. The American call for a hemispheric defensive alliance was continuously countered by the agreement upon consultation.[40] Washington's anxiety with the growing signs of

[35] Whitaker, *Western Hemisphere Idea*, p. 106.
[36] *Ibid.*
[37] The latter goal had been one of the main reasons for the U.S. interest in an extraordinary conference. The bloody Chaco War had broken out again, and existing machinery had proved inadequate to deal with the problem. See Slater, "Role of the O.A.S.," p. 76.
[38] *Ibid.*, p. 77.
[39] *Ibid.*
[40] *Ibid.*, pp. 77–79.

Nazi infiltration and subversion in the Latin American countries was not mirrored by the Latin American delegations. The general approach of the Latin American countries to the problem of the growing European hostilities is perhaps best illustrated by the resolution of the American Foreign Ministers, meeting after the outbreak of the war in Europe. The Panama Conference of 1939 created a 300-mile-wide zone of neutrality around the American republics. What has sometimes been called the "Pan-American chastity belt" was justified by the U.S. delegate, Sumner Welles, in terms that smacked of pure isolationism: The American republics, he declared, have "a right inherent in their position as peaceful and independent powers, constituting an entire continent . . . to protect themselves . . . from . . . the repercussions of a war which has broken out thousands of miles from their shores and in which they are not involved."[41]

Fortunately, as later proved to be the case, the U.S. military was not nearly so isolationist as the Latin American diplomatic corps. Two of the military's activities during the late 1930's later proved pivotal in U.S.– Latin American relations. The first was the expansion of the military mission system in the Latin American countries. It is notable that the impetus for the expansion of the military missions did not come from the American military itself but from the State Department.[42] From the military point of view the Latin American military could offer minimal assistance in the defense of the hemisphere or the continent. But American diplomats took a broader view of the possible benefits to be derived from military assistance:

> Alarmed by the increasing volume of German Nazi and Italian Fascist activity in Latin America, the Department of State, rather than the armed services, took the initiative in convening an informal interdepartmental conference on 10 January 1938 to discuss ways and means of providing greater military assistance to the other American republics. After this meeting, the Department of State proposed such limited measures of cooperation as training additional Latin American students in United States service schools; more frequent visits of naval vessels and demonstration flights of service aircraft in Latin America; visits by high-ranking Latin American officers to the United States; and providing Army and Navy publications to military libraries in Latin America.[43]

A month later the State Department added to its recommendation that additional military attaches should be sent to Latin American capitals.[44]

---

[41] Quoted in Whitaker, *Western Hemisphere Idea*, p. 150.
[42] Conn and Fairchild, *Hemisphere Defense*, p. 173.
[43] *Ibid.*
[44] *Ibid.*

One year later these "limited measures of cooperation" were in full swing. One example was the mass flight of U.S. bombers to Argentina in February of 1939. On the day that Roberto M. Ortiz was inaugurated as president of Argentina the American bombers shared the skies over Buenos Aires with Italian-made planes—a situation that led one Argentine writer to comment: "Among more enlightened savages, it is customary to leave your guns behind you, when you come in friendship."[45] By the time of the mass flight, which was made possible by the cooperation of Pan-American Airways (to recall an old friend), the U.S. army had twenty-two officers assigned to Latin American countries.[46] By the end of the year both aviation and naval missions were beginning to multiply.[47] Professional instruction was being offered at all levels at less than cost, if necessary to underbid the Axis powers.[48] By the time of Pearl Harbor there was not an Axis mission left in Latin America.[49]

Among the duties of the military missions was that of promoting the sale of U.S.-made munitions, but in this area much had to be sacrificed to the preservation of congressional consciences. In March 1939 the War, Navy, and State Departments had supported a House resolution to "assist the governments of the American republics to increase their military and naval establishments" by making war materiel available at cost. But the Senate had refused to go along with the measure.[50] A measure authorizing military cooperation with the other American republics did not pass the Senate until May 29, 1939, but in June 1940 both houses of Congress passed an authorization which was to break the back of the European armaments monopoly in Latin America.[51] Joint Resolution Number 367 had as its stated purpose "to authorize the Secretaries of War and of the Navy to assist the governments of American republics to increase their military and naval establishments, and for other purposes."[52] But the State Department analysis of the bill probably comes closer to indicating its true purposes:

> The title of the resolution does not quite suggest what it means. It deals solely with war vessels, aircraft guns, and coast-defense weapons. It does not deal with arms and ammunition in the sense of rifles, and things of that kind.
>
> Several of the American republics are desirous of increasing the strength of their naval armament and the strength of their coast defense in order that

[45] Beals, *Coming Struggle*, p. 316.
[46] Lieuwen, *Arms and Politics*, p. 191.
[47] *Ibid.*
[48] *Ibid.*
[49] *Ibid.*
[50] *Ibid.*, p. 192.
[51] Epstein, "Military Influences," p. 284.
[52] Quoted in *ibid.*, p. 284.

they may be better prepared to resist any possible attack on their territories by the armed forces of non-American powers. Those American republics do not have the facilities within their own jurisdiction to manufacture modern coast defense and antiaircraft artillery. Most of them do not possess shipyards suitable for the construction of modern vessels of war without foreign cooperation. In these circumstances the Governments of the American republics in question find it necessary in order to carry out their armament programs to purchase the necessary artillery and ammunition abroad and either to purchase the necessary vessels of war abroad or to obtain foreign cooperation in their construction at home. They would prefer to make these purchases and to obtain this cooperation in the United States, but when they approach American arms manufacturers they find that these manufacturers are not equipped to manufacture artillery or ammunition of the types desired, and when they approach American shipbuilders they find that those shipbuilders cannot construct or cooperate in construction of vessels of war except at prices which compared with prices charged by European manufacturers appear exorbitant.[53]

Under Secretary of State Sumner Welles explained why it was important that the Latin Americans "buy American": "Should the proposed Joint Resolution result in the construction of military equipment . . . the relationship thereby established would facilitate the continuation of technical collaboration in military and naval matters."[54] What is important to remember is the reasoning that underlay the State Department's concern for military collaboration: it was that military collaboration was one approach to the problem of internal subversion in the Latin American countries.

A second area in which the military went beyond the political isolationism of the period was that of military planning. In April 1938 the Standing Liaison Committee was created to deal with problems of hemispheric security. It was composed of the under secretary of state, the chief of staff, and the chief of naval operations. Among the first problems discussed by the Liaison Committee were those of the German and Italian military missions, the German control of the Brazilian and Colombian airlines, and the German arms shipments to Brazil, Uruguay, and Argentina.[55] From its formation to the close of the war the Standing Liaison Committee was to serve as a clearing house for all plans and operations dealing with the problems of defense and internal security in Latin America.[56]

[53] Quoted in *ibid.*, pp. 285–86.
[54] Quoted in *ibid.*, p. 286.
[55] Langer and Gleason, *Challenge to Isolation*, I: 40.
[56] To my knowledge, there is no single work which deals with the work of the Liaison Committee; but examples of its operation can be found in Langer and Gleason, *Challenge to Isolation;* and by the same authors, *The Undeclared War* (New York: Harper and Brothers, 1953), *passim.*

But by far the most important pre-hostilities work of the military was done in the area of the broader aspects of defense planning. It has already been indicated that until 1939 the American armed forces were operating on the basis of the old "color" plans. But as the prospect of a two-ocean war grew ever more imminent, military planners became ever more dissatisfied with the state of defense planning, which continued to envision a Pacific war with Japan. In April 1939 the planners of the Joint Board submitted a report on the possibility of a two-ocean war. Their general conclusion was that priorities in defense had to go to the vital positions in the Western Hemisphere, such as the Panama Canal and the Caribbean.[57] It was decided that the United States and the Panama Canal Zone could be subject to invasion or large-scale attack only if such an attack was backed by airpower. "Airpower in strength could not be projected directly across the oceans, but it could be launched from land bases within the Western Hemisphere. Therefore, the primary objective of the hemisphere defense policy, from the Army's point of view, was to prevent the establishment of any hostile air base in the Western Hemisphere from which the continental area or the Panama Canal might be bombed or from which a surface attack or invasion might be supported."[58] It was assumed that if Britain and France opposed the Axis in the Atlantic, the defense of the approaches to the Caribbean could easily be assured. But if they did not, "the security of the South Atlantic would become the major concern of U.S. forces, and the active cooperation of the Latin American states the indispensable prerequisite for political and military action."[59] It was further agreed that the sensitive area in Latin America was the Brazilian "bulge," which was subject to possible aerial attack from Africa. It was here that the Axis could hope to gain a foothold in the Western Hemisphere by direct projection of their airpower.[60]

Eventually a whole new set of military plans was created to deal not with specific enemies but with specific defensive situations. The five Rainbow plans that finally evolved from the planners efforts were defined by the Joint Board as follows:

RAINBOW I assumed the United States to be at war without major allies. United States forces would act jointly to prevent the violation of the Monroe Doctrine by protecting the territory of Western Hemisphere north of 10° South Latitude, from which the vital interests of the United States might be threatened. The joint tasks of the Army and Navy included protection of the

---

[57] Louis Morton, "Germany First," in Kent Roberts Greenfield (ed.) *Command Decisions* (New York: Harcourt, Brace and Company, 1959), pp. 13–14.

[58] Conn and Fairchild, *Hemisphere Defense*, p. 15.

[59] Morton, "Germany First," pp. 13–14.

[60] *Ibid.*, p. 14.

United States, its possessions, and its sea-borne trade. A strategic defensive was to be maintained in the Pacific, from behind the line Alaska–Hawaii–Panama, until developments in the Atlantic permitted concentration of the fleet in mid-Pacific for offensive action against Japan.

RAINBOW II assumed that the United States, Great Britain, and France would be acting in concert, with limited participation of the U.S. forces in Continental Europe and in the Atlantic. The United States could, therefore, undertake immediate offensive operations across the Pacific to sustain the interests of democratic powers by the defeat of enemy forces.

RAINBOW III assumed the United States to be at war without major allies. Hemisphere defense was to be assured, as in RAINBOW I, but with early projection of U.S. forces from Hawaii into the western Pacific.

RAINBOW IV assumed the United States to be at war without major allies, employing its forces in defense of the whole of the Western Hemisphere, but also with provision for United States Army forces to be sent to the southern part of South America, and to be used in joint operations in eastern Atlantic areas. A strategic defensive, as in RAINBOW I, was to be maintained in the Pacific until the situation in the Atlantic permitted transfer of major naval forces for an offensive against Japan.

RAINBOW V assumed the United States, Great Britain, and France to be acting in concert; hemisphere defense was to be assured as in RAINBOW I, with early projection of U.S. forces to the eastern Atlantic, and to either or both the African and European Continents; offensive operations were to be conducted, in concert with British and allied forces, to effect the defeat of Germany and Italy. A strategic defensive was to be maintained in the Pacific until success against the European Axis Powers permitted transfer of major forces to the Pacific for an offensive against Japan.[61]

With regard to hemispheric defense, there was little difference between the various Rainbow plans. They all called for the defense of the hemisphere north of 10° south latitude. But politically this aspect of the planning carried broad implications. By choosing "quarter hemisphere defense" over the defense of the entire hemisphere the planners essentially cordoned off Argentina and Chile from the area that was considered to involve vital security interests for the United States. No single aspect of hemispheric relations during the war goes further toward explaining the indifference that the United States could continue to show toward the apparent Axis sympathies of the Argentine and Chilean governments. Only Rainbow IV called for the defense of the entire hemisphere, and that plan envisioned American defense against an Axis attack upon the continental portions of the Americas. Because it assumed the absence of operations in the Atlantic or the Pacific, Rainbow IV simply extended the old principle of concentra-

---

[61] Summary taken from Morton, "Germany First," p. 15.

tion of force to its hemispheric extreme. The principle of a centrally located "strategic reserve" had long played an important role in American military planning.[62] That same principle was now extended to the hemisphere. Rainbow IV, like the other Rainbow plans, recognized the importance of the Brazilian bulge to the defense of the hemisphere and the continental United States, but it allowed for a situation in which an enemy force freed of other considerations would be able to launch an attack on the bulge from the south as well as the east.

As might be imagined, the tactical implementation of Rainbow IV showed precious little regard for the nonintervention commitments. As early as the winter of 1940 troop divisions were being trained for the possible necessity of invading the area in the vicinity of the Brazilian bulge.[63] Fortunately Rainbow IV proved not to be the relevant plan for American participation in World War II, but the attitude which it evidenced was to find numerous expressions during the course of American–Latin American wartime relations. Probably the best expression of that attitude came from President Roosevelt himself in 1944: the President sent extra arms and "advisers" to the Brazilians to enable them to station "two or three divisions near the Argentine border" in order to impress "the present military gang in control of Argentine."[64] The irony of the President's idea is that it consisted of using the "present military gang" in Brazil to impress their Argentine counterparts, who at least had a great deal of popular support in their country.

The Rainbow plans naturally raised the question of acquiring bases in the southern part of the hemisphere. The whole problem was accentuated in March 1939 by the results of naval and aerial exercises in the Caribbean. After these exercises the Department of the Navy was particularly concerned with the problem of safeguarding the Panama Canal.[65] Its report indicates the extent to which the area affecting the security of the canal had been extended in military thinking: "This problem brings home the absolute necessity for a base of operations in or near the eastern extremity of South America in case the South Atlantic is to be controlled by any force."[66] The problem of bases was further complicated by the fear that British, French, or Dutch defeat in a war with Germany might result in the transfer of Caribbean territory to the Germans. In military planning, the problem of transfer took priority. Joint Task No. 1 of the joint army and navy Rainbow IV plan was to "establish United States sovereignty

---

[62] Conn and Fairchild, *Hemisphere Defense*, p. 16.
[63] *Ibid.*, p. 88.
[64] Quoted in Lieuwen, *Arms and Politics*, p. 193.
[65] Langer and Gleason, *Challenge to Isolation*, p. 136.
[66] Quoted in *ibid.*

in British, French, Dutch, and Danish possessions in the Western Hemisphere."[67] In domestic politics the possibility of German possession of territory in the hemisphere also received attention. Early in 1940 both houses of Congress passed resolutions declaring that transfer of new world territory to any non-American power would be regarded as dangerous to the peace of the United States.[68]

## Nonintervention in Wartime

By the time the American ministers met in Havana in 1940, American military missions and arms suppliers were rapidly taking over the function earlier fulfilled by the American marines. Latin American military establishments were dependent upon the ability of their respective military missions to supply them with requested armaments, and their governments were dependent upon their respective military establishments. But this gradual penetration of the political integrity of the individual Latin American states was the least of the American ministers multiple problems at Havana. Far more important was the prospect of the Germans gaining a foothold in the Western Hemisphere through the transfer of the remaining European territories in the new world. Second, with the fall of France and the deterioration of the British positions, there came the unpleasant prospect of actual German aggression in the Western Hemisphere. Accordingly the Havana Conference issued two resolutions. The first was a declaration to the effect that if any of the remaining European territories were in danger of changing hands, "the American nations might establish a regime of provisional administration with the understanding that the possessions would ultimately either be made independent or restored to their previous status."[69] Declaration No. XV constituted the final recognition by the American states that their individual fates were indivisible with respect to the Allied–Axis war. That resolution declared:

> That any attempt on the part of a non-American State against the integrity or inviolability of the territory, the sovereignty or the political independence of an American State shall be considered as an act of aggression against the States which sign this declaration.
>
> In case acts of aggression are committed or should there be reason to believe that an act of aggression is being prepared by a non-American nation against the integrity or inviolability of the territory, the sovereignty or the political independence of an American nation, the nations signatory to the present declaration will consult among themselves in order to agree upon the measure it may be advisable to take.

[67] Quoted in Conn and Fairchild, *Hemisphere Defense*, p. 48.
[68] Dexter Perkins, *The United States and Latin America* (Baton Rouge: Louisiana State University Press, 1960), p. 28.
[69] Mecham, *Inter-American Security*, p. 187.

All the signatory nations, or two or more of them, according to circumstances, shall proceed to negotiate the necessary complementary agreements so as to organize cooperation for defense and the assistance that they shall lend each other in the event of aggressions such as referred to in this declaration.[70]

At Havana and at subsequent meetings the unity of inter-American security was reaffirmed *ad nauseam*, but the truth was that inter-American security meant U.S. security, and the United States would have to assure that security itself. The Havana Act and subsequent legitimizations of unilateral actions merely added the cast of respectability to actions that the United States was already taking in its own defense.[71] Throughout the war the unalterable fact of the inter-American system was that it was not a collective system of hemispheric security but a shelter under which the United States could effect needed bilateral arrangements with certain Latin American governments. It is notable in this respect that when an inter-American defense board was proposed at the Rio Conference in 1942, one month after the bombing of Pearl Harbor, the proposal was opposed by both the U.S. army and navy, who opted for the simpler bilateral arrangements for arms and raw materials.[72] By the end of the war all Latin American countries except Argentina had entered into bilateral defense arrangements with the United States. Under these circumstances the Inter-American Defense Board—the only institutional structure that even approached a collective security arrangement—"was able to play no vital role in World War II."[73]

The bilateral arrangements, legitimized by the inter-American resolutions, had three major purposes in U.S. strategy: (1) to assure the supply of

[70] Quoted in Samuel Flagg Bemis, *The Latin American Policy of the United States: An Historical Interpretation* (New York: Harcourt, Brace and Company, 1943), pp. 369–70.

[71] A good example of this tendency to legitimize U.S. action was afforded by another section of the Act of Havana which declared: "Should the need for emergency action be so urgent that action by the committee cannot be awaited, any of the American Republics, individually or jointly with others, shall have the right to act in the manner which its own defense or that of the continent requires. Should this situation arise, the American Republic or Republics taking action shall place the matter before the committee immediately, in order that it may consider the action and adopt appropriate measures" (quoted in Bemis, *Latin American Policy*, p. 371).

At the time this declaration was signed, the United States was preparing to occupy the French island of Martinique rather than have it fall into German hands. The Martinique invasion proved unnecessary; but in November of 1941, American and Brazilian troops did occupy Dutch Guiana, rather than tolerate a violation of the no-transfer principle by the Allied governments (see Conn and Fairchild, *Hemisphere Defense*, pp. 49–51).

[72] See Mecham, *Inter-American Security*, for a discussion of the various attempts to set up some collective security system.

[73] Lieuwen, *Arms and Politics*, p. 194.

raw materials from Latin America; (2) to facilitate American use of Latin American air and naval bases; and (3) to root out Nazi subversion in the hemisphere. The first of these objectives was fully achieved. During the war Latin America supplied the United States with all of its quinine, balsa wood, and rotenone. Eighty-three percent of copper imported into the United States came from other American countries. In addition, Latin America accounted for 77 percent of U.S. Manila fiber, 56 percent of its tin, 76.7 percent of its imported vanadium, and 43.2 percent of its crude rubber.[74]

The success of the attempt to control Nazi subversion in the hemisphere is more difficult to assess. In the first place, control of fifth column activity in Latin America was a U.S. requirement not a request. Early in 1941 some U.S. government officials became very concerned lest a Nazi-inspired revolution lead to establishment of a government unfriendly to the United States in one of the countries near the Panama Canal.[75] The approved army plan for such a contingency consisted of an earmarked airborne division based in Panama under the command of Lt. General Daniel Van Voorhis. It was envisioned that such a force would be able to come to the aid of friendly governments in time to suppress any attempted overthrow of the government. Although the official army history maintains that this unit was to be used only at the request of a besieged government, in the one instance that the plans were almost invoked there does not appear to have been any such request.[76]

A second important factor to remember with respect to Nazi subversion in the hemisphere is that "because German minorities in Latin America engaged in subversive activities under the express direction of official German representatives, the most effective countermeasure was the breaking of relations with the Axis."[77] With the severance of diplomatic relationships after Pearl Harbor, most of the German espionage networks in Latin America were thrown into disarray. The major exception to this rule was Argentina, but the geographical position of that country made the exception tolerable. Although the United States did attempt to use the Committee for Political Defense to force Argentina into a position of conformity with the rest of the continent, the attempt proved fruitless except for provoking the Argentine resignation from the Committee.

American use of Latin American bases proved to be another kind of problem. "To the disappointment of United States military men, Latin

---

[74] Perkins, *United States and Latin America*, p. 31.
[75] Conn and Fairchild, *Hemisphere Defense*, pp. 186–91.
[76] The instance was the outbreak of hostilities between Peru and Ecuador in the summer of 1941 (see *ibid.*, p. 190).
[77] Edgar S. Furniss, Jr., *American Military Policy* (New York: Rinehart, 1957), p. 265.

America's officer corps tended to view the matter from the angle of advantages that might accrue to their own military establishments."[78] Securing bases from the Latin Americans became next to impossible until the extension of Lend Lease to Latin American allies lubricated the nationalistic friction that the earlier base negotiations had tended to engender.[79] In 1942, after the extension of Lend Lease to Latin America, the desired facilities were secured from Brazil, Mexico, Cuba, Panama, and Ecuador.

But the problem of bases in Latin America cannot be dismissed so simply. In the first place, it is necessary to point out that the U.S. need for bases in Latin America was largely satisfied by the so-called Destroyer-Base Agreement of 1940, whereby the United States traded Britain fifty old destroyers for bases in the Caribbean.[80] Second, where the need for bases was considered critical, as in the area of the Panama Canal, the United States proved itself willing to take bases by armed force, in spite of its commitment to nonintervention. In the autumn of 1940, for example, the U.S. army was occupying base sites in Panama, despite the passive opposition of the Panamanian government.[81]

Most importantly, the Department of State had already developed a unique plan for getting around Latin American objections to the construction of American air bases within their territories. The U.S. government negotiated with Pan-American Airways to do the air base construction that it could not do itself.[82] By 1939 the Pan-American system was already developed to the point that the United States could fly medium and heavy bombers to Natal on the Brazilian hump, but to permit movements of shorter-range aircraft it was necessary to develop a more comprehensive network of airfields.[83] Lt. Colonel Robert Olds described the importance of the Pan-American system in a report to General Headquarters Air Force in late 1939: "The economic and military value of the Panagra-Pan American Airways System to the United States in its broad concept of hemispherical defense cannot be over-estimated. . . . The

---

[78] Lieuwen, *Arms and Politics*, p. 194.

[79] *Ibid.*

[80] For the details of the destroyer deal, see Langer and Gleason, *Challenge to Isolation*, II: 742–46.

[81] Langer and Gleason, *Undeclared War*, pp. 148–50. The illegality of the American occupation of the Panamanian sites is by no means a settled matter; but the American claim to the legality of the occupation based upon the 1936 Canal Treaty seems tenuous in the extreme. Even if the subsequent exchange of notes, which authorized unilateral action in cases of dire necessity, is taken into consideration, it would be difficult to show that dire necessity of the type envisioned was present in 1940.

[82] Details of the Airport Development Program can be found in Conn and Fairchild, *Hemisphere Defense*, pp. 249–59.

[83] *Ibid.*, p. 250.

concentration . . . of Air Force units from North America into South America will depend solely under existing circumstances upon the full utilization of Pan American facilities. . . . Whether in the form of a government subsidy or in the form of direct installations on a rental basis, it is mandatory that certain existing facilities of the Pan American System be augmented along the east coast of South America to insure the rapid concentration of American Air Forces in the defense of the critical Natal area."[84] The military and the diplomats took the Colonel's advice. In September 1940 the government concluded a contract with Pan-American in the amount of $12,000,000 for the development of a network of airfields to fit the specifications of the army and navy. One year later the contract was revised upward to $19,000,000. This increase was to allow Pan-American to extend the airport program to Bolivia and Paraguay. Notably, the War Plans Division of the army opposed this extension as unnecessary under existing defense plans, but the Department of State insisted upon it for political reasons.[85]

By using Pan-American Airways as its negotiating front the United States was able to get around the technical neutrality of the Latin American nations. But more importantly it was able to get around the popular nationalistic reactions to the official presence of American military might. In any case, the Airport Development Project was a military success. By 1942, "a screen of air and naval bases open to, or actually occupied by, United States troops covered the continent from Mexico to Uruguay, from Brazil to Ecuador's Galapagos Islands. In Panama alone upwards of one hundred installations were turned over, ranging in size from small anti-aircraft sites to the large Rio Hato airfield."[86]

U.S.–Brazilian relations offer a felicitous example of the general nature of U.S.–Latin American cooperation in the defense of the hemisphere. All of the Rainbow plans recognized the importance of the defense of the Brazilian bulge to the defense of the hemisphere. In fact, by 1940 it was axiomatic that Nazi penetration of Northwest Africa would make it "imperative for the United States to anticipate such action by the preventive occupation of the air fields and ports in northeastern Brazil."[87] And the Pan-American contract was designed largely to facilitate the accessibility of the Brazilian northeast to the U.S armed forces. In June 1940 the army sent Lt. Colonel Lehman W. Miller, who had previously served with the Military Mission in Rio de Janeiro, to conduct staff discussions with the Brazilian military. Miller's instructions were explicit as to the goal of

---

[84] Quoted in *ibid.*, p. 250.
[85] *Ibid.*, pp. 256–57.
[86] Furniss, *American Military Policy*, p. 259.
[87] Conn and Fairchild, *Hemisphere Defense*, p. 274.

U.S.–Brazilian military collaboration; that goal was "the maintenance in Brazil of a Government, both determined and able, to preserve its territorial integrity and freedom from European control, and to cooperate fully with the United States in hemisphere defense."[88] The staff discussions took place, and in January 1941 the Brazilian military presented their request for needed armaments. It was calculated that the Brazilian requests would have cost about $250,000,000.[89] That price was steep even for collaboration in the vital area of the bulge, but eventually a more reasonable figure of $100,000,000 was settled upon and credits were arranged through the Import–Export Bank.[90] But it proved impossible to supply these minimum Brazilian demands; the critical supplies requested by Brazil were needed by other allied countries as well and could not be spared. Even after the attack on Pearl Harbor, President Vargas of Brazil made it quite clear to Sumner Welles that the stationing of U.S. ground forces in Brazil was contingent upon the delivery of substantial quantities of military equipment.[91]

The Brazilians were as good as their word. When the Lend lease allocations of January 1942 made even more equipment available to them at cheaper rates, the Brazilians were ready to negotiate the stationing of American troops again. The final Lend lease agreement called for delivery of military equipment valued at $200,000,000; some of that equipment was so scarce that it had been removed from the existing defenses of New York City.[92] But on March 3 President Vargas announced "a wide reaching program for Northeast Brazil" that included the stationing of 800 U.S. army maintenance personnel, new construction, and unrestricted flight privileges for U.S aircraft.[93]

With minor variations, depending upon the military sensitivity of the area, this was the story of inter-American cooperation in the defense of the hemisphere. It was the story of sovereignty bought by guns and tanks. It could not quite be called intervention, but it was an unfortunate second-best. The success of the American hemispheric defense effort depended upon the possibility of bribing the Latin American military establishments with weapons that they would never use in the defense of the hemisphere but that they might very well use in defense of their own interests in the Latin American societies. But from the immediate American point of

---

[88] *Ibid.*, pp. 276–77.
[89] *Ibid.*, p. 279.
[90] *Ibid.*, pp. 293–96.
[91] *Ibid.*, p. 314.
[92] See *ibid.*, pp. 312–20, for details of these negotiations.
[93] *Ibid.*, p. 317.

view it undoubtedly seemed as if the United States had found the touchstone to the successful unification of its policies of nonintervention and of hemispheric security. "Because of their key political role, the armed forces in most Latin American countries largely determined the extent of their nation's support of the United States during World War II."[94] And that support could be bought with a few palliatives thrown to the military from America's large supply of modern weaponry. The real fruits of these policies were not reaped until the postwar era and therefore will be discussed later. Let it suffice here to say that even in 1945 the cure for intervention was already looking worse than the disease.

[94] Lieuwen, *Arms and Politics*, p. 195.

# VII.

# The Consolidation of the Inter-American System

THE CONSOLIDATION of the inter-American system in the form of the Organization of American States was perhaps the inevitable result of the apparent success of the system in meeting the wartime crisis. The problem was that it was not the formal aspects of the system, as embodied in the Charter of the O.A.S., that were responsible for that success. Far more important were the bilateral arrangements with the Latin American military establishments, which allowed a large degree of U.S control of the internal political situation in strategically sensitive areas of the Western Hemisphere—particularly in the Caribbean area. In consequence, the nonintervention articles of the Charter were an exercise in creative fiction from the day they were written.

Bilateral military arrangements that assured American control of hemispheric security during World War II were perpetuated even into the present day by a series of mutual defense and mutual security agreements.[1] Such arrangements have of course coexisted with various programs of economic assistance—most notably loans and credits financed through the Export–Import Bank—which in terms of dollars far exceed expenditures for military assistance and which have their own history of manipulation in the service of what were and are perceived as U.S. interests in the hemisphere. But it is in the area of military assistance that those interests have been most blatantly identified and where their articulation

---

[1] The details of the postwar U.S. military program in Latin America can be found in Edwin Lieuwen, *Arms and Politics in Latin America* (rev. ed.; New York: Frederick A. Praeger, 1961).

is least cluttered by the patina of humanitarian rhetoric.[2] And in postwar history it has usually been the failure of subsidized Latin American militaries to preserve an acceptable political configuration in domestic politics that has signaled the perceived necessity of direct U.S. intervention. In short, however devoutly it may have been desired from time to time that the economic assistance programs would result in the kind of social and political security in Latin America that would render dependence upon military instrumentalities, direct and indirect, unnecessary, those programs have not proved sufficiently successful to allow the eschewal of even direct military intervention as a means of preserving minimal hemispheric security.[2a]

Therefore, the bilateral military programs remained a kind of indispensable core—the ultimate safety valve—of U.S.–Latin American policy even in periods of postwar diplomatic history in which programs of economic and technical assistance held the center stage. The enemy, of course, changed. The specter of Nazi invasion yielded to the phantom of Soviet lodgment that in turn gave ground to the presiding demon of communist subversion. And it was in response to this last perceived threat that the bilateral military assistance technique proved, in the U.S. view, inadequate.

## The Structure of Consolidation

In early 1945 the hemispheric Ministers of State met at Chapultepec to assess the future of the inter-American system. This conference produced the Act of Chapultepec, the most important provision of which declared

[2] It has been pointed out to me that my strong emphasis upon U.S. military assistance programs in the postwar era yields a misleading portrait of contemporary U.S.–Latin American policy, which since the middle 1950's has made increasing use of economic aid and investment incentives. I would concede the fact of the resulting distortion and make appropriate references to the shortness of life and the limits of printing space. The reason for choosing to focus on the military assistance programs is simply that within such programs the bureaucratic perception of "essential" U.S. interests is usually more explicit. For example, it is one thing to be told by Hubert Humphrey that in 1963 one of the motives for U.S. participation in the Alliance for Progress was that the success of the Alliance would "thwart the spread of communism in the Western Hemisphere." It is another to know that under the Kennedy administration counterinsurgency measures assumed increasing importance in the military aid program. The latter data suggests a shift of military concern from external attack to internal political opposition. The former statement informs us only of Humphrey's acceptance of the conventional political wisdom of the period, to the effect that communism is the child of poverty.

[2a] In the early 1960's, the distinction that I am drawing was usually phrased in terms of immediate threats versus long-range progress. For example, in his Report on the Alliance for Progress, 1963 (Washington: GPO, 1963), Hubert Humphrey justified the massive counterinsurgency aid then flowing to the Betancourt government in Venezuela as "designed to provide a shield of security behind which the Alliance for Progress can develop. They are essential to repulse the immediate threat to the stability and internal security that are necessary if the long-term Alliance for Progress economic programs are to succeed."

that an attack on an American state by any state, American or foreign, would be considered an attack against all of them, warranting collective measures to repel the aggression. Notably, Latin American acquiescence in the mutual defense arrangement resulted not so much from their involvement in World War II as from mutual fear and suspicion among the Latin Americans themselves. The inter-American wars of the 1930's were hardly forgotten, and Peron's Argentina provided a ready-made threat for several South American countries. Finally, the traditional enmities among the Central Americans had abated not in the least. In contrast, the German threat was perceived by Latin Americans as relatively unimportant. As Mexican diplomat Jose Reuben Romero put it: "Certainly, we Latin Americans are not winning the war, possibly because it is far away and we have not suffered its privations, because it has not awakened our enthusiasm, our confidence, our fate, which every war requires."[3]

One of the most pregnant consequences of the Chapultepec meeting went relatively unnoticed at the time. It was there decided to make the Inter-American Defense Board a permanent organization with generalized powers of recommendation to all participating governments.[4] Within the year the IADB issued its first such recommendation—the standardization of equipment, organization, and training among all participating countries.[5] Hence, through a seemingly insignificant consolidation of the formal structure of inter-American cooperation, the United States took a giant step toward accomplishing one of the main goals of its military policy since 1938. Standardization of military weaponry in 1945 had the same significance as it had for the Germans and Italians during the 1930's—the long-range dependency of the standardized military upon a single source of supply.

For a time it appeared that these gains would be lost to an apathetic Congress. In both 1946 and early 1947 Congress delayed action on the administration's request for a continual funding of inter-American defense efforts. Upon the demise of the Lend-Lease program, almost all subsidized provisioning of the Latin American militaries came to an end, and out of necessity the Latin Americans began to turn to sources of supply outside the hemisphere.

But times were rapidly changing and old allies were becoming new enemies and a threat to American security wherever they might be found. U.S.–Latin American policy has always borne an intimate relationship to developments in other parts of the world, and at no time in U.S. history has this relationship been more apparent than in the period of the Cold

---

[3] Pan American Day Speech, April 14, 1943.
[4] Lieuwen, *Arms and Politics*, p. 197.
[5] *New York Times*, May 7, 1946.

War. In the first place, the impending activation of the United Nations made increased U.S. attention to its Latin American fences mandatory if U.S. influence in the hemisphere was to be maintained within the framework of the international organization. The U.S need for Latin American votes in the General Assembly gave the Latin Americans a bargaining power vis-à-vis the United States which they had not enjoyed for years. Second, the almost paranoid anticommunism that was becoming prominent in government circles in the late 1940's and early 1950's became an instant ally of the Latin American military, whose requests for arms and provisions were increasingly predicated upon the necessity of defending the hemisphere from possible communist attack and the protection of supplies of strategic materials in the event of global conflict.[6]

Against this background of growing anticommunism as the centerpiece of U.S. foreign policy, the consolidation of the inter-American system continued apace. In June 1947 the State Department dropped its misguided struggle with Argentina's Peron, whereupon Brazil invoked a conference at Rio for August. The Rio Conference produced the inter-American Treaty of Reciprocal Assistance (the Rio Treaty), whereby the American nations agreed to submit their controversies to peaceful settlement within the inter-American system before resorting to the United Nations (Article II), to consider an *armed* attack by any state on an American state as an attack on all of them and consequently, to "assist in meeting the attack," although each state may determine what form its assistance will take until the appropriate organ of consultation has met (Articles III and XX). In such a crisis the "organ of consultation" must meet at once to determine collective measures, which may range from breaking diplomatic relations to use of armed force (Articles II and VIII). However, no state can be obligated to use armed force without its consent.

Even at its inception the Rio Treaty was viewed by the United States as the formalization of an anticommunist alliance. At Rio, President Truman used the communist threat as a justification for hemispheric cooperation: "We find that a number of nations are still subjected to a type of foreign domination which we fought to overcome. . . . I need not tell you how important it is to our success that we have your understanding, support, and counsel".[7] Latin Americans, on the other hand, generally hoped for something more—e.g., Marshall-plan type economic aid to alleviate the chronic poverty of the area.[8] Of course, as the Alliance for Progress was to illustrate

[6] See Edgar S. Furniss, Jr., *American Military Policy* (New York: Rinehart, 1957), pp. 235 and *passim*.

[7] Department of State, *Bulletin* (September 14, 1947), pp. 498–500.

[8] See the statement of Mexican Foreign Minister Torres Bodet in *New York Times*, August 17, 1947.

some years later, the two views are not and were not mutually exclusive. But in 1947 the connection between a successful communist offensive and economic and social conditions in the target country was only dimly perceived. Communist takeovers were still viewed as a process of infiltration, propaganda, and peaceful seizure of the reins of power.

This early Cold-War *Weltanschauung* was evidenced in Article VI:

> If the inviolability or the integrity of the territory, sovereignty, or political independence of any American state should be affected by *an aggression which is not an armed attack* or by an extracontinental or intracontinental conflict, *or by any other fact or situation that might endanger the peace of America*, the organ of consultation shall meet immediately in order to agree on the measures which must be taken in case of aggression to assist the victim of the aggression or, in any case, the measures which should be taken for the common defense and for the maintenance of the peace and security of the continent (italics added).

Behind the vagueness of Article VI lay a multifaceted compromise relating both to the position of the inter-American system vis-à-vis the United Nations and to the consistency of hemispheric ideology. The problem of preserving a regional defense system within the United Nations was one that had plagued hemispheric diplomats since the announcement of the first Dumbarton Oaks proposals. In fact, the Chapultepec meeting had been held largely at the insistence of Latin Americans, fearful that collective security in the hemisphere would be eviscerated by absorption into a universal system of collective security.[9] Again in San Francisco the Latin Americans were forced to fight to preserve hemispheric autonomy. The result of their efforts was Articles 51, 52, and 53 of the United Nations' Charter, providing for the maintenance of regional organizations with primary peacekeeping responsibility and the right of collective self-defense. However, under Article 53 of the U.N. Charter, no enforcement action could be taken under regional arrangements without the authorization of the Security Council.

To the extent that Article VI of the Rio Treaty provides for immediate determination and execution of collective measures in response to an "aggression" or "situation" that is not an armed attack, it nullified the import of Article 53 of the U.N. Charter and effectively took the problem of "subversion and penetration" out of the United Nations. At a later date this effective nullification was to become highly important. In both the Cuban and Dominican crises, the United States and the O.A.S. were able to by-pass the Soviet veto power in the Security Council on the somewhat

---

[9] Furniss, "The United States, the Inter-American System, and the United Nations," *Political Science Quarterly* (September 1950).

dubious grounds that measures short of armed force—i.e., "quarantine" and "humanitarian intervention" for the protection of nationals—did not constitute "enforcement action" within the meaning of Article 53.

Article VI of the Rio Treaty also covered some basic ideological differences in the hemisphere. In 1947 the issue of dictatorial governments in Latin America was very much alive. The wave of right-wing military takeovers that had accompanied the depression was subsiding, and a number of the military regimes then in power were reformist in tenor. It was one of those brief interludes in the long history of Latin American dictatorships during which hopes were running high for democratic institutions. Accordingly, three democratic regimes—Guatemala, Uruguay, and Venezuela—proposed to convert the Rio Treaty into an antidictatorial alliance by including a provision that "violations of the essential rights of man or the departure from the democratic system shall require joint and solidary action."[10]

Since this resolution was ultimately voted down by a showing of hands in committee, it did not evoke a great deal of revealing debate.[11] The United States opposed on the grounds that the introduction of such a controversial issue into the treaty negotiations would unduly delay the ratification and signing of an effective treaty. Undoubtedly, a number of Latin American states opposed on the simple grounds that such a provision would have converted the treaty into an alliance against their governments. But the resolution dramatically posed the real issues at stake in the negotiation of the treaty. For the United States, stability within the hemisphere was simply a more important goal than the fulfillment of democratic ideals. If stability meant supporting dictatorial military regimes, then such regimes would be supported. This much may be comfortably encompassed within an arguably shortsighted view of "national interest." But the view held notable dangers at a time when leftist or "communist" governments were increasingly identified as inherently "unstable" in terms of the American national interest.

In any event, Article VI—along with Article IX's authorization of the organ of consultation to characterize acts other than armed attack as "aggression"—gave something to both sides of the controversy. "Any other fact or situation that might endanger the peace of America" could presumably cover a dictatorial or a communist regime so long as a two-thirds majority could be mustered.

Clearly, the Rio Treaty contemplated the possibility of internal political upheaval as an alternative to armed attack and recognized the potentiality

---

[10] Rio Conference, *Analysis and Comparative Compilation of the Projects* (Washington: Pan American Union, 1946), p. 16.

[11] Rio Conference, *Original Minutes and Documents*, Minutes of Committee II.

of a coordinated defense program for the coercion of internal political conformity. However, the relative weight of this consideration within the panorama of military objectives apparently contemplated by the Rio Treaty can only be assessed by reference to the overall U.S. diplomatic effort in Latin America following the war. The Bogotá Conference came close on the heels of the signing of the Rio Treaty, and it was there that the pivotal importance of the U.S. concern with "international communism" came strongly to the forefront.

In April 1948, the American ministers met again—this time in Bogotá—for the purpose of realizing the century-old dream of an effective regional organization. The Charter of the Organization of American States attests to the results of their efforts. But both the Charter and the Bogotá Conference offer something of a microcosm of U.S.–Latin American relations during the major portion of the postwar era: The Latin Americans remained intensely concerned with their national sovereignties and with protecting themselves both from one another and from the United States. The United States was introducing the paean of anticommunism that was to remain the central theme of U.S. foreign policy for the next decade and beyond. The Latin Americans emphasized the problems of economic assistance, while the United States—already heavily committed in other parts of the globe—wished to rely upon private investment and internal economic development to solve the multiple problems of underdevelopment.

The result of these conflicting interests—as in the case of the United Nations—was a formal regional structure with negligible powers of enforcement or independent decision. This is not to say that the O.A.S. has not been an effective peacekeeping organization with respect to conflicts between Latin American states. In the Honduras–Nicaragua territorial dispute of 1957–61, the Nicaraguan invasion of Costa Rica in 1955, and, apparently, in the Salvadoran–Honduran War of 1969, the O.A.S. proved a valuable forum for settlement, though even in these cases U.S. efforts outside of the O.A.S. were of at least equal importance.[12] It is rather in the area of internal politics that the O.A.S. has proven ineffective, in the sense that it has either rubber-stamped U.S. policy or, as in the case of the Bay of Pigs invasion, been incapable of providing an alternative to U.S. armed intervention. The underlying divergence between U.S. and Latin American interests that has made this the case were evident as early as the Bogotá Conference.

[12] Jerome N., Slater, "The Role of the Organization of American States in United States Foreign Policy, 1947–1963," Ph.D. dissertation (Princeton University), pp. 63–77.

The first area of U.S.–Latin American differences that emerged at Bogotá was that of the importance of the communist threat in the hemisphere. Almost immediately upon its arrival, the U.S. delegation, led by Secretary of State Marshall, had begun lobbying for a strong anticommunist resolution from the Conference. Even before the Conference, Marshall had argued that the primary U.S. interest in creating a regional organization such as the O.A.S. was that of gaining the cooperation of the American states in meeting the threat to world peace posed by the Soviet Union.[13] But the Latin Americans appeared obstinate in their refusal to recognize the threat.[14]

Then on April 9, in the midst of the Bogotá Conference, the assassination of Jorge Eliecer Gaitan, a popular Colombian nationalist, touched off the most serious urban riots in Latin American history. Approximately 1,500 Colombians lost their lives and large sections of Bogotá were completely destroyed. Delegates to the Conference were forced to disperse to the suburbs of the city. In retrospect the *Bogotázo* is probably most accurately viewed as "a Latin American Watts riot."[15] The conservative regime of Laureano Gomez had been as antipoor as it was antiurban, and unrest was already running high in the urban *barrios* of Bogotá. Gaitan had long been identified as the champion of Colombia's lower class as a result of his defense of coastal plantation workers. His death had a psychological effect quite similar to that of the later assassination of Martin Luther King in the United States.

Despite the obvious social and political causes of the riots, Secretary Marshall, from the safety of a suburban high school, flatly blamed the riots on the Soviet Union and began to press for a resolution condemning "international communism." The Colombian hosts of the Conference were more than delighted to agree with the characterization of the riots as part of a communist plot to disrupt the Conference. The result was a resolution entitled "The Preservation and Defense of Democracy in America" which declared that "by its anti-democratic nature and its interventionist tendency, the political activity of international Communism or any other totalitarian doctrine is incompatible with the concept of American freedom." The resolution went on to suggest that cooperative measures should be undertaken to prevent the agents of international communism from distorting the true will of the Latin American people. This resolution

---

[13] Department of State, *Bulletin* (April 11, 1948), p. 470.
[14] J. Floyd Mecham, *The United States and Inter-American Security, 1889–1960* (Austin: University of Texas Press, 1961), p. 429.
[15] This characterization of the *Bogotázo* was suggested by U.S. ambassador to Colombia, Covey Oliver, in a conversation with the author during the summer of 1966.

passed unanimously, but only after Venezuela and other nations had forced the extension of the original anticommunist resolution to cover all types of totalitarianism.[16]

The political significance of this resolution can be vastly overrated if one fails to take adequate account of the context in which it was promulgated.[17] A major diplomatic meeting had just been disrupted by a lower class riot in a principal Latin American capital. To suggest that the riots had simply been the result of many years of governmental repression of the Colombian poor would have aborted the entire hemispheric undertaking. For the incumbent Colombian regime to admit such a thing would have been political suicide. The theory of an international communist conspiracy offered everyone an easy way out. A better measure of the Latin American concern with international communism was probably shown during the Korean War, when only one country—Colombia—sent troops to help in the fight.

The second major difference between the United States and the Latin Americans at Bogotá related to economic aid. Under Article 5(i) of the Charter, the United States did commit itself to cooperate with other American nations in achieving just and decent living conditions for the population of the hemisphere; but it was to be thirteen years before the U.S. interpretation of the meaning of this commitment was to even closely approximate that of the Latin Americans.

In simplistic terms the Latin American critisicm of the U.S. aid program can be summed up as "not enough" and "not the right kind." What little U.S. aid came to Latin American countries in the years following the war came in the form of loans and private investment. From 1945 to 1948 Latin America received only about $200 million from the Export–Import Bank.[18] In comparison, the Latins came to Bogotá asking for a program funded at $5 billion, under which loans would be made for thirty years at 1 percent per annum.[19] In 1948 such a plan had no chance of passage in the U.S. Congress and was largely brushed aside by the U.S. delegation. The economic agreement that was finally signed at Bogotá was so inane that it was never taken seriously and received only three ratifications.

In retrospect, the divergence of U.S. and Latin American opinion on the problem of economic aid may be viewed as a distinct difference of goals. The prime interest of the United States in the area was to maintain political stability. To this end an informal alliance had been formed with the Latin American military establishments and, to a lesser extent, with

---

[16] *New York Times*, May 3, 1948.
[17] See e.g., Mecham, *Inter-American Security*, p. 429.
[18] *Ibid.*, p. 314.
[19] *Ibid.*

the Latin American ruling classes. Economic aid on the scale suggested by the Latin Americans would have severely disturbed political stability in the hemisphere and have represented an unprecedented undertaking for the U.S. Congress. It was not until the disastrous Nixon tour of Latin America in 1958 that the connection between economic development and political stability was officially made; and in 1948 large-scale economic aid was still viewed as primarily a postwar recovery measure. It was in fact not until the Alliance for Progress was launched in 1961—on the theory that economic aid might be an alternative to military aid as a means of fighting communism—that the aid and cooperation portions of the O.A.S. commitment were implemented on more than a nominal scale.

It is of course conventional wisdom that the primary accomplishment of the Bogotá Conference was the drafting of the first Charter of the Organization of American States. The formal structure of the O.A.S. has been dealt with at length elsewhere, and we will refer to it only as a necessary part of our description of its activities. For our purposes attention may be conveniently focused upon the Charter's incorporation and extension of the nonintervention norms of previous inter-American treaties and agreements.

Articles 15, 16, and 17 of the Charter of the O.A.S. provided the most lyrical statement to date of the prohibition of intervention in the hemisphere:

ARTICLE XV. No State or group of States has the right to intervene, directly or indirectly, for any reason whatever, in the internal or external affairs of any other state. The foregoing principle prohibits not only armed force but also any form of interference or attempted threat against the personality of the State or against its political, economic, and cultural elements.

ARTICLE XVI. No State may use or encourage the use of coercive measures of an economic or political character in order to force the sovereign will of another state and obtain from it advantages of any kind.

ARTICLE XVII. The territory of a State is inviolable; it may not be the object, even temporarily, of military occupation or of other measures of force taken by another State, directly or indirectly, on any grounds whatever. No territorial acquisitions or special advantages obtained either by force or by other means of coercion shall be recognized.

Despite the stunning finality of these provisions, Article XIX took away with the left hand a good part of what Articles XV and XVII had given with the right by declaring that "measures adopted for the maintenance of peace and security in accordance with existing treaties do not constitute a violation of the principles set forth in Articles XV and XVII." Since most of the members of the O.A.S. had already signed both the Rio Treaty and the United Nations Charter, Article XIX, in effect, drew a legal dichotomy between "legal" collective intervention and "illegal" unilateral intervention. There was, of course, no dearth of Latin American delegates arguing that collective as well as unilateral intervention had been outlawed under Article XV, but Article XIX provided a possible legal characterization of interventionary acts of the kind that the Latin Americans sought to prohibit—a characterization that the United States was to overwork in later years.

Consequently, the Bogotá Conference may be viewed as something of a microcosm of future inter-American relations. The Latin Americans remained intensely concerned with protecting themselves from intervention by the colossus of the North. The United States was introducing the paean of anticommunism, which was to remain the central theme of American foreign policy for the next decade and beyond. Finally, the formal structure of the inter-American system left open the channel of multilateral action— real and apparent—as a means of by-passing the nonintervention norm.

*Military Aid*

Of course, the formal structure of the inter-American system was meaningless apart from available arrangements for military aid. The Department of State had consistently resisted all Latin American pleas for Marshall aid money and for an overall plan of hemispheric economic development. Whatever mutual aid and development was possible under the O.A.S. Charter was, at best, a future hope and not a present reality. Reality, however, did consist of millions of dollars of military aid being shipped to Latin America on an interim basis under the Surplus Property Act. This program, which took the place of lend-lease, provided armaments to various Latin American countries at about 5 percent to 10 percent of cost.[20] With the President's authority under the Surplus Property Act running out and the U.S. Congress refusing to appropriate additional funds under the Arms Standardization Act, the pressure was on the Latin Americans in 1948 to agree to almost any form of structure and ideological orientation which would have assured them of continued U.S. support for their bloated armed forces.

The pressure was finally relieved by the passage of the Mutual Defense Assistance Act of 1949, allowing for the purchase of surplus weapons and equipment at low prices to any Latin American nation willing to assure that the material would be devoted to hemisphere defense requirements. With this additional aid the U.S. military was able to hold the military mission front until the Mutual Security Act of 1951 authorized bilateral military assistance agreements that under one name or another were to dominate our Latin American relations up to the present time.

[20] *Ibid.*, p. 338.

When in 1937 Sumner Wells suggested sending warships to Latin America, Eduardo Santos, Colombian journalist and political leader, wrote: "Don't do this evil thing to us. The use of armaments is like the vice of morphine. Once begun, the cure is almost impossible. You will ruin us with cruisers and create for us new problems . . . because there is always someone with the desire to try out the armaments and obtain from them some advantage."[21] To continue Santos's metaphor, the military assistance agreements under the 1951 Act were a nearly lethal dosage of the narcotic of military armament.

The Military Assistance Agreements appear to have been drawn with three principal purposes: (1) diplomacy; (2) leverage; and (3) profits. As for diplomacy, it was clear by 1951 that the United States could not afford to ignore its deteriorating relationships in Latin America. The Korean War was under way, and the United States needed Latin American support and materials. The securing of leverage was by now becoming a relatively familiar process. A stranglehold on the army of a Latin American nation was, in fact, a stranglehold on the nation itself. The profit motive is by far the most ambiguous. By 1951 U.S. armament suppliers, private and public, were on their way to becoming the largest provisioners of arms in the world.[22] Even in the bite of the Korean War, large stocks of World War II surplus equipment and armaments still lay in the hands of the armed forces and private brokers. At a minimum it may be suggested that the Latin American militaries offered a tempting possibility for recouping some of the cost of this excess equipment.

The agreement between the United States and Honduras was fairly typical of the bilateral assistance agreements. It provides that the United States may call upon Honduras to provide "raw and semi-processed materials required by the United States of America as a result of deficiencies or potential deficiencies in its own resources." (Article VII). Further, the government of Honduras is obligated to cooperate with the United States to undertake any measures designed to control trade with nations which "threaten the security of the Western Hemisphere" (Article VIII). Finally, the agreement provides for U.S. specification of the purposes for which equipment provided under the agreement may be used; and if the assistance is no longer needed for the specified purposes the equipment is to be returned to the United States (Article I, Par. 3).

Apart from the potentiality for international arms-dumping that is apparent within the agreements themselves, the timing of their execution also gives some flavor of the underlying intentions of the agreements. Up to the present, twelve nations have signed such agreements with the

[21] Quoted in John Gerassi, *The Great Fear* (New York: Macmillan, 1963), p. 296.
[22] See Sheenan, series in the *New York Times* July 19, 20, and 21, 1967.

United States. The last was Guatemala, which in December 1954, received the first U.S. armament shipment "to modernize" her army.[23] One imagines, however, that the newly—and somewhat precariously—installed Armas regime was more in need of the stable items of a military dictatorship than it was of modernizing its army. One of the early agreements was signed by Cuba, whose recently returned military dictator, Batista, was likewise in need of insurance for his own position in the country. In Colombia the initial aid received under the agreement emboldened the army sufficiently for it to revoke its established pledge and growing tradition of noninvolvement in civilian politics and to establish a brutal military dictatorship which used the same U.S. military equipment to institute a reign of terror over members of the opposition. In short, the military assistance agreements from the beginning played a role not unlike that played by U.S. recognition policy—through the granting, withholding, and execution of military assistance agreements the disfavored might be destroyed, the favored rewarded, and the friendly manipulated. As Professor Lieuwen put it, "the objectives of the U.S. military programs in Latin America are primarily political, although it has seemed wiser to express in military not in political terms."

Of course, the mutual defense assistance agreements were only as valuable as the appropriation which backed them. Congressional authorization for the program took the form of the Mutual Security Act of 1951, which, in large part, was the result of the growing enchantment in Washington with the theory of a worldwide communist conspiracy. Under the act, "military assistance may be furnished to other American republics only in accordance with defense plans which . . . require the recipient nations to participate in missions important to the defense of the Western Hemisphere." The expansive reading which the administration was willing to give this part of the act is indicated by the fact that even before the act was officially passed President Truman had already called the American foreign ministers together in consultative meeting to request Latin American cooperation in the Korean conflict. Ultimately, one country—Colombia—actually sent troops to Korea. But the instance does illustrate the degree to which the theory of an international communist conspiracy was dominating American thought on U.S. relationships within the hemisphere.

Between 1950 and 1965 when the United States began to feel the budgetary pinch of the Vietnamese war, over $580 million in grant military aid was sent to Latin America. In addition, well over $1 billion was spent by the Latin Americans in direct purchases of U.S. military equipment.[24]

---

[23] Mecham, *Inter-American Security*, p. 337.

[24] Edwin Lieuwen, *The United States and the Challenge to Security in Latin America* (Columbus: Ohio State University Press, 1966), p. 15.

But even this does not tell the whole story. To these figures must be added an indeterminate but sizable portion of the so-called "economic aid" programs, which in fact have gone for supportive items in the military programs.[25] This has been particularly the case since 1961, when the main emphasis in the U.S. military aid program shifted to counterinsurgency and civic action projects. For example, it would be nearly impossible to separate the military and economic portions of the police-training program operated by the Agency for International Development.

Why this sizable expenditure for maintaining the Latin American military establishments? The perennial justification for the military aid program in Latin America has been stated in terms of protecting the U.S. supply of Latin American raw materials. As Assistant Secretary of State Henry F. Holland stated in 1954: "In time of war we would rely heavily on Latin American raw materials to maintain our economy in full production, and the Latin Americans would in turn rely on us for imports which they would require to maintain the stability of their economies. The maintenance of this vital trade in time of war will be dependent on protection of the inter-American sea and air routes of communication and certain strategic installations. The purpose of this program, then, is to provide Latin American countries with the type of equpiment and training they will need in order to assume a part of the burden of safeguarding such lines of communication and installations."[26]

This then was a restatement of the "lines of communication" argument used by Mahan over half a century earlier—an argument questionable in 1895, ridiculous in World War II, and ludicrous by 1954. In the first place, the idea that the uncoordinated and inefficient Latin American militaries could defend themselves against conventional armed attack by one of the major powers falls within the realm of the comic. In 1955, less than a year after Holland was putting forth the "lines of communication" argument to Congress, the total strength of the Latin American armed forces numbered about one-half million men.[27] Most of these establishments were equipped with castaways and museum relics. The majority of their enlisted men were inadequately trained and of low combat effectiveness because of ill health and illiteracy.[28] In short, in a conventional land war the combined Latin American militaries could probably be quickly destroyed by a modern army one-half as large. Second, even by 1951 the possibility of an attack by the Soviet Union upon Latin America was a contingency to be

[25] Richard J. Barnet, *Intervention and Revolution: The United States in the Third World* (New York: World Publishing Company, 1968), pp. 19–20.

[26] Hearings before the Committee on Appropriations on Mutual Security Appropriations for 1955, Senate, 83rd Cong., 2nd sess., p. 248.

[27] Lieuwen, *Arms and Politics*, p. 210.

[28] *Ibid.*, p. 211.

classed with invasions from outer space and similar military threats, and the probability was to grow even more remote in future years.[29] The only feasible route of such an attack would have been by way of the Pacific, where the logistical requirements of a land war on the South or Central American continents would have required a prior assault on U.S. Pacific possessions. On the other hand, a jet or missile attack would have by-passed the Latin American militaries entirely, since no Latin American country has developed a significant air force, and only Argentina, Brazil, and Chile have even marginal navies.[30]

Of course, the "lines of communication" arguments is two-pronged: lines of communication under the theory must be protected from internal sabotage as well as external attack. In the wake of the Castro takeover in 1960, the emphasis of the U.S. military aid program in Latin America shifted from hemispheric defense to internal security. At present, about 70 percent of the military aid program is specifically earmarked for programs such as counterinsurgency training, antiguerrilla equipment, civic action plans, and the like.[31] In addition, the United States, working through the Inter-American Security Committee, has conducted an intensive program to curtail travel and propagandizing by persons considered "subversive."[32] Consequently, although rarely officially articulated, the preservation of internal security might be considered the main justification for the military aid program in Latin America. Indeed, some authors have put the proposition more broadly. Studying the entirety of the U.S. aid program in the "third world," Richard Barnet concluded as follows: "Indeed, from the Truman Doctrine on, the suppression of insurgent movements has remained a principal goal of U.S. foreign policy. It has been the prime target of the U.S. foreign-assistance program, most of the funds for which have gone for civic-action teams, pacification programs, support for local police, and, above all, military aid to the local army."[33]

The factual legitimacy of the internal security justification for the military aid program must rest upon some assessment of the present threat of internal subversion in the Latin American countries. This will be dealt with in the following chapter. From the point of view of inter-

---

[29] See George Fielding Eliot, "The Defense of Latin America," *American Mercury* (October 1954).

[30] Lieuwen, *Arms and Politics*, p. 211.

[31] Maurice J. Mountain, "United States Military Assistance in the Caribbean Area," in A. Curtiss Wilgus (ed.), *The Caribbean: Current United States Relations* (Gainesville: University of Florida Press, 1966), p. 188. A detailed exposition of the various facets of the internal security program in Latin America can be found in Williard F. Barber and C. Neale Ronning, *Internal Security and Military Power: Counterinsurgency and Civic Action in Latin America* (Columbus: Ohio University Press, 1966).

[32] Lieuwen, *Challenge to Security*, p. 16.

[33] Barnet, *Intervention and Revolution*, p. 9.

national law the internal security program raises even more difficult questions. Aid in the form of conventional weaponry undoubtedly strengthens the power and prestige of the recipient armed forces within a given Latin American country. If the armed forces throw their support behind one political group or the other, then such aid indirectly strengthens the favored group. But the training and equipment involved in the counterinsurgency programs is highly discriminatory. It is directed against groups labeled "subversive"—an eminently expandable concept, as the old House Un-American Activities Committee and the Senate Internal Security Subcommittee have demonstrated. This point would remain valid even if the Latin American militaries chose their own "subversives." But the practice is even more highly subject to U.S. direction. A major part of the internal security program has consisted of the training and political indoctrination of Latin American officers, under the supervision of the U.S. Army Forces Southern Command at Fort Gulick, in Panama.[34] Hence, an opportunity is given the U.S. military establishment to participate in the identification of the subversive groups that the counterinsurgency training is designed to suppress. Second, under the 1958 Morse Amendment to the Mutual Security Act,[35] arms and equipment received by Latin America under the mutual defense agreements could be used for internal security purposes—i.e., civil strife—only with presidential authorization; and the President's determinations were classified as "secret." To the degree that this prohibition is effective, a discretionary determination of a U.S. policymaker guides the actions of the Latin American military. The initial results of this internal security package were summarized by James Reston in 1962: "It is conceded that subversion is the problem, that our arms are now intended to maintain internal order, that President Kennedy has formally authorized their use in this way. The trouble is that everybody wants to maintain 'order,' the bad guys as well as the good guys—both with our weapons."[36]

Because the Latin American militaries operate as relatively independent political groups, it is no answer to the interventionary issue raised by the internal security programs that incumbent governments must acquiesce in the assistance. For civilian political leaders in Latin America, there is often no safe path of nonacquiescence, as President Goulart of Brazil found out. In the early 1960's Goulart, following the lead of his predecessor Janio Quadros, attempted to reorient the external politics of Brazil by seeking aid from the socialist countries to build up the state sector of the Brazilian

---

[34] See Richard R. Clark, "U.S. Military Assistance in Latin America," *Army Digest* (September 1966).

[35] Mutual Security Pact of 1959, § 105(b)(4).

[36] *New York Times*, August 3, 1962.

economy. Goulart's policy was apparently approved by a large majority of the Brazilian people, who gave him an overwhelming victory in a 1963 plebiscite. By and large, Goulart ignored thinly veiled threats that all U.S. aid would be denied him, but his army lent a more sympathetic ear. In 1964 the army threw Goulart out of the government to the accompaniment of high praise from the U.S. ambassador to Brazil, Lincoln Gordon.[37] The victorious military men immediately arrested over 7,000 "communists and extremists," and carried on a purge of "extremist influences" from the Congress (44 congressmen), the unions, the educational system, and the government bureaucracy.[38] All this in a country whose Communist party was then estimated to include only 40,000 members.[39]

The actual degree of U.S. complicity in the overthrow of Goulart will not be known until the present military regime is replaced, but several indications should be noted. Under Goulart, the United States had openly used its financial assistance program to attempt to strengthen the anti-Goulart faction in the Brazilian government.[40] One of the first acts of the newly appointed "president" of Brazil, General Humberto Castello Branco, was the reorientation of Brazil's foreign policy toward a pro-U.S. line, and that was immediately followed by the reestablishment of the aid program on the basis of direct intergovernmental dealings.

Of course, this thumbnail sketch of the Brazilian coup is oversimplified in that it ignores important domestic factors—inflation, attempts to prevent tax evasion, and the President's attempt to appeal to the enlisted men over the head of the officer corps—that predisposed the military against Goulart. But the fact remains that apart from any conscious and direct attempt to influence the Brazilian military to intervene against Goulart, any move by the civilian government that threatened the bilateral arrangement between the U.S. and the Brazilian militaries was bound to generate the opposition of a military establishment possessed, in effect, of its own foreign policy arrangements and of decisive power in domestic politics. To the extent that the interests of U.S. policymakers and Brazilian military men could be made to coincide, the bilateral military assistance program again became the functional alternative to armed intervention as a means of assuring desired political outcomes in Brazilian foreign policy.

[37] J. P. Morray, "The United States and Latin America," James Petras and Maurice Zeitlin (eds.), *Reform or Revolution?* (New York: Fawcett, 1968), pp. 106–7.
[38] Lieuwen, *Challenge to Security*, p. 54.
[39] *Ibid.*, p. 53.
[40] Robert N. Burr, *Our Troubled Hemisphere* (Washington: The Brookings Institution, 1967), p. 141.

# VIII.

## Militarism and the Myth of Communist Subversion

THUS FAR IT HAS BEEN SUGGESTED that the peculiar relationship between the United States and the Latin American militaries developed almost sub rosa as a functional alternative to direct intervention as a means of securing what U.S policymakers perceived as a minimal level of political stability in strategic Latin American areas. This is not to deny the importance of other programs aimed at economic and social development that were supposedly responsive to the same perceived threat of communism in the hemisphere. But the military programs, as Humphrey pointed out, were thought to constitute the sine qua non of the long-range success of programs that were to eliminate the "conditions" of communism. Without short-term political stability the long-term economic programs, such as the Alliance for Progress, could not even be undertaken.

As is generally recognized and as we will detail in the next chapter, the military relationship proved inadequate to achieve even minimal acceptable conditions, and a return to direct armed intervention was immediately forthcoming—the rhetoric of collective action notwithstanding. But before proceeding to the fact of failure, a digression is warranted to examine some of the facts of Latin American political life—as compared to U.S. perceptions of them—that made failure inevitable.[1] It will be noted that,

[1] In the spirit of full disclosure it should be stated that the author's own bias is that the active attempts to manipulate the Latin American militaries in order to influence domestic and foreign policy in Latin American countries is both morally indefensible and a clear violation of the nonintervention provisions of the O.A.S. Charter, even if one assumes the accuracy of American perceptions of the communist threat in the hemisphere. But here I wish to make only the more limited argument that the policy fails in its own terms, because the assumptions that underlie it are not in accord with anything in the real world—however cloudily perceived.

quite apart from the moral and legal objections to a policy that consciously or inadvertently attempts to strengthen the hand of a local military establishment as against other political groups, reliance upon the military arrangement evidences a failure to understand both the nature of Latin American militarism and the diversity and thrust of Latin American leftist movements.

Militarism in Latin America has been as dynamic as it has been long-lived. Even by 1945 it was no longer possible to describe that phenomenon in terms of the old alliance of Church–Land–Soldier; although the long tradition of military involvement in domestic politics continued unabated and thereby lent a patina of continuity to the military's political role.[2] In reality the Latin American soldier—specifically the officer class—had changed radically. While the "democratization" of the Latin American armies during the 1930's took control of the military out of the hands of the landed aristocracy, the growing professionalization of the military— influenced in part by training in U.S. military methods—produced what may be called the "technological soldier," interested in the modernization of his country and convinced of the peculiar capability of the military for its accomplishing.[3] In short, the Latin American militaries were developing an autonomous interest in intervening in civilian politics—an interest that existed quite independent of any desire to maintain the status quo in the social structure and sometimes directly hostile to such preservation. In terms of the dubious labels of the 1950's, left-wing military intervention became theoretically as possible as right-wing military intervention. Modernization, after all, can be approached in many different ways.

Just as the interventionists changed, so there were subtle shifts in the rhetoric of military takeovers. Domestically, there was increasing reference to the peculiar position of the military as a receptacle of "pure" nationalism. Internationally, until the mid-1960's military intervention was usually justified in terms of the opposition of the military to "communist" influences in the civilian government. In the two-dimensional world of Dulles diplomacy it was only this second justification that received any scrutiny, and even that analysis was severely hampered by the demonology of U.S. anticommunism. For Eisenhower's State Department the new-found concern of the Latin American military establishments with the "communist threat" was adequately justified. Just as Mexican intractability had been labeled Bolshevism by Secretary of State Kellogg, the

---

[2] The various stages of transition through which the Latin American military have passed are documented in John J. Johnson, *The Military and Society in Latin America* (Stanford: Stanford University Press, 1964).

[3] See Victor Alba, "Latin American Militarism," in John J. Johnson (ed.), *The Role of the Military in Underdeveloped Countries* (Princeton: Princeton University Press, 1962), pp. 172–74.

constant problems for American policy presented by Latin American politics could only be attributable to that new-found villain of international diplomacy, the international communist conspiracy. That the theory did obvious violence to both history and reality in Latin America seemed to go largely unnoticed. And if the question of the desirability of military dictatorship was raised at all, it was usually answered by reference to the necessity of choosing between the evils of military dictatorship and of communism—a forced choice that the militarists inevitably won.

The problem, of course, was and is with the definition of the word "communist" and the very definite differences in the understanding of that term by Latin Americans and U.S. policymakers. For a Latin American leader to state that he is an *anticomunista* is for him to state his political opposition to a definable political group; he does not necessarily make any statement about the attractiveness or desirability of communist economic models. The official U.S. policy of anticommunism has generally meant something less specific and certainly more inclusive. In his ground-breaking study of anticommunism in America, Michael Parenti described the American definition of communism this way: "A fear of this dimension tends to reify the feared object; communism becomes a political force divorced of the historical, national, ethnic, cultural, organizational, material, indeed, human, substances which give it form and identity."[4] Indeed, U.S. notions of the communism to be feared in Latin America have been so lacking in form and identity as to render rational identification of the interests sought to be secured by the anticommunist policy impossible. But the divergence between the U.S. and Latin American views have made practicable a situation in which it is quite possible for an *anticomunista* to be a communist. In fact, when Venezuela's Betancourt declared his own opposition to communism in 1959, he was quite sincerely considered a communist by many in the State Department. And more recently a military regime in Peru was declaring its anticommunist position while expropriating American-owned properties— an act that some years earlier had constituted the basis for a charge of communist domination leveled at the Guatemalan government.

Consequently, to the extent that U.S. support of the Latin American militaries is predicated upon some notion of providing a bulwark against communism, while viable democratic governments can be established in a context of improving social and economic conditions, an unreal portrait of Latin American politics becomes the framework for policy. In the first place, the supposed threat is either nonexistent or almost all-inclusive. If the communist threat is meant to refer to orthodox party adherents, then

---

[4] Michael Parenti, *The Anti-Communist Impulse* (New York: Random House, 1969), p. 32.

support of the military is simply unjustified. Even in 1960, when Castro's popularity was at its apex, it is generally estimated that hard-core party membership in all of Latin America did not exceed 250,000. Out of a population of over 200,000,000 the number is insignificant, and in some Central American countries it meant that only a few dozen communists were to be found. If, on the other hand, the threat is supposed to come from all those Latin Americans who subscribe to some variant of Marxist economic models and who would be inclined to the use of force for their establishment, then many Latin American military men—along with a majority of Latin American students and untold numbers of Marxist intellectuals—would have to be considered communists. In the second place, support of Latin American military establishments as protectors of acceptable civilian political regimes misses the point that the military is often a principal competitor of alternative political groups for positions of leadership in the process of modernization.

*Communism in Latin America: Threat or Myth?*

Since 1947 the stock justification of U.S. aid programs in Latin America—whether military or economic—has been phrased in terms of resisting the threat of international communism. The support given the Batistas and Trujillos of the hemisphere by the Truman and Eisenhower administrations was largely grounded upon a kind of theory of "second best"— the theory underlying the notion that Batista was a dictator but better than the communist alternative. Central to this scheme of thought is the view of the social and political upheavals of Latin America as reflective of a global Cold War. Richard Barnet has described this view, which he argues is the predominant mental set of the U.S. foreign policy bureaucracy:

> The National-Security Manager is a global thinker. In themselves, local problems of other countries are not worthy of his attention; it is the transcendent importance of local revolutionary struggles that warrants intervention. Interference in purely domestic matters is still unjustified as a matter of law and sound policy. Unfortunately, he hastens to add, the line between domestic and foreign matters has blurred. When political factions struggle with one another in far-off places, their conflict is an expression of a single worldwide struggle.[5]

This global view has lain close to the surface of U.S.–Latin American policy since 1947—rising and falling in intensity in accord with events in the hemisphere. Upon Castro's takeover in Cuba it reached manic pro-

---

[5] Richard J. Barnet, *Intervention and Revolution: The United States in the Third World* (New York: World Publishing Company, 1968), p. 28.

portions. With specific reference to Latin America, Senator Thomas Dodd wrote in 1965: "In the long run, communism aims to subjugate the world, and we should not refrain from reminding ourselves that, by its own words and deeds, the international Communist movement is a world conspiracy. Their goal does not change. However, policies and techniques of subversion vary with regional, national, or local circumstances. This is what causes confusion in the West and the Free World."[6]

As previously noted, if the number of avowed communists in Latin America is any measure of the communist threat, then Senator Dodd's concern with the subjugation of Latin America by the communists would have to be considered a paranoic dream. Outside of Cuba, the combined strength of the severely fragmented communist parties amounted to only one-thousandth of the population in 1963.[7] And since that time the communists are generally considered to have lost ground.

But the specter of international communism in Latin America is not so easily banished from the minds of U.S. policymakers. In part, the mythology of the communist threat rests not on numbers but upon the unsupported speculation that communists—few though they may be—are peculiarly adept at turning indigenous unrest and fervent nationalism to their own ends. Even the most fervid anticommunists have ultimately been forced to the position of the U.S.-dominated Consultative Committee on Security Against the Subversive Action of International Communism:

> Lacking sufficient numerical strength and without Soviet and Chinese Communist military forces close enough to this hemisphere to give them support, the Communists are dangerous only to the extent that they usurp the strength of others; that is, the students, the workers, rural workers, writers, and even political leaders. Since the great majority of the citizens of the Americas believe in the ideals of national independence and individual liberty, and reject intervention and dictatorship, the Communists can strengthen themselves, and even come into power, only through a program of deceit that assumes many and varied forms. Only thus can Communist subversion triumph.[8]

For the Latin American students, writers, and political leaders whose power is supposedly being usurped by the communists, this is the stuff that political rhetoric is made of and, like the rhetoric of some senators, is not to be taken seriously. But for U.S. leaders, like Senator Dodd, the commu-

---

[6] U.S. Senate, Committee on the Judiciary, *Organization of American States Combined Reports on Communist Subversion*, 89th Cong., 1st sess. (Washington: GPO, 1965), p. iv.

[7] Edwin Lieuwen, *The United States and the Challenge to Security in Latin America* (Columbus: Ohio State University Press, 1966), p. 50.

[8] *Organization of American States Combined Reports on Communist Subversion*, pp. 3–4.

nist "program of deceit" is a Cold War reality which must be countered by effective American action. As the following chapter will demonstrate, his view has frequently been shared by the State Department. For the observer of Latin America with no political or economic interests in having a powerful communist opponent in the area, the position that any leftist political or social group is suspect as being subject to use and abuse by communist conspirators raises probative problems more typical of the theological, as opposed to the political. In simplest terms, the proposition that Latin America faces a severe internal threat from organized communism is one that has not and cannot be proved.

Historically, communism in Latin America began as a belated reaction to the Russian Revolution of 1917.[9] The process of development was exceedingly slow and largely confined to the urban laboring classes of Argentina, Brazil, Chile, Mexico, and Uruguay.[10] It was not until 1942 that every Latin American country could claim an existing communist party, and even then no party equaled its political rivals in strength or numbers. The communists enjoyed some local successes in the mid-1950's, but overall membership rolls were badly mauled by the rise of more broadly based reformists parties in Guatemala, Venezuela, Brazil, Colombia, and Chile. That is the dismal story of Latin American communism up to the Cuban Revolution.

Even where local parties were successfully established, they could hardly be called pawns of international communism. The first call for obedience to Moscow was included in Lenin's Twenty-One Points, and it produced almost immediate fragmentation of the Latin American parties. In Peru, for example, Victor Raul Haya de la Torre broke away to establish the eminently more successful American Popular Revolutionary Alliance (APRA). The Sino–Soviet split and the rise of Castro has produced similar splintering. Of most importance, the local parties have never been able to successfully oppose popular nationalist leaders. Even in Cuba, with its heavy economic dependence upon the Soviet Union, the attempt of orthodox communists to gain power within the Partido Unificado de la Revolucion Socialista Cubana (PURSC) finally resulted, in 1965, in a purge of major communists, such as Carlos Rafael Rodriguez of the Agrarian Reform Institute. In Chile and Venezuela communist electoral opposition to Frei and Leoni virtually decimated the parties in 1965—a blow from which they have still not fully recovered. In short, the communist parties of Latin America function in obedience to the dictates of the inter-

[9] Rollie E. Poppino, *International Communism in Latin America: A History of the Movement* (London: Collier–MacMillan, 1964), pp. 24–35.

[10] Edwin M. Martin, "Communist Subversion in the Western Hemisphere," Dept. of State, *Bulletin* (March 11, 1963), p. 34.

national communist movement only at grave risk to their continued existence. Under these circumstances, most local communists have found more political profit in nationalism than in attempting to unite the world under a red banner.

In their weakness, Latin American communists have been forced to align themselves with various dominant political groups on the Right and Left; often in opposition to popular nationalists who threatened to mobilize apathetic masses for national purposes and to undercut the potential source of any future communist strength. Consequently, when Brazil's Quadros ran against Marshall Lott, a traditional militarist, the communists unsuccessfully supported Lott. In Colombia the communists have for years supported an intellectual oligarch, Lopez Michelsen, against both the ruling Frente Nacional and a mass-based nationalist movement led by Eugenia Rojas. Both Trujillo and Batista counted upon organized communist support in their better years. Even Castro was initially opposed by the communists, who went so far as to betray Castro supporters to Batista's secret police.[11]

But alignment does not mean control. Nowhere in Latin America—with the arguable exception of Guatemala, which will be discussed presently—have orthodox communists successfully gained control of a larger nationalist movement with which they have allied. In Argentina the Peron–communist coalition—before it went underground due to the army's takeover—was firmly in control of the Peron faction. In Cuba, Castro was able to purge most of the important communists from the government within a year. In Venezuela, Betancourt—once himself widely denounced as a communist—banned the party from legal participation in national politics. In short, the communists, rather than subverting and controlling the nationalist movements with which they have aligned, have more often been the tools of the same movement.

If it is not the orthodox communist parties, with their presumed ties to foreign powers, that constitute the "communist threat" in the hemisphere, who then is the anticommunist policy supposed to oppose? By the late 1960's that question could be answered with some assurance by observing the direction of the military and economic aid programs. In Venezuela, Bolivia, Peru, Colombia, Brazil, Guatemala, and Uruguay, the United States was actively supporting attempts to suppress a variety of rural guerrilla movements styled in part after Castro's successful campaign in the Cuban *campo*. Similar support was going to the Dominican military to aid in the suppression of the urban-based pro-Bosch Constitutionalists,

[11] In fact, the purge of communists from Castro's government, in 1965, was initiated in March of 1964, when Marcos Rodriguez, a communist, was tried and found guilty of betraying a plot to kill Batista by a group of students to Batista police.

after they had lost a U.S.-supervised election that had been characterized by an anti-Bosch terror campaign.[12] Apart from certain similarities in method, the only characteristics shared by these various groups were their Marxist ideological orientation and their opposition to U.S. support of existing and allegedly suppressive governmental regimes. Even if the Dominican Constitutionalists are excluded as a special case, the question would remain as to why these "communists" present the same threat as foreign-dominated traditional communist parties and as to whether the strengthening of local military units is an appropriate response.

While no means clear, apparently the official view of the various rural guerrilla movements is that they are the result of "Castro-supported subversion and insurgency."[13] The occasional discoveries of Cuban arms in the hands of some of the guerrillas and the well-publicized escapades of Che Guevara in Bolivia have lent a certain superficial credibility to the view. But unfortunately life is not so simple. In Colombia the rural guerrilla movement pre-dates Castro by some ten years and reached its height of numbers and power long before Castro came down from the Sierra Maestra. In Guatemala Castro supported one guerrilla movement (FAR) over another (MR–13), and the Castro-supported movement was advocating election participation, while the excluded group was moving toward more violent measures. In Brazil the origins of one of the guerrilla movements date back to the splintering of Getulio Vargas' Brazilian Labor Party, while another faction, associated with Francisco Julião's Peasant Leagues of the Northeast has a strong domestic economic and political base. Even in Venezuela, where Cuban support has been most apparent, the guerrilla movement is clearly traceable to a badly handled and violent attempt to suppress student adherents of the MIR (Movement of the Revolutionary Left).[14] In fact, the only guerrilla movement that might arguably be stamped with the label "Made in Cuba" was Che Guevara's group in Bolivia; and that, if the Guevara *Diary* is to be credited, failed for lack of local support.

If the guerrilla movements are not a threat to U.S. interests because they constitute proxy forces for Castro, they must be a threat because of ideological and material support from Cuba and the resulting suspicion that a successful guerrilla movement would produce a government closely aligned with Cuba in hemispheric politics. In the first place, it may be doubted

[12] *Christian Science Monitor*, May 13, 1967.
[13] Statement of Secretary of State Dean Rusk, Dept. of State, *Bulletin* (May 29, 1967), p. 828.
[14] James Petras,"Revolution and Guerrilla Movements in Latin America," in Petras and Maurice Zeitlin (eds.) *Reform or Revolution?* (New York: Fawcett, 1968), pp. 338–40.

how significant Cuban support in the form of material can be. Ten years
after the Revolution Cuba is still a desperately poor nation, dependent
upon Soviet subsidies amounting to between $350 and $400 million a
year.[15] And one of the main sources of contention between Castro and the
Soviets has been the question of fomenting insurgency in other Latin
American countries. Without Soviet aid for the purpose, it is at least clear
that Cuba can never export the kind and quantity of sophisticated armaments that would allow a small group of unpopular agents to overwhelm
even the average Latin American police force. If, on the other hand,
popular support for these guerrilla movements has reached such proportions as to make feasible Cuban aid a meaningful factor in the outcome of
civil conflict with established governments, then military assistance is no
longer responsive to an external threat, but is placed in opposition to an
internal revolutionary movement. And, parenthetically, the multilateral
justification for opposition to communism as an influence foreign to the
hemisphere collapses entirely.

In the second place, the argument that the Marxist or communist leanings of the guerrilla movements and their more peaceful adherents renders
them peculiarly susceptible to foreign domination—whether Cuban,
Russian, or Chinese—simply fails to appreciate the central role played by
populist nationalism in these movements. Nationalism in Latin America
takes many forms—one of which will be discussed in relation to the
military, another of which is best represented by the remaining oligarchy;
but for most of the twentieth century by far the most important variant
has been populist nationalism, with its peculiar fusion of nationalism and
social revolution. Throughout Latin America, populist nationalism has
served to call into question the whole heritage of Latin American society,
both from the standpoint of social structure and of basic community
values. Indeed, the major structural changes in Latin American society in
this century have resulted from nationalist, not communist or purely
socialist, movements taking over the reins of authority. Castroism—if one
may use that term to blanket the amalgam of Marxist intellectuals, dis-
enchanted middle class, and radicalized peasants and students that constitute the Jacobin left in Latin America—has not somehow been im-
munized against the necessity of making the same nationalist appeal in
order to accomplish major social alterations.

It is, of course, precisely this strong infusion of populist nationalism
into the various movements of the Jacobin left that has resulted in their
strongly xenophobic and usually anti-U.S. quality. But what is too fre-

[15] See, Viator, "Cuba Revisited After Ten Years of Castro," *Foreign Affairs* 48
(January 1970): 312.

quently forgotten is that the very same characteristics make these movements unlikely targets for the kind of foreign domination that is supposed to constitute the main threat of communism in the hemisphere. Castro— whose supposed subjugation to Soviet interests will be discussed in the next chapter—has, in large part, pinned the recent drive toward agricultural diversification upon the nationalistic necessity of freeing Cuba from economic dependence upon the Soviet Union. The leadership of the Bolivian MNR, which presided over an extensive social revolution between 1952 and 1964, openly rejected Trotskyite members of their own party, as well as international communism, on the grounds that the communist ideology was internationalist and "contrary to national sentiments."[16] And the Mexican Revolution, while profoundly anti-United States at various stages of its development, has never been even seriously threatened by foreign direction of any kind.

If foreign domination is not to be feared from the success of the Jacobin left in Latin America, it is difficult to understand how the activities of the various guerrilla groups and Marxist intellectuals are supposed to threaten U.S. interests, apart from the loss of private investments due to expropriation. As we have already pointed out, the strategic zone arguments are transparently fallacious. In terms of Cold War prestige, surely the United States has lost more than it has gained from its support of right-wing dictatorships and from episodes such as the Bay of Pigs and the Dominican invasion. Even the previously sacrosanct Panama Canal has been officially assigned a low strategic priority since World War II; and defense of the Canal has been merely skeletal since the mid-1950's.[17] Perhaps, to men schooled in the Dullesian rhetoric of the Cold War the mere fact of an anti-United States orientation and an ideology based upon identifiably Marxist models might suffice to justify opposition to the point of armed intervention, on the theory that there is no middle ground for those opposing U.S. hegemony short of enlistment in the international communist conspiracy. Dulles himself, it is often said, thought neutralism immoral. But even if it were thought that such world views still held sway in Washington it would be necessary to seek an explanation of why a Frei, a Leoni, or a Peruvian military junta should not be similarly opposed and upon the same grounds.

It is possible, of course, to oppose communist revolutionaries not so much on the grounds that they are communists as on the grounds that they are revolutionaries. Indeed, the thesis has been advanced by both

[16] Arthur P. Whitaker and David Jordan, *Nationalism in Contemporary Latin America* (New York: Free Press, 1966), p. 148.
[17] Martin B. Travis and James T. Watkins, "Control of the Panama Canal: An Obsolete Shibboleth?" *Foreign Affairs* 37 (April 1959): 407–18.

Richard Barnet and Michael Parenti, each writing from a different perspective, that U.S. policy in the Third World, including Latin America, is explicable in terms of an intense desire for "world stability" and peaceful development, coupled with the assumption by the United States of a policeman's role in the preservation of world order.[18] In this view U.S. policymakers could well be in sympathy with the reformist goals of the radical Latin American left, but still object to the use of violent methods, tending to disrupt the political stability of the hemisphere. Hence, a distinction could be made between a Frei seeking radical reform through peaceful means and a Turcios resorting to violent revolution. The theory also goes far toward explaining what Dominican Constitutionalists have in common with Guatemalan guerrillas in the eyes of U.S. policymakers. But the question of whether support of local military establishments and/or direct armed intervention is a rational method for preserving some desired minimal level of internal stability would remain; and to answer it, it is necessary to look first at the military groups to which the United States is lending its support.

## Modern Latin American Militarism

If U.S. perceptions of who and what are the communist enemies are faulty, perception of the nature and identity of our natural allies in Latin America borders on the pathological. For over two decades, U.S. aid policies have been based upon either of two models of the Latin American military. The first is that of the loyal professional group. Under this model, support is given to the militaries of reformist-democratic regimes, such as that of Betancourt–Leoni in Venezuela, on the theory that a strong military will provide needed protection from communist subversives until liberally supported reforms can achieve the "elimination" of the conditions of poverty and social upheaval without which the communist revolutionaries would loose their mass appeal. The second model—which is usually brought forward after a U.S.-supported military has toppled a reformist regime—is that of the embattled second best: "The United States would prefer a constitutionally elected regime; but if the present military leaders are not supported, the communists will take over the country." Or alternatively, "Given the degree of communist infiltration of the toppled regime, the military did the only thing possible and should now be given U.S. support." What is usually overlooked is the degree to which modern Latin American militarism produces a tendency toward military intervention into civilian politics, quite independent of the relative success of reformist civilian regimes or of the existence of any actual communist

[18] See, Barnet, *Intervention and Revolution;* and Parenti, *Anti-Communist Impulse.*

threat. Second, there has been an almost irrational assumption that the ideological leanings of intervening militaries will be preferable from the standpoint of U.S. interests to those of the feared communists.

Modern Latin American militarism may be conveniently described as a nationalistic movement within a nationalistic movement. While military interventionists traditionally have wrapped themselves in the national flag, they share that propensity with all other successful Latin American political groups. As Johnson has pointed out, "Nationalism in its broadest sense is manifested in such a variety of ways that it would be impossible to determine with certainty whether civilians or the armed forces (which are at all times likely to have militantly nationalistic elements) are the more nationalistic."[19]

But military nationalism is distinguishable in that, apart from asserting the unique cultural features of a particular Spanish-American heritage, it further asserts the peculiar competence of the military to carry forward the realization of national aspirations. As the Grupo de Oficiales Unidos (GOU), the fraternal organization of Argentine military activists, put it in April 1943: "Civilians will never comprehend the grandeur of our ideals and for this reason it is necessary to eliminate them from the government and give them the only mission which befits them: labor and obedience."[20] Or, as Juan Peron expressed the same proposition: "Government is a battle, and battles, whether military or economic, are governed by the same principles. . . . We are better prepared than any other group to triumph in this struggle . . . the others may have intelligence, but the fighting spirit, the will to conquer, is further developed in the soldier than in the members of any other profession."[21]

The Latin American soldier's conviction of his peculiar competence to direct the nation is a product of both his society and his training. Again, the degree of diversity among Latin American nations makes generalizations hazardous, but a few remain within the realm of academic decency.

Foremost among the elements of modern Latin American militarism is the simple absence of a "constitutional habit." The history of almost every Latin American country is rife with incidents of military interference in civilian politics; and this fact has two consequences: The first and most obvious is that there is ample precedent for military intervention whenever the military feels that its professional or ideological interests are threatened. Less obvious, but equally important, is the resulting propensity of civilians

[19] John J. Johnson, *The Military and Society in Latin America* (Stanford: Stanford University Press, 1964), p. 141.

[20] German Arcienegas, *Entre la Libertad y el Miedo* (Mexico, 1952), pp. 59–60.

[21] Robert Alexander, *The Peron Era* (New York: Columbia University Press, 1951), p. 117.

to seek the aid and support of the military for their own aspirations. The problem was well formulated in 1959 by Rafael Caldera, the presidential candidate of the Venezuelan Social Christian party in the 1958 elections. "Venezuelans," he said, "are so accustomed to seeing the army as a factor in their daily lives, so accustomed to make the army the arbiter of their political contests, that at each moment the most varied groups for the most dissimilar ends attempt to involve the army in new adventures to change our political reality."[22] It is not that the military has intervened at the behest of one group or the other, but that it has intervened at the behest of different groups. Thus, the Peruvian military coup of 1948 was clearly designed to maintain the status quo for the benefit of the landed oligarchy. In Guatemala, however, the military intervened in 1944 to throw out a military dictator aligned with the traditional ruling classes and to undertake a social revolution of major proportions.

Second, the very political environment of Latin America since the 1930's has been highly conducive to military intervention. The prevailing shift of political power to the middle sectors of Latin American society has not been an easy one, and the modern day bid of the lower classes for increased power promises even greater violence. In a polarized political situation the Latin American military has often been faced with the choice of assuming the reins of government itself or of sitting by while the nation falls into what the military perceives as chaos. For example, in Colombia, Rojas Pinillas assumed power in 1952 only after the traditional political parties had engaged in a bloody civil war for over ten years. And Castillo Branco's coup in Brazil occurred in the midst of a tension-spawning attempt by civilian leaders to align themselves with a lower-class popular movement and against traditional party oligarchs. In such situations the army, as the main receptacle of authoritative force in the country, often feels that intervention is desirable for the purpose of restoring some semblance of order, regardless of the ideological equities of the political conflict.

This emphasis upon order as a prerequisite for modernization is closely related to another characteristic of the Latin American military—its relative technological orientation, as compared with other segments of Latin American society. In vivid contrast to periods of the nineteenth and early twentieth centuries, when the prime role of Latin American military was to preserve the particularized interests of the upper classes, the modern-day Latin American military man has his own special interest in the modernization of Latin American society. In the first place, U.S. equipment and training have resulted in a radical upgrading of the technological

---

[22] Quoted in Johnson, *Military and Society*, p. 120.

abilities of the military man. In a country in which rugs are still woven with a hand-thrown shuttle and fields still plowed with oxen and wooden plowshares, a soldier may still be required to be relatively familiar with the workings of complex mechanical and electronic devices, including rockets, tanks, and computer guidance equipment. Increasingly, the military man finds (1) that his skills are primarily designed for the modern world and (2) that the military is the primary, if not the only, consumer of those skills in a backward society. Hence, modernization becomes the only route by which the modern Latin American soldier may increase his own social importance as a military man and open alternative avenues to himself as a future civilian.

The attraction of the ideal of modernization is further exaggerated by what may be called the "internal" upgrading of the Latin American militaries. All the Latin American states now provide some kind of advanced training for officers in war colleges, command schools, and universities.[23] Usually this training is a prerequisite to promotion. To the degree then that the military career becomes an alternative to university training as a means of social advancement, military men can be expected to share the ideal of modernization with their university counterparts. Finally, the movement toward opening officer ranks to young men of the lower and middle sectors of Latin American society has produced an officer less bound by traditional structures and ideas than his predecessor of two generations.

The contact between U.S. and Latin American military officers may contribute to militarism in a less technological way. That is by means of an emulative process which, for lack of a better word, might be called a "military-industrial complex." Latin American military officers trained in the United States or by U.S. military missions normally derive their image of the social role of the U.S. military from U.S. military officers. In numerous conversations with Colombian military officers during 1966 and 1967 we were increasingly impressed with the disparity between the image of this role held by Latin American military officers and that subscribed to by most Americans. It was not at all infrequent to hear that the influence in national policymaking wielded by the Latin American military was not greatly different from that wielded by the American military—the differences being those of form rather than substance. In the view of these Colombian officers, intervention into civilian politics was simply an alternative to the more structured pattern of influence in the United States and was simply another route by which the legitimate concerns of the Latin American military could be accorded their due weight in national decision-making.

[23] *Ibid.*, p. 102.

The reasons that this distorted view of the role of the American military should be so prevalent in Latin America are not difficult to find. For the Latin American officer whose main contacts with the United States are by way of military bases or local U.S. advisers, American society approximates the "garrison state." The paraphernalia of modern nuclear warfare must appear to one raised in the rural areas of Latin America as obtainable only by a political group yielding deciding power in national decision-making. Central to this distortion is the Latin American's view of the military, not as the military but as a political party. And this impression is reinforced by the fact that all of the officers' official dealings with the U.S. government are through other military officers who can only appear to them to have the final say in an official decision.

It is also possible to speculate that the prevailing rhetoric of American military society itself has provided reinforcement for the Latin American view of U.S. society at large. Since the army–McCarthy hearings of the early 1950's—and especially since the Kennedy liberalism of the early 1960's—the position of the military in American society has been, at best, equivocal. It is only to be expected that the debate surrounding the proper role of the American military has generated defensive attitudes within the military itself. For the Latin American officer those rash attitudes—expressed in the liturgy of self-importance so common in American officers' clubs around the world—may represent his principal source of information on the U.S. decision making process. For him, this rhetorical "puffing" may well become the truth of American society.

Finally, as Victor Alba has pointed out, neomilitarism in Latin America may itself be a form of psychological compensation. The express function of the Latin American militaries—that of cooperating in hemispheric defense—has never been more than a political fiction. In the nuclear age the combined forces of all the Latin American militaries would be inconsequential as against any attack on the hemisphere by a major power. The changing nature of warfare has simply made the Latin American military an anachronism in the modern world.

> Given this reduced capability and lack of a meaningful and legitimate function, many Latin American military men find themselves in a state of mind comparable to what Alfred DeVigny said of the Napoleonic army: "The army is a nation within a nation. It is ashamed of itself and it knows not what it does nor what it desires. It asks itself ceaselessly whether it is a slave or owner of the state and its body searches everywhere for its soul and does not find it!"[24]

[24] Alba, "Latin American Militarism," p. 178.

All of the above elements, of course, lie in the ethereal realm of the psychological and are little subject to concrete evidence. Nevertheless, the essential point remains that strong sociological and psychological predispositions toward intervention into civilian politics exist among most Latin American militaries. And the essential criticism that may be made of all U.S. military aid programs to Latin America since World War II relates to their failure to take adequate consideration of these ephemeral predilections. It is precisely this failure—in conjunction with a heavy reliance upon the military assistance program as a means of assuring a desirable political configuration in Latin America—that accounts for the depth and frequency of U.S. involvement in Latin American civil strife. The simple fact is that most of the Latin American militaries more closely approximate political rather than military institutions, and cheap weapons procurement increases the likelihood of their "political" success in the same way that provision of aid to any other internal political institution would do the same.[25]

In this regard, the modest proportions of the U.S. military assistance program to Latin America, when compared to similar programs in Asia and Europe, is deceptive. The relative position of power held by the military in a given Latin American country—if it can be viewed quantitatively at all—will depend upon the capacity of the individual foot-soldier to apply violence relative to the "average civilian's" ability to resist. That capacity will in turn be effected by a number of variables, including cumulative allocations of funds to different types of weaponry, the per capita civilian income in the country, and the internal solidarity of the military. For example, a small amount of money spent on automatic weapons increases the military's ability to coerce the civilian population much more than a larger money allocation for the purpose of buying a battleship. But automatic weapons give the military a decisive advantage over civilian groups only in a country where the per capita income is too low for the civilians to be able to similarly arm themselves.[26] Hence, simplistic correlations of total dollar amounts of aid and the incidence of military intervention in civilian politics give a misleading picture.[27]

It is with this view toward specific allocations of military aid that it can be said that the U.S. military aid program has made an increasing contribution to neomilitarism in Latin America. The shift, late in 1961, to counterinsurgency and civic action as the centerpieces of American

[25] Cf. Edwin Lieuwen, *Generals vs. Presidents* (New York: Frederick A. Praeger, 1964), p. 95.

[26] This line of analysis is fully developed in John Duncan Powell, "Military Assistance and Militarism in Latin America," *Western Political Quarterly* 18 (1965): 382.

[27] See e.g., Charles Wolf, *United States Policy and the Third World* (Boston: Little, Brown and Company, 1967), pp. 90–111.

military aid policy in Latin America added ominous techniques and equipment to the repertoire of the recipient Latin American militaries and increased their involvement in the social and political upheavals in their respective countries. Even by 1963 Latin America was bearing the fruit of Kennedy's "new look." In the Dominican Republic the U.S.-trained riot police and antiguerrilla units aided the army in overthrowing President Bosch and went on to hunt down Bosch's noncommunist supporters in the name of anticommunism. In Guatemala, Ecuador, and Honduras counterinsurgency forces were similarly used as a branch of the secret police to eliminate opposition to incumbent governments. And in Peru U.S.-trained antiguerrilla units led the overthrow of Manuel Prado.[28]

But there is an important distinction to be made between the tendency to intervene in domestic politics and the ideological content of military intervention. All of the factors mentioned thus far are ideologically neutral in that they increase the propensity of the military to intervene without giving any necessary direction to what the military may do after intervention. Since military figures are no more immune to the ideological currents of the time than are other Latin Americans, there is no real assurance that an incoming military regime will be any more reliable a protector of U.S. interests than any of the alternative political groups, including those of the left. Alternatively, to the extent that groups within the military share the goals of revolutionary modernization of the radical left, the effectiveness of the military establishment as a bulwark against radical leftist elements is diminished. The first possibility is well illustrated by the latest Peruvian coup, which was immediately followed by expropriations of U.S.-owned properties and moves toward the establishment of trade relations with the Soviet Union. The second alternative is suggested by both the Cuban and Dominican examples in the following chapter. In Cuba in 1959 and in the Dominican Republic in 1965, the total collapse of the military was due in no small part to the effective defection of numerous junior officers. Thus even if the rationality of opposing the Latin American radical left were to be conceded, it would still not be proved that the support of Latin American military establishments is the way to go about it.

Of course, it may still be contended that as long as the communists or the radical left are viewed by Washington as a threat to essential U.S. security interests that continued reinforcement of the Latin American military establishment is preferable to more intensive modes of U.S. intervention into the domestic politics of the other countries of the hemisphere. Thus, the practitioner of *Realpolitik* might argue that—however irrational—anticommunism and the identification of nationalist revolutionaries as communists is so firmly embedded in the U.S. national psyche

[28] Lieuwen, *Generals vs. Presidents*, p. 127.

as to deny immediate extirpation. Consequently, it is preferable to depend upon maintaining some influence over local military establishments than to do nothing until left-wing activity in Latin America provokes another Santo Domingo. The fallacy here is that close reliance upon the domestic military may in the end prove as damaging to U.S.–Latin American relations as direct armed intervention. And, as the next chapter will seek to demonstrate, in some instances that same heavy reliance may ultimately foreclose the option of nonintervention. An example of the first tendency was seen in Bolivia.

Throughout the year 1967 the Bolivian government of Rene Barrientos had been plagued by guerrilla activities in the hinterlands. In response, what appears to have been a sizable counterinsurgency program, using U.S. special forces units as advisers and possibly participants, was undertaken by the U.S. military and intelligence services. This effort paid off in October 1967, when a guerrilla unit led by Che Guevara was ambushed in the *campo* and Guevara was killed—whether in the ambush or subsequently murdered by intelligence agents. Thus far, we had had a successful counterinsurgency operation which had eliminated one of the main threats to the incumbent Bolivian government. Only later did it become evident what this program had cost in terms of Bolivian sovereignty.

In July 1968 Bolivia's minister of the interior, Antonio Arguedas, fled to Chile after having forwarded a copy of Guevara's diary to Cuba. The ensuing scandal precipitated a crisis in the Bolivian cabinet, which resigned en masse at the end of July 1968. The country's military leaders immediately went into conference and began making arrests of prominent Bolivian politicians.[29] Barrientos, a former air force officer, immediately named an all-military cabinet on the grounds that it was "necessary to prevent the nation from falling into anarchy."[30] The commander of Bolivia's armed forces, General Alvredo Ovando Candia, describing the role of the armed forces as a "watch dog," warned that the army would intervene if there were a "complete" breakdown in the democratic processes.[31]

Then on August 17 Arguedas returned to Bolivia to "give the Bolivian people the full truth" about alleged interference in their sovereignty by the United States.[32] Arguedas publicly declared that he had been an agent of the U.S. Central Intelligence Agency since 1965 and named two military attachés of the American embassy as being involved in C.I.A. activities in Bolivia. Arguedas explained that in 1965 he had been forced to abandon his post in the government by C.I.A. agents accusing him of being a communist infiltrator and threatening to cut off all American aid to Bolivia un-

[29] *New York Times*, July 26, 1968.
[30] *New York Times*, July 29, 1968.
[31] *New York Times*, July 30, 1968.
[32] *New York Times*, August 19, 1968.

less he resigned. He was reinstated only after he had submitted to four days of interrogation and had been subjected to drugs and a lie detector tests by the C.I.A. Subsequently, he claimed, that he had been given money by the agency for the purpose of corrupting officials of political parties, unions, and the press.[33]

The point is not that Arguedas's declarations constitute solid proof of C.I.A. involvement in the Bolivian government, but that the previous involvement of both the intelligence agencies and the military in the counterinsurgency program lent and continued to lend considerable credibility to these charges. By the time the Bolivian army began to make its first moves toward a new intervention into Bolivian politics, it was impossible to separate the actions of members of the indigenous military from those of American intelligence agents and military attachés who were by that time heavily implicated in domestic politics. In effect, the United States role in the counterinsurgency program had become an integral part of Bolivian domestic politics.

Another dimension of the Bolivian problem involves the relationship between two branches of the armed forces. The rivalry between Barrientos, as head of the air force, and Ovando, as head of the army, dated back to their initial appointments as co-presidents of the military junta that took control of the Bolivian government in 1964. The involvement of the U.S. intelligence agencies in the Barrientos government not only strengthened the hand of Ovando but also increased the probability that the new junta would strike in an anti-U.S. direction.

The Bolivian example illustrates the heavy costs of U.S. reliance upon bilateral military arrangements to obtain a desirable level of internal security in Latin American countries. Even in the precounterinsurgency era, pacification of the area could only be purchased at the expense of strengthening the position of the militaries of the various Latin American countries receiving aid and of promoting mini-arms races in the hemisphere. The turn to counterinsurgency has served primarily to increase the intimacy of the involvement of the U.S. military and intelligence establishments in the domestic politics of Latin America. Against the background of the purist conceptions of nonintervention popular in the hemisphere, these involvements suffice to raise xenophobia to hysterical heights and to severely damage the prestige of the United States as a law-aiding member of the inter-American community. But even apart from international legal considerations, the method has by and large proved a failure and has served only to pave the way to more noxious violations of of the nonintervention norm in the form of armed intervention, whether direct or by proxy.

[33] *Ibid.*

# IX.

# Three Interventions: The Early Demise of Multilateral Security

THREE TIMES SINCE THE CONSOLIDATION of the inter-American system in 1947 the United States has resorted to major use of armed force in Latin America, either directly or by proxy—in Guatemala, Cuba, and the Dominican Republic. In all three instances, the multilateral machinery of the O.A.S. was either by-passed or roughly overridden. By the end of 1965 it was clear to almost everyone that cared to look that U.S.–Latin American policy was reverting to the era of "marines and latrines" to which the nonintervention commitment and the O.A.S. structure was supposed to be an alternative. As early as April 1961, shortly following the Bay of Pigs disaster, President Kennedy was voicing what was to become the "new candor" in U.S.–Latin American relations:

> Any unilateral American intervention in the absence of an external attack upon ourselves or an ally would have been contrary to our traditions and to our international obligations. But let the record show that our patience is not exhaustible. Should it ever appear that the inter-American doctrine of non-interference merely conceals or excuses a policy of inaction; if the nations of this hemisphere should fail to meet their commitments against outside Communist penetration, then I want it clearly understood that this government will not hesitate in meeting its primary obligations, which are the security of our nation.[1]

Kennedy's thought was to reach full fruition in Johnson's sending marines to the Dominican Republic, accompanied by the announcement of a new

---

[1] Speech to the American Society of Newspaper Editors, *New York Times*, April 21, 1961.

184

view toward the nonintervention commitment: "The first reality is that old concepts and old labels are largely obsolete. In today's world, with enemies of freedom talking about 'Wars of National Liberation,' the old distinction between 'Civil War' and 'International War' has already lost much of its meaning."[2]

If one is to take the President seriously, the clear implication of the Baylor statement is that the brief era of nonintervention in the hemisphere was at an end. If all civil strife is international war, then every outbreak of left-wing rebellion in Latin America justifies "counterintervention" on the part of the United States—every Latin American nationalist with a gun justifies a Green Beret similarly equipped. Even before the President's speech, this was precisely the conclusion that had apparently been reached in Washington. As Richard Rovere put it: "Practically no one, in the government or out, nowdays seems to regard nonintervention as a defensible principle. No one has tried to square our policy with the O.A.S. Charter; the common view, even among those who have criticized the policy on other grounds, is that Article Fifteen should never have been in the Charter in the first place, or that it has become passe. Whether this reveals a new cynicism or a new sophistication, it is part of the prevailing mood."[3]

How in such a short period of time had the principle of nonintervention within the inter-American system become obsolete? To some the answer is to be found in atavistic "knee-jerk anticommunism" left over from the early period of the Cold War.[4] For others, the Cuban and Dominican interventions are miniature Vietnams, to be explained as an example of a powerful nation overcompensating for political failures by abusing the military instrument.[5] There is, of course, a great deal of truth in both these explanations, but they both fail to take into account the basic continuity of U.S. military intervention in Latin America. In a sense, the U.S. interventionary policy never ended in Latin America; there was merely an attempt to carry it out by proxy—it was hoped that Latin American military establishments, controlled by bilateral aid arrangements, would replace U.S. marines. In this view, recent U.S. invasions of Latin American territory do not constitute failures of the supposed multilateral security system represented by the O.A.S., since no real multilateral security system ever existed.

This latter analysis is readily borne out by close examination of the three occasions on which armed force was visibly utilized by the U.S.

[2] Lyndon B. Johnson, speech at Baylor University, *New York Times*, May 29, 1965.
[3] "Letter from Washington," *New Yorker* (May 15, 1965).
[4] Richard J. Barnet, *Intervention and Revolution: The United States in the Third World* (New York: World Publishing Company, 1968).
[5] Theodore Draper, *Abuse of Power* (New York: Viking Press, 1966).

government. On all three occasions, force was necessary to reassert what was apparently perceived as a "minimum" degree of U.S. control over domestic politics in a Latin American country, after U.S. control of the local military establishment had been lost or after the military establishment itself had lost control of local politics.

## Guatemala

As the war came to a close and low-visibility plans were being laid for the hemisphere, Guatemala was marching to the tune of its own particular drummer. In 1944, after nearly thirteen years as dictator, Jorge Ubico was overthrown by a coalition of young army officers and university students.[6] Thus began one of the most exciting periods of political productivity in the history of the small republic. Democratic reforms were immediately instituted by Juan Jose Arevalo, a radical ex-school teacher who became President in 1945. A new constitution was adopted, similar to the Mexican Constitution of 1917. It assured basic labor rights, gave the traditional individual guarantees, and, most importantly, authorized land reform. The remainder of Arevalo's term was largely spent in implementing the first two elements—educational facilities were expanded, organized labor received legislative protection, and some social welfare reforms were instituted. The all-important issue of land reform was, for the most part, held in abeyance for the time being.

Even these relatively minor reforms were, however, sufficient to strain the uneasy alliance that had brought the government into power. The army split into two factions—headed on the left by Colonel Jacobo Arbenz and on the right by Colonel Francisco Javier Araña. In spite of the subsequent official characterization of Arbenz as a leftist fellow-traveler from the beginning, the split between these two men had more to do with temperament and background than with their respective political affiliations. Underlying their dispute was the issue of what position the army should occupy in relation to the government. In any case, the unsolved murder of Araña in 1949 assured Arbenz of the presidency in the 1950 elections, but it also assured the fatal division of the revolutionary coalition that had brought him to power.

Although representing the left of the military coalition, Arbenz was viewed by many observers at the time he came to the presidency as a "centrist" by comparison to the radical Arevalo. He was, after all, a professional army officer of many years and a substantial property owner. He was married to the daughter of a wealthy Salvadoran plantation owner

---

[6] A full account of the 1944 revolution is contained in Medrado Mejia, *El movimiento obrero en la revolucion de octubre* (Guatemala City: Tipograffia Nacional, 1949).

and, at no little cost, had achieved some degree of respectability in Guatemalan "society." Had the land reform issue not been ripe for decision, he would probably have represented normalcy for Guatemalan politics. In terms of his personal politics, the most prodigious investigations have failed to yield any more damaging evidence than the fact that his library included Marx and Lenin and that his wife participated in the salon society of post-1944 Guatemala. Consequently, one is forced to view the official charges of communist affiliation against Arbenz as more a product of excess Dullesism in the State Department than anything approximating proven fact.

The problem of assessing the degree of communist involvement in the Arevalo and Arbenz administrations is likewise complicated by official excesses. The only serious full-scale study of communist penetration was published by Praeger in 1959, as part of a series of the Foreign Policy Research Institute of the University of Pennsylvania.[7] The author, Ronald Schneider, relied primarily upon materials provided by the National Committee for Defense against Communism (Comité Nacional de Defensa contra el Comunismo), an arm of the Guatemalan executive branch that in less chauvinistic times might be called the secret police. Much of the evidence is photographic and without meaning or reference except for the official commentary. Given the vested interests involved in the Committee and the added likelihood that the Committee was as much controlled by American intelligence operatives as was the Castillo Armas invasion the authenticity of the evidence—and, hence, the validity of the Schneider study—is open to serious question. It is at least certain that the State Department version of communist penetration of Guatemalan society— citing 4,000 as a likely figure for party membership in the country— is a specious fabrication, designed as an after-the-fact justification for a failure of foreign policy.

Perhaps the most dependable assessment was that provided by Basque Professor Jesus de Galindez, a fervent anticommunist and an advocate of democratic reform throughout Latin America. In the spring of 1953, prior to his murder, presumably by Trujillo henchmen, de Galindez wrote of the danger represented by the communists in Guatemala. With a membership of approximately 500—including 4 members of the legislature and none in the government—the Guatemalan communists represented only

---

[7] Ronald M. Schneider, *Communism in Guatemala, 1944–1954* (New York: Frederick A. Praeger, 1959). At the time of preparation of the study, the Foreign Policy Institute was under the direction of Dr. Robert Strausz-Hupé, and the published study bears the imprint of many of his ideas on the nature of the communist conspiracy. See, Strausz-Hupé et al., *Protracted Conflict* (New York: Harper & Row, 1963).

a potential force that might become important, if rabid anticommunism were to lead to the frustration of needed reforms in Guatemala.[8]

The necessity of reform in Guatemalan landholding is best indicated by the 1950 Guatemalan census (Censo Agropecuario). It shows that in 1950 small farmers representing 72 percent of the country's agricultural workers held 9 percent of the arable land; 2 percent of the owners of farm land held 78 percent of the arable land; and 22 plantation-owners (latifundistas) owned 13 percent of the arable land. What these figures do not show is the central importance of the United Fruit Company's holdings in the area. Alone the company held more than 400,000 acres of uncultivated land; it had long been politically powerful in the internal politics of the country, and it was untiringly represented by the U.S. Department of State. With the postwar rise of Latin American nationalism, the company inevitably became the target of the Guatemalan reformers.[9] On the other hand, even the most radical reformer would have anticipated that any dispute with the company might very easily escalate to the level of international diplomacy. John Foster Dulles had drawn up the original contracts between the company and the Guatemalan government in 1930 and 1936. Allen Dulles, then head of the C.I.A., was a one-time president of the company, and Henry Cabot Lodge was one of the company's largest stockholders. Whether or not these personal ties played any actual role in subsequent events, they served at least to endow the company with a formidable aspect of the sacrosanct.

The Agrarian Reform Law of June 1952 was a predictable compromise between these two moving forces in Guatemalan politics. The expropriation provisions of the law were aimed at uncultivated lands contained in holdings of more than 667 acres; no holding was subject to seizure where the land was fully cultivated. Compensation was to be based upon the declared value of the land for tax purposes, and payment was to be made in agrarian reform bonds bearing 3 percent interest and carrying a maximum maturity of twenty-five years.[10] On the whole, the reform measure was palpably less radical than its Mexican predecessor and occasioned no official protest, either from the U.S. State Department or the United Fruit Company, upon its promulgation.

Trouble for the Arbenz administration began almost a year later, in March 1953, when the government made its first expropriation of United Fruit lands in Tiquisate on the Pacific coast, with the seizure of 219,160

[8] *Argentina de Hoy* (May 1953).

[9] On the course of nationalism in Latin America, see generally, Arthur P. Whitaker and David Jordan, *Nationalism in Contemporary Latin America* (New York: Free Press, 1966).

[10] Ley de Reforma Agraria (Dec. 900), *El Guatemalteco*, June 17, 1952.

acres of uncultivated lands for which the government planned to pay 627,583 quetzales—twice the company's cost and precisely the evaluation that the company itself had placed on the land for tax purposes. Apparently in advance of the filing of any formal claim by the company, the State Department protested the amount and nature of the compensation offered.[11] The Guatemalan embassy in Washington rejected the protest as unfounded.

No formal claim was filed by the State Department until April 20, 1954,[12] but in the intervening period the Department undertook a virtual diplomatic offensive designed to beat the drums over the danger of communist penetration of the Guatemalan government. On October 6, 1953, the United States requested that the O.A.S. Council include "Intervention of International Communism" on the agenda of the upcoming Tenth International Conference of American States, scheduled for the following March. Given the anticommunist line taken by the United States at the Bogotá Conference and the convulsive McCarthyism then sweeping the country, the request could have remained a concession to national peculiarities and a potential historical curiosity. But as the time for the Caracas Conference approached, it became more and more evident that the State Department meant to hang the communist tag on Guatemala alone.

On October 13, 1953, John M. Cabot, then assistant secretary for inter-American affairs, publicly complained of the communist line being followed by the official Guatemalan press and issued an unmistakable warning:

> With any regime's purpose of social reform, insofar as it is sincere, we have no quarrel. . . . But when we are resisting Communist aggression and subversion all over the world, no regime which is openly playing the Communist game can expect from us the positive cooperation we normally seek to extend to all of our sister Republics. We know indeed that despite its hypocritical appeals on behalf of the underprivileged, communism does not give a snap of the fingers for the welfare of the masses. It will liquidate them or send them to slave labor camps by the millions to advance its tyrannical power.[13]

In Cabot's mind—and probably in that of other members of the Dulles staff—the communist danger was linked with assaults upon American private investment in Latin America. It was an article of faith following

---

[11] This first State Department protest is not mentioned in any of the official literature in the *Bulletin*, but is reported in the Guatemalan literature. See, Gregorio Selser, *El Guatemalazo* (Buenos Aires: Ediciones Iquazu, 1961), pp. 40–41. The Guatemalan version seems more plausible, since on June 26, 1953, the Guatemalan embassy did present the State Department with a responsive memorandum.

[12] Department of State, *Bulletin* (May 3, 1954), p. 678.

[13] Address made before the General Federation of Women's Clubs (October 14, 1953), Department of State *Bulletin* (October 26, 1953). p. 556.

Korea that the communists were attempting only to exploit "the unthinking emotions of the still backward people," and one of the ways they went about it was to keep them backward. Thus Cabot explained "the vicious propaganda against American companies operating in the Caribbean area."

> By their attacks the Communists seek, of course, to discredit the United States. But they have other objectives too. They want to prevent the development of these republics and the improvement of living standards in them, and they know that increasing foreign investments will endanger their objectives. They seek to turn the Caribbean nations against foreign investment and foreign investors against the Caribbean nations. But if in one Carribean country a misguided government is dancing to their tune, in all the other independent countries they have little enough to show for their efforts.[14]

By February 1954, less than one month before the 10th Inter-American Conference in Caracas, the identification of Guatemala's land reform program with international communism was complete, and high State Department officials were referring directly to Guatemala as a country "deeply penetrated with the virus of international communism."[15]

The growing bitterness of the rhetoric between Guatemala and the United States had its own escalatory effect. Guatemala had not yet ratified the Rio Pact, and with relations ever more embittered the Guatemalan Senate withdrew its formal ratification. This meant that Guatemala was not eligible for military assistance under the Mutual Security Act of 1951. The lack of armament left Guatemala vulnerable to her traditional enemies—Nicaragua and Honduras—who were in turn known to be harboring ex-Ubico supporters, violently opposed to the Arbenz regime. Exacerbating the situation was the fact that U.S. agents were thought to be interfering with Guatemalan purchases of arms in Denmark. And in January 1954 a shipment of antiaircraft ammunition from Sweden and Switzerland was seized by U.S. Customs while awaiting transshipment in New York. The seizure was made on the highly unusual grounds that the transshipment had no export license for Guatemala.

What in retrospect must be considered the final break between the United States and Guatemala—at least so far as the Guatemalans were concerned—came in February 1954 with the formal accusation by Arbenz's press secretary that the United States was deeply involved in a plot to

---

[14] Address before the Conference on the Caribbean at the University of Florida (December 3, 1953), Department of State, *Bulletin* (December 21, 1953), p. 857.

[15] Under Secretary Smith, address before the Chicago World Trade Conference (February 23, 1954), Department of State, *Bulletin* (March 8, 1954), p. 360.

invade Guatemala and overthrow the Arbenz regime.[16] The press release was accompanied by a great deal of documentation, but the most important item was a letter to General Anastasio Somoza, president of Nicaragua, from one Carlos Centeno, an alias used by Castillo Armas on his Honduran passport. It revealed the details of an invasion plan that was being carried on with the agreement of the "Government of the North" and involved the governments of El Salvador, the Dominican Republic, and Venezuela. The main training base was at Momotombito, an island belonging to Nicaragua. Training operations were under the direction of Colonel Carl Studer, U.S. Army retired, and the documentation included a copy of Colonel Studer's passport. Secret radio stations for the coordination of the invasion were said to be operating from the home of a Mr. H. Faith in Tegucigalpa, Honduras. According to the Guatemalans all of this information had been gained from a defector from Samoza's government.

In a press release, interestingly dated January 30, 1954, the State Department denied all of the charges of U.S. complicity, suggested that the publication of the release was connected with the recent change of Guatemalan foreign ministers, and called the accusation an attempt to disrupt the forthcoming Caracas Conference and inter-American solidarity.[17] According to the Department of State, "It is the policy of the United States not to intervene in the internal affairs of other nations. That policy has repeatedly been reaffirmed under the present administration."[18]

A judgment as to the date of active U.S. complicity in the Guatemalan invasion cannot but color one's interpretation of subsequent events—particularly in the absence of "hard" information from the intelligence services. Even the apologists for U.S. involvement usually date that involvement from a later date—when the Arbenz regime began receiving shipments of Soviet arms. But what evidence there is strongly suggests that the Guatemalan version of U.S. complicity at an early date is probably the closest to the truth. Apart from the fact that the invasion closely followed the lines revealed by the captured plan, journalistic revelations from the postinvasion victors closely coincide with the Arbenz press release. After the invasion two Costa Rican supporters of Castillo Armas, with declared access to top figures in the invasion plot, reported how the invasion had been delayed over a month and a half by the traitorous defection of a Nicaraguan named Isaac (Chaco) Delgado.[19] According to the story, Delgado had photocopied documents and confidential papers that had

[16] Yvan M. Désinor, *Bombes sur le Guatemala* (Port-au-Prince: Imprimerie de L'Etat, 1960), pp. 85–87.
[17] Department of State, *Bulletin* (February 15, 1954), p. 253.
[18] *Ibid.*
[19] *La Nación* (Costa Rica), July 7, 1954, p. 4.

gone through him while the invasion was being prepared and sold the copies to Arbenz for $20,000. The fact that Delgado was Nicaraguan and supposedly entered the plot by befriending a Central American president supports the conclusion that it was he who provided the Armas–Samoza letter publicized by the Guatemalans.

If it is true that unilateral U.S. efforts to bring about the downfall of the Arbenz regime were under way as early as February 1954, if not before, then subsequent attempts by the United States to use the O.A.S. to bring pressure against the Arbenz regime must be viewed as part of a larger strategy. As Slater puts it:

> Therefore, the administration decided, the Arbenz regime had to be removed. If this could be done through the OAS, so much the better; if not, then other measures were available. Initially, then, a multilateral approach was adopted and the administration decided to seek an OAS statement of policy clearly prohibiting the establishment of Communist regimes in the Western Hemisphere. Optimally, such a declaration would encourage the anti-Communist forces inside Guatemala and bring about the internal collapse of the Arbenz regime. That failing, the way would be paved for later, more substantive multilateral actions. And if worse came to worse, an OAS statement could at least help legitimize unilateral United States measures.[20]

The Latin American delegates to the Tenth International Conference of American States at Caracas were not unaware of the U.S. strategy; there was simply not much to be done about it. Nicaragua, El Salvador, the Dominican Republic, Venezuela, and Peru were all firmly controlled by right-wing dictatorships. Most American countries were in dire need of economic aid due to falling commodity prices, and the United States was the only possible source of such aid. Only Argentina and Mexico were in a position to resist U.S. pressures—which they did with some success. The overall situation was best described by a Panamanian delegate to the Conference: "If the United States had wanted to badly enough, it could have a resolution declaring that two and two are five."[21]

Even so, the desired anticommunist resolution did not come cheaply. Dulles, who began the Conference in the Bogotá tradition, denying that large-scale economic assistance to Latin America was necessary, ultimately was forced to agree to a special conference for consideration of Latin American economic problems.[22] More importantly, the U.S.-proposed resolution was substantially watered down by a Mexican amendment.

[20] Jerome N. Slater, "The Role of the Organization of American States in United States Foreign Policy, 1947–1963," Ph.D. dissertation (Princeton University), p. 117.

[21] *New York Times*, March 8, 1954.

[22] Compare *New York Times*, March 5, 1954 (Dulles speech on economic aid) with *ibid.*, March 14, 1954.

In its final form the Resolution on the Preservation of the Political Integrity of the American States against International Communist Intervention stated in relevant part "that the domination or control of the political institutions of any American state by the International Communist movement, extending to this hemisphere the political system of an extracontinental power, would constitute a threat to the sovereignty and political independence of the American States, endangering the peace of America, and would call for appropriate action in accordance with existing treaties."[23] But also adopted was the Mexican amendment which declared that "this declaration of foreign policy made by the American republics in relation to dangers originating outside this hemisphere is designed to protect and not to impair the inalienable right of each American state freely to choose its own form of government and economic system and to live its own social and cultural life."[24] Even this watered version of the original proposal was further qualified, as the delegations of the democratic regimes registered their understanding that the resolution would not serve as a grounds for collective or unilateral intervention in the internal affairs of any state.[25]

Despite Dulles's subsequent nonsensical claim that the resolution had "multilateralized" the Monroe Doctrine,[26] the Caracas Conference clearly signaled the impossibility of multilateral action against the Arbenz regime. Juridically the great majority of Latin American nations sided with Guatemala's minister of foreign affairs, Toriello, in the position that the nonintervention norm applied equally to collective and unilateral intervention and that without the nonintervention norm the O.A.S. would collapse.[27] Consequently the United States proceeded with the other half of the two-pronged strategy—unilateral intervention.

As the planning and training of the invasion force continued in Honduras and Nicaragua, Arbenz was faced with a shortage of arms and ammunition. Since no U.S. military aid was possible, he was forced to turn to the Soviet bloc for the first time in the course of his regime. In mid-May approximately 2,000 tons of small arms—principally rifles and machine guns— arrived in Guatemala by a circuitous route aboard a Swedish ship, the *Alfhem*. The United States immediately began the motions for seeking another O.A.S. conference, in hopes of gaining authorization for a naval blockade of Guatemala in case the planned invasion were to fail.[28]

---

[23] Tenth Inter-American Conference, *Chronological Collection of Documents* (Washington: Pan American Union, 1954), Document 110.

[24] *Ibid.*

[25] *Ibid.*, Documents 368–81.

[26] Department of State, *Bulletin* (March 22, 1954), p. 429.

[27] Selser, *El Guatemalazo*, p. 75.

[28] Slater, "Role of the O.A.S.," p. 122.

On June 18 Armas led a band of 150 mercenaries across the border with Honduras in accordance with the original invasion plan. Air cover was provided by three C.I.A.-supplied P–47 Thunderbolts flown by American pilots.[29] Then tragedy set in for Armas. Two of the planes upon which the prevention of civilian opposition depended were lost, and the invasion bogged down.

On the same day President Eisenhower met with C.I.A. Chief Allen Dulles, Assistant Secretary of State for Latin Affairs Henry F. Holland, and Secretary of State Dulles. They debated whether or not to replace the desperately needed planes—with the Dulles brothers arguing for replacement. Holland, who was probably uninformed as to the extent to which the United States was already involved in the invasion, argued that supplying the planes would violate the U.S. commitment to nonintervention. But the President had the final say:

> I realized full well that the United States intervention in Central American and Caribbean affairs earlier in the century had greatly injured our standing in all of Latin America. On the other hand, it seemed to me that to refuse to cooperate in providing indirect support to a strictly anti-Communist faction in this struggle would be contrary to the letter and spirit of the Caracas resolution. I had faith in the strength of the inter-American resolve therein set forth. On the actual value of a shipment of planes, I knew from experience the important psychological impact of even a small amount of air support. In any event, our proper course of action—indeed my duty—was clear to me. We would replace the airplanes.[30]

While the planes were being shipped, Guatemala made a last desperate attempt to save itself by prosecuting a dual appeal to both the Security Council and the Inter-American Peace Committee. This last step was a mistake since although Guatemala quickly withdrew its request for a meeting of the regional body the United States would later be able to argue that the Security Council should not usurp the jurisdiction of the O.A.S. Consequently all that the Arbenz regime was ever able to achieve in the Security Council was a relatively innocuous cease-fire resolution.

The interplay between the O.A.S. and the Security Council was particularly significant, since it proved that the costs of regional organization

---

[29] D. Wise and T. B. Ross, *The Invisible Government* (New York: Random House, 1964), p. 177n.

[30] Eisenhower, *Mandate for Change* (Garden City: Doubleday, 1963), pp. 424–26. A less self-serving statement of how the planes came to be sent was given by Eisenhower to the American Booksellers' Association in 1963: "There was one time when we had a very desperate situation, or we thought it was at least, in Central America, and we had to get rid of a Communist government which had taken over, and our early efforts were defeated by a bad accident and we had to help, send some help right away" (quoted in Wise and Ross, *Invisible Government*, p. 166).

could be high for the Latin Americans. In a sense, the Guatemalans found themselves locked in the juridical cage that the Latin Americans had built in hopes of containing U.S. intervention. On June 22 Guatemala requested further action by the Security Council on the grounds that the cease-fire was being violated. Henry Cabot Lodge, then serving as president of the Council, delayed action on the Guatemalan request on the grounds that the fighting in Guatemala was merely a "civil war."[31] Lodge even went so far as to warn that usurpation of the jurisdiction of the O.A.S. would "destroy" the United Nations. In the end it was decided that the Guatemalan complaint would not be considered, and the matter was effectively left with the O.A.S.

On June 26, with Arbenz's downfall already assured, the United States joined with nine other American nations to request an emergency conference of American ministers to consider "the demonstrated intervention of the international communist movement in the Republic of Guatemala."[32] The meeting was set for July 7, but was postponed *sine die* when Arbenz was replaced by a military junta, including Armas.[33] In the end, the O.A.S. had served only to prevent pressure being brought against the U.S.-sponsored invasion effort in the United Nations.

The subsequent history of Guatemala is fairly well known. Armas, after being hailed as democratic freedom fighter by members of the U.S. Senate, was to institute a brutally repressive regime and to repeal ten years of liberal reforms in Guatemala. Three years later he was assassinated by one of his own bodyguards. But by that time massive U.S. aid had put the army's conservative faction firmly in control. But for our purposes, the prior history of Guatemala is more salient. Specifically, it is necessary to ask why Armas and his occupation by proxy of Guatemala was ever necessary in the first place, when in most Latin American countries an acceptable level of internal security had been achieved by more peaceful subsidization of the local military establishment.

In the first instance there is an element of historical freakishness to the Arevalo–Arbenz regime. Thirteen years of traditional military dictatorship had split the Guatemalan army between young and old officers, and this split never healed during the ten years after the revolution. Once the reform regime had been effectively "demilitarized" under Arevalo, the army lacked the internal cohesiveness to move against any regime—whether of the right or the left. Second, it must be remembered that the Guatemalan revolution progressed in a period of inter-history—after the large-scale

---

[31] United Nations Security Council, *Official Records*, 676th Meeting, June 25, 1954.
[32] *Inter-American Treaty of Reciprocal Assistance Applications*, Volume I, 1948–1959 (Washington: Pan American Union, 1964), pp. 159–60.
[33] *Ibid.*, pp. 161–62.

military aid programs of wartime had ended and before the MAP program had gotten under way. Consequently the Guatemalan Congress's refusal to enter the Rio Pact effectively cut the lines of control that U.S. policymakers were exercising over other Latin American military establishments.

But the neutralization of the Guatemalan army under Arevalo and Arbenz left the country with virtually no means of self-defense, even against the relatively small force of Armas. At the eleventh hour Arbenz did devise a plan to arm a quickly formed people's militia, but the army, including those units loyal to Arbenz, refused to distribute the arms. The remaining loyalist units that did oppose Armas—and initially brought the invasion to a halt—were forced to back down in the face of U.S. air cover. For example, in Guatemala City Colonel Enrique Diaz announced his intention to defend against Armas. The following day a U.S. plane bombed both the radio station which he was using for communications and his headquarters. In the face of potential annihilation his junior officers, with advice from U.S. Ambassador Peurifoy, arrested Diaz and dropped the defense of the city—proving, one would suppose, the accuracy of Eisenhower's views on the psychological importance of air power. In fact, the appearance of U.S planes over Guatemala City merely confirmed for the young Guatemalan officers what most of Latin America already suspected: it was not Armas but the United States against which they would have to defend. In the face of that opposition most of the loyalists found prudence the better part of valor.

The larger question raised by the Guatemalan incident is simply that of what U.S. policymakers thought they had to gain. The simple answer that Dulles was an anticommunist paranoid who shared his affliction with most of the Latin American experts in the State Department is appealing but unsatisfactory to one who suspects that the nation's capital was not completely devoid of intelligent life. Further, the timing of the American discovery that Guatemala was teeming with communists suggests that the label was more propaganda than reality. The more likely explanation was given by Dulles to the British government, when he informed them that the U.S. navy had established what amounted to a blockade of arms shipments to Guatemala and requested British cooperation. As Sir Anthony Eden described the source of Dulles's concern: "Guatemala was weak in arms, and the United States Government watched and worried over President Arbenz' attempt to build up his arsenal. In their view, the situation in Guatemala was a threat to the security of other Central American republics, and above all to the Panama Canal, seven hundred miles away."[34]

[34] Anthony Eden, *Memoirs: Full Circle* (Boston: Houghton Mifflin, 1960), pp. 150–51.

It is of course true that such a preoccupation with the security of the Canal was absurd in the early 1950's. The Canal was still one of the best fortified installations in the world, and the armed forces of the United States were larger than the entire Guatemalan population. But the factual point misses the essential irrationality of American strategic concern with the Canal since 1914. The fear of German lodgment in the hemisphere during World War II was no less absurd; yet, that fear too had prompted major interventionary activity. What happened in Guatemala was but a reflection of what was happening in a global context: strategic assumptions that were at least half a century outdated were becoming wedded to equally untenable assumptions concerning the nature of international communism. This wedding march was to become a recurring theme in U.S.–Latin American relations for the next fifteen years.

For Latin Americans the Guatemalan intervention—perhaps more than any other event in the last twenty years—signaled the failure of the O.A.S. to contain U.S. interventionary policies in the hemisphere.[35] But for U.S. policymakers the very success of the venture carried its own tragic consequences. In large part, Guatemala established the pattern for attempting to deal with popular nationalist governments in the hemisphere, and it was a pattern that was to lead to disastrous results elsewhere.

## Cuba

The relations of the United States with Cuba during the late 1950's and throughout the 1960's make for a dreary repetition of the pattern of U.S. Guatemalan relations a few short years before. But while the story line is similar, the climax and denouement have been drastically changed. Castro did not follow Arbenz into exile; and refugees of the Bay of Pigs, rather than being hailed as the defenders of peace and democracy, have been conveniently forgotten by the U.S. State Department and Central Intelligence Agency alike. The failure of U.S. policy and might in Cuba is itself revealing of the underpinnings of the nonintervention policy, for it was in Cuba—even more than in Guatemala—that the instrumentality of a controlled internal military was unavailable as an alternative to direct intervention.

The story of this phase of U.S.–Cuban relations actually began in 1933, when a barracks revolt under the leadership of a sergeant named Batista replaced one military dictatorship with another. For the next eleven years Batista and the army ran Cuba under a tight rein. Puppet presidents who resisted army-sponsored programs were impeached. The size of the army was increased by one-third, and pay raises and recreational facilities for the

[35] *New York Times*, June 27, 1954.

military were the order of the day. The armed forces share of the national budget increased to 22 percent (up from 15 percent in 1932). So powerful was the army's position in Cuban society that even during the eight-year interlude of civilian rule, from 1944 to 1952, the army's hold on the national treasury was never seriously questioned.

By 1952 the stakes in the game of Cuban presidential chairs were reaching new heights. Cuba was negotiating for a share of the $38,000,000 for Latin American military aid appropriated by the U.S. Congress in 1951, and under the Mutual Security Act of 1952 an additional $65,000,000 was appropriated. Batista, running a poor third in the constitutional elections, in March of 1952 organized and executed a new army coup and again took control of the government. Cuba, however, was not immune to the growing social unrest that characterized Latin America throughout the 1950's. Batista found it increasingly difficult to govern the island and was forced into ever more severe coercive measures to suppress a series of student riots, army and navy conspiracies, and guerrilla operations in the *campo*.

Exacerbating the dreary rule of a military dictatorship were the unresolved social and economic problems that had plagued the island since before the sinking of the *Maine*. The 1953 census indicated that the severe illiteracy problem was growing even worse. Cuba's economy was still centrally dependent upon sugar exports to the United States, which in 1951 accounted for 88.1 percent of all Cuban exports. Approximately 40 percent of the profits from such exports still went to American-owned companies.[36] The patterns of land ownership remained little changed since the days of the Spaniards. Hence, a sizable portion of the rural population consisted of migrant laborers. In short, outside the somewhat more prosperous urban areas, Cuba was not a place for Cubans.

All of this, however, is not meant to suggest that the revolution that ultimately toppled Batista and made Fidel Castro the central villain of American foreign policy was a "social" revolution on a scale with those of the French or Russians. As Theodore Draper has amply pointed out, Cuba before the revolution—for all its rural poverty and economic problems—was well off in comparison to other Latin American nations. In terms of percentages it had one of the largest urban middle classes in Latin America. Its universities were among the best in Spanish–American academia. And the revolution, when it came, was led not by starving peasants and urban workers, but by lawyers, doctors, and economists. Batista fell not because the strength of the revolting masses overwhelmed him, but because he was

[36] Robert F. Smith, "The United States and Cuba," in Marvin Bernstein, ed., *Foreign Investment in Latin America* (New York: Knopf, n.d.), p. 153.

deserted by the middle class to which he had so carefully catered for over twenty-six years.

What then accounts for the sudden demise of Batista as Cuba's strong-man and sole dictator? The answer is as complicated as the question is simplistic, but at least three elements should be familiar to observers of modern-day student unrest in the United States. In the first place, the Cuban constitution of 1940—suspended by Batista immediately following the 1952 coup—served as a constant reminder to the young and the politically active of the vast disparity between Cuban constitutional goals and Batista practice. Second, Batista's increased reliance upon coercive measures for the suppression of opposition—doubtlessly exaggerated in the mythology of the revolution, but no less real—was largely directed against the middle class itself and tended to shatter the complacency of the otherwise well-established. Finally, the total corruption of the Batista regime, as well as rendering the public treasury a disaster area, undermined all respect for the legitimate authority of the government among the young and disillusioned.

About the constitution of 1940 little can be said that is not apparent from a brief perusal of the document. It is one of the most advanced social instruments of its kind, incorporating reforms in criminal procedure and civil rights that were only to come in later years in the United States. It outlawed discrimination with regard to race or sex, provided special protection for female and children workers, and made specific provision for maximum hours and minimum pay, paid vacations, and accident compensation. But apart from the intrinsic appeal of the document a generation of Cuban students had grown up amidst the mythology of loyalty to country and adherence to the constitution. Consequently the suspension of the constitution in 1952 brought an immediate reaction from the university students, who defied Batista's military intelligence service to hold a four-day wake on the university steps.[37] It was inevitable therefore that a revolutionary elite led by professional men and intellectuals would take as their avowed aim the re-establishment of the constitution.

The phrase that Batista kept himself in power "only by a mounting use of oppression, corruption, and violence" is one often repeated but subject to little solid documentation.[38] In 1960, while mass graves were still being discovered all over the island, the revolutionary government estimated that Batista and his henchmen had murdered an estimated 20,000 Cuban citizens. However one may assess the accuracy of this figure, there appears

[37] Samuel Shapiro, "Cuba: A Dissenting Report," *New Republic* (September 12, 1960), p. 8.

[38] Arthur M. Schlesinger, Jr., *A Thousand Days* (Boston: Houghton Mifflin Co., 1965), p. 216.

to be little doubt that thousands of Cubans—particularly middle-class students—were eliminated by Batista forces between 1952 and 1959. What is more important is that the belief was widespread within the Cuban middle class that murders were committed on such a scale. Further, it was apparent to all save Washington officialdom that the United States was a principal participant in maintaining Batista's army in power. As Herbert Matthews was to write in the *New York Times* sometime later: "History will prove that the dictator did have United States support for much of the greater part of his second seven years as sole ruler. . . . The United States sold President Batista the arms that permitted him to stay in power."[39] So complete was U.S. involvement in the Batista regime in the eyes of Castro's revolutionaries that while marching on Havana Castro felt compelled to warn the United States that the sending of troops would result in bloody fighting on the beaches.[40]

Importantly, Castro and his followers came to power over the ruins of a military establishment closely identified with the United States. This is not to say that Castro's victory entailed the physical destruction of the army. On the contrary, as Draper has pointed out, "the collapse of Batista's army was far more a political and psychological than a military phenomenon." In April 1958 Castro called for a general strike from his hideout in the Sierra Maestra. When the strike failed—due in part to the lack of Communist participation—Batista launched a general offensive designed to wipe out Castro and his followers in the mountains. The problem was that once the repressive machinery of the Batista government was put into play there was little way to maintain its direction. The army and secret police launched a campaign of counterterror, the impact of which fell not on Castro's dispersed mountain forces but upon the rebellious middle-class students and their parents in the urban areas. In the last days of the regime Batista forces are said to have killed 19,000 members of the urban resistance movement, as compared to only 1,000 *barbudos* fighting with Castro in the mountains.[41] In part this was simply the result of greater concentrations of population in the urban area, but on the whole it was indicative of where the real opposition to the Batista regime lay. But because the official terrorism of Batista's regime fell mainly on the urban areas, it fell mainly on the middle-class families from which Cuba's junior officers came. In many cases this meant that a Cuban soldier might be stalking the mountains for pro-Castro supporters at the very moment that his younger

[39] *New York Times*, January 4, 1959.
[40] Maurice Zeitlin and Robert Scheer, *Cuba: Tragedy in Our Hemisphere* (New York: Grove Press, 1963), p. 52.
[41] Draper, *Castro's Revolution: Myths and Realities* (New York: Frederick A. Praeger, 1962), p. 15.

brother was being tossed into a mass grave outside Havana. The effect was to totally demoralize the military while swelling the ranks of the Resistencia Civica—the urban-based resistance organization.

Seventy-one days after it began, Batista's mountain offensive collapsed and for all practical purposes the Batista regime collapsed with it. By late 1958 the ranks of the guerrillas had swelled from approximately 500 at the time the mountain offensive was launched to nearly 8,000. In a final effort to prevent Castro from taking power the U.S. ambassador, Earl Smith, attempted to work out a plan whereby Batista would turn over power to a military junta headed by General Eulogio Cantillo, a former Batista henchman.[42] But the Castroites would have none of the plan. The Cuban military, in effect, had no bargaining position left—the desertion rate was high in the enlisted ranks and the navy could not be depended upon not to revolt. Finally, in late December Castro forces attacked Santa Clara, and Batista fled the country. On New Year's Day 1959 Castro entered Santiago as the new leader of his nation.

The first major undertaking of the Castro regime was to finish the destruction of the Cuban military and to order the U.S. military mission out of the country. Many of the *Batistianos* had fled the country with their leader, but the middle-class officer caste remained, including many who had been involved in counterterror activities against suspected pro-Castroites. Both political expediency and public clamor in Cuba demanded the elimination of the officers. The now-celebrated revolutionary trials were a part of Castro's strategy.

While still in the Sierra Maestra, in February 1958, Castro had promulgated the Cuban War Crime Law which purported to authorize summary courts-martial for murder, arson, theft, and looting committed by any person, especially members of the armed forces or persons in the service of the Batista regime. At the time of the law's promulgation, Batista had been frantically enlisting and sending into the field poorly trained *casquiots* who were not adverse to supplementing their barely adequate salaries; and it was hoped that the law would cut down on this minor theft and looting as well as the more serious violence practiced by Batista's secret police. Beginning in late January 1958 the law formed the legal basis for completing the destruction of the entrenched military. Of all defendants tried under the War Crime Law 450 were executed while about 1,000 were released—a remarkable record in light of the intensity of public passions involved.[43] Approximately 20,000 persons had died at the hands of Batista's hench-

---

[42] New York Times, January 5, 1959; Earl E. T. Smith, *The Fourth Floor: An Account of the Castro Communist Revolution* (New York: Random House, 1962).
[43] Zeitlin and Scheer, *Tragedy in Our Hemisphere*, pp. 67–68.

men—most leaving family and friends who were now seeking blood venge-
ance.

In spite of this background U.S. public opinion was outraged. There were
congressional demands for intervention, economic embargo, and a cut in
the sugar quota; and the new U.S. ambassador, Philip W. Bonsal, publicly
criticized the trials. The Cubans were of course outraged by the outrage.
Batista had operated in a much more high-handed fashion for years without any official reaction from the U.S. government. The result was the
first indication of hostility between the United States and the new Cuban
government, when on January 21, 1959, Castro accused the United States
of "interference" in Cuban domestic affairs.

There is little to be gained here by going into the dreary account of the
deterioration of U.S.–Cuban relations or by adding to the hundreds of
pages that have been written on the question of whether or not Castro was
a communist from the beginning or merely forced into the arms of the
Soviet Union by inept U.S. policy.[44] What is essential about the U.S.–
Cuban relationship following Castro's takeover is that the previous singular
reliance upon Batista and the army to effect U.S. preferences in Cuban
politics left the United States with no alternative means to influence Cuban
policy—short of interventionary behavior outlawed by the Charter—once
Batista and the army were destroyed. In 1959 the Alliance for Progress was
still two years away, and no large-scale economic aid was forthcoming.
The State Department had been as closely tied to Batista as had the
military. And the O.A.S. had already proved something of a rubber stamp
for the United States in the Guatemalan controversy. The only real influence that the United States could exert on the Castro regime was
through the sugar quota.

For Castro, of course, the reconstruction of the bilateral military relationship was unthinkable as well as unnecessary. The only alternative
available to the United States was the same program of massive economic
aid that U.S. diplomats had been rejecting in the councils of the O.A.S.
Castro himself proposed such a program in May 1959, while in Buenos
Aires for the Sixth Plenary Session of the Economic Council of the O.A.S.
In advocating a $50 billion "Alliance for Progress," Castro repeated the
arguments that were already standard in the hemisphere:

> The people of the United States have made sacrifices to provide foreign
> aid, but that foreign aid has not been directed to the peoples that are most
> closely linked to the United States by tradition, by policy, and by their
> economic situation. Why can't the peoples of Latin America look forward to

[44] Those interested in these questions might compare the treatment given in *ibid.* with
that in Draper, *Castro's Revolution.*

receiving from the United States the kind of backing and the kind of facilities that they have extended to other parts of the world?

We are not asking for a gift of capital for our industrial development. We are proposing that we borrow initial capital, to be repaid with interest. So the sacrifice of the United States taxpayer will actually benefit the future generations of the United States.[45]

Whatever inclination there might have been in Washington to consider the Castro proposal was effectively ended with the promulgation of the first Agrarian Reform Law on May 17, 1959. Like its Guatemalan predecessor, the Cuban Agrarian Reform Law limited ownership to 30 caballerias (995 acres), with exceptional increases to 100 caballerias (3,316 acres). Compensation for land taken under the act was to be based upon the evaluation put on the land by the owners themselves for tax purposes.[46] Payment was to be made in twenty-year bonds in Cuban currency, maturing at an annual rate of 4.5 percent interest. As had been the case in Guatemala, the promulgation of the Agrarian Reform Law launched a progressive deterioration in U.S.–Cuban relations, with the State Department reiterating its demand for "prompt, adequate and effective compensation" and with Cuba pleading its inability to pay more.[47] In the meantime Senators Keating and Mundt began warning of communist infiltration in Cuba, and Ambassador Bonsal was recalled to Washington.

By March 17, 1960, U.S.–Cuban relations had deteriorated to a point at which Eisenhower was willing to accede to a proposal by Vice-President Nixon that he attempt to repeat his Guatemalan success. On that date he authorized the C.I.A. to begin collecting and training Cuban exiles for guerrilla action against the Castro regime.[48] Appropriately, the training base chosen for the operation was at Retalhuleau, Guatemala, where General Miguel Ydigoras Fuentes—with firm U.S. backing—was in control.[49] Recruitment was centered principally in Miami, Florida, where

[45] Quoted in Zeitlin and Scheer, *Tragedy in our Hemisphere*, p. 85.

[46] Ironically, when Castro requested American landowners to reassess their property for tax purposes they submitted the same low figures.

[47] The plethora of notes moving between the two governments can be most conveniently traced through the *New York Times*.

[48] The principal sources of information on the planning and training stages of the Bay of Pigs debacle are to be found in the memoirs of President Kennedy's administrative associates. Most of the information which follows is derived from Schlesinger, *Thousand Days* and Theodore Sorensen, *Kennedy* (New York: Harper & Row, 1965).

[49] Some months later, while the training of Cuban exiles was in progress, the Retalhuleau Base was to provide an interesting example of the "contagiousness" of intervention. In November 1960 a revolt of army officers nearly unseated Ydigoras Fuentes, who in an intercepted radio message ordered the Guatemalan ambassador in Washington to apply to the State Department for help. By-passing the O.A.S. entirely, the United States dispatched warships to the Guatemalan coast, and the rebellion fell apart. Since the conservative army officers in rebellion offered no danger of communist takeover, it

refugees from the Castro regime—first *Batistianos* and later others—had tended to congregate. Within a short time the expeditionary brigade numbered over 1,400.[50]

The planning and training stages of the operation were among the worst kept secrets in Washington. As early as July 11, 1960, the *Wall Street Journal* indicated that something was afoot:

> But in hush-hush deliberations there are government officials already engaged in considering just how Mr. Castro's downfall might be hastened by promoting and discreetly backing opposition to him within Cuba, if, as U.S. strategists hope, his prestige and popularity should begin to wane. . . . Such undercover stuff, to be sure, is unacknowledged and no responsible official would be likely to admit it. But the U.S. has taken a hand in just such situations before, when it backed rebel forces against a Communist government in Guatemala in successful revolution in 1954.[51]

By October 30 a principal Guatemala City newspaper had broken the story of the base with all its lurid details.[52] Finally, *The Nation* broke the base story on November 19, but by that time Washington was in the interregnum between two administrations and little responsive to public disclosure.

Passive U.S. involvement in rebel attacks on the Castro regime predated Eisenhower's authorization of the invasion scheme. One of the principal causes of the progressive deterioration of U.S.–Cuban relations during the latter half of 1959 was a series of continued bombings of military and agricultural sites in Cuba by planes flying out of Florida bases. As early as October 1959 Ambassador Bonsal conceded that the flights were taking place but maintained that the United States was unable to halt them.[53] To Cubans—and indeed to many Americans— this was scarcely credible. In the first place, the United States was committed under the Convention of the Rights and Duties of States

---

is interesting to speculate how much of the U.S. concern with maintaining Ydigoras Fuentes in power was actually concern with preventing the exposure of the Cuban training base. See John Gerassi, *The Great Fear* (New York: Macmillan, 1963), pp. 184–85.

[50] A sidelight to the operation was the apparent changeover from the initial concept of a guerrilla force to the final plan for a full-scale invasion on the Anzio model. Both Sorenson and Schlesinger indicate that Kennedy was under the impression that the guerrilla operation was what he was approving; but the contention contains a certain element of black humor. Sorensen, for example, maintains that "the President thought he was approving a quiet, even though large-scale, reinfiltration of fourteen hundred Cuban exiles back into their homeland." *Kennedy*, p. 302. How one would quietly "reinfiltrate" 1,400 men by landing them on a guarded coast boggles the imagination.

[51] Philip L. Geyelin, *Wall Street Journal* (July 11, 1960).

[52] *La Hora* (Guatemala City), October 30, 1960.

[53] Zeitlin and Scheer, *Tragedy in our Hemisphere*, p. 104.

in the Event of Civil Strife "to use all means at (its) disposal to prevent the inhabitants of their territory, nationals or aliens, from participating in, gathering elements, crossing the boundary or sailing from their territory for the purpose of starting or promoting civil strife" and "to prevent that within their jurisdiction there be equipped, armed or adapted for warlike purposes any vessel intended to operate in favor of the rebellion." This commitment was buttressed by a provision of the federal law making it a crime to promote, finance, or take part in "any military or naval expedition or enterprise to be carried on from thence against the territory or dominion of any foreign prince or state, or of any colony, district or people with whom the United States is at peace."[54] Consequently the entire military and investigatory machinery of the United States was theoretically at the disposal of the government for the control of the bombing flights.

It was not until March 23, 1960, that the State Department took any overt action to halt the flights. At that time it was announced that a new Flight Information Center was to be established at the Miami headquarters of the Immigration and Naturalization Service, which was to receive "voluntary information on proposed flights by privately operated planes to foreign countries from the southeastern United States."[55] These measures were described by the State Department as "the most rigorous and elaborate system of controls ever adopted by the United States Government in time of peace."[56] Needless to say, those planning bombing flights over Cuba were not diligent in giving "voluntary" reports of their activities.

In Cuba the persistent bombing raids and the occasional landing of guerrilla fighters obviously raised the problem of armaments for Castro's restructured militia. U.S. military aid to Cuba, which had slowed to a trickle after the revolution, was cut off altogether on July 1, 1960.[57] Furthermore, the United States had intervened to prevent sales of British planes to Castro.[58] Hence, Castro found himself in the unenviable position of having to defend his country against repeated attacks with a diminishing supply of weapons and ammunition. Like Arbenz before him, he was forced to turn to foreign sources. Interestingly, his first move was to Western Europe and, in particular, to Belgium, where he bought 100,000 automatic rifles.[59] But by the spring of 1960 due to U.S. pressures and lack

[54] 18 U.S.C.A. § 960 (1948).
[55] *New York Times*, March 24, 1960.
[56] U.S. Department of State, *Memorandum for the Press*, No. 366, June 29, 1960. Quoted in Zeitlin and Scheer, *Tragedy in Our Hemisphere*, p. 149.
[57] *New York Times*, February 26, 1960.
[58] *New York Times*, October 17, 1959.
[59] *New York Times*, March 10, 1960.

of foreign exchange, these sources were becoming unavailable. It was at this point in time—the summer of 1960—that Castro turned to the Soviet bloc for military aid.[60]

The timing of the Cuban recourse to Soviet arms is important, since it post-dates what the Department of State apparently considered to be the final break in U.S.–Cuban relations—the refusal of the oil companies to refine Soviet oil. In May 1960 the Cuban government demanded that the American and British oil refineries process about 1,000,000 tons of Soviet crude oil, in place of the Venezuelan crude that the companies were then supplying for Cuban consumption. The Cuban demand was based upon the country's 1938 Mineral Fuel Law which provided in relevant part:

> Petroleum refineries existing or which are established in the Republic must meet the following precepts:
> . . . Their plants shall be obligated to refine petroleum for the Nation when the Government so resolves, the respective proration being established among them if the amounts to be refined so demand or so require, in such manner that all petroleum necessary can be refined at a price which does not exceed the cost of operation, plus a reasonable industrial profit.[61]

According to Ambassador Bonsal, the companies would "probably have reluctantly gone along with the government's request" had they not been strongly urged by the Secretary of the Treasury to refuse.[62] On June 29 Texaco Oil did refuse a shipment of Soviet oil and was intervened by the Cuban government. On the same day the United States accused Cuba before the O.A.S. Peace Committee of carrying on a campaign of lies and slander against the United States,[63] and a week later the Cuban sugar quota was cut by executive decree. The journey to the Bay of Pigs was officially begun.

Virtually the only difference between the course of events from this point on and the course of events in the Guatemalan crisis lay in Cuba's immediate attempt to get the crisis into the Security Council and out of the O.A.S. cage. On July 18 Cuba charged the United States with economic aggression and intervention and requested a meeting of the Security Council to consider its charges.[64] This precipitated an immediate Peruvian

[60] Edwin Lieuwen, *Arms and Politics in Latin America* (rev. ed.; New York: Frederick A. Praeger, 1961), p. 269.

[61] Ley de Minerales Combustibles (May 9, 1938), Cap. X, Sec. 44(3), reprinted in *Legislacion de Minas y Minerales Combustibles* (Habana: Editorial Lex, 1942).

[62] Philip W. Bonsal, "Cuba, Castro and the United States," *Foreign Affairs* 45 (January 1967): 272.

[63] "Provocative Actions by the Cuban Government," Department of State, *Bulletin* (July 18, 1960), pp. 79–88.

[64] U.N. Security Council, *Official Records*, 874th Meeting (July 18, 1960).

request for a meeting of O.A.S. ministers—which request provided a basis for adjourning debate of the Cuban charges pending an O.A.S. report. Cuba was back in the cage and the United States was faced with roughly the same situation that had been present before the Caracas Conference.

The Sixth and Seventh Meetings of Consultation at San José, Costa Rica, bear the mark of a dreary replay. Since it was apparent that U.S. influence could probably not withstand another turndown on the economic aid issue, in preparation for the event President Eisenhower requested Congress to appropriate $600,000,000 in economic assistance for Latin America.[65] Further, the United States acquiesced in a condemnation of the Trujillo regime for an attempted assassination of Venezuela's Betancourt. Still, the anti-Castro resolution that the United States was finally able to obtain from the San José Conference was far short of what had been hoped for—in fact, it failed to mention Castro or Cuba.

The Declaration of San José, which the Secretary of State was to laud as a great victory for the U.S. position,[66] was in every sense a compromise. Articles 1 and 2 condemn "the intervention or the threat of intervention . . . by an extracontinental power in the affairs of the American Republics and declares that the acceptance of a threat of extracontinental intervention by any American state endangers American solidarity and security" and further condemn the attempts of the Sino–Soviet powers to exploit the difficulties of any American state as a danger to peace and security. But Article 4 merely restated the incompatibility of the inter-American system with any form of "totalitarianism"—presumably left or right. Article 3, on the other hand, was directed at the United States and reaffirmed "the principle of nonintervention by any American state in the internal or external affairs of the other American states, and reiterates that each state has the right to develop is cultural, political, and economic life freely and naturally." This result has been adequately described with a view to the negotiations of the Conference as a whole, as "a defeat for the United States." Says Jerome Slater: "Not only was no collective action taken, but the United States had been denied even symbolic Latin American support for its own increasingly severe anti-Cuban actions. Even the administration's more limited hope that by going through the motions of a conference it might appease its domestic critics was not fulfilled; on the contrary, the tepidness of the OAS response only increased the clamor for drastic United States action."[67]

[65] Department of State, *Bulletin* (August 29, 1960), p. 326.
[66] Department of State, *Bulletin* (September 12, 1960), p. 408.
[67] Slater, "Role of the O.A.S.," p. 149.

The clamor for drastic action mentioned by Slater was due in part to the presidential campaign then in progress in the United States. One of the future President's main criticisms of the Eisenhower administration was that it had been soft on Castro and had failed to strengthen the *Batisti-anos*—to whom Kennedy dubiously referred as "fighters for freedom."[68] Possibly in anticipation of this charge, Eisenhower had announced on August 24, 1960, that the United States would act in its own interests under the Monroe Doctrine should the San José Conference fail to take multilateral action against communist penetration of the hemisphere.[69] Once Kennedy launched his campaign on the issue, Eisenhower undertook new unilateral action against Cuba. On October 19, Eisenhower announced an embargo on goods exported to Cuba with the exception of medical supplies and most foodstuffs. Domestically, the embargo was an effective reply for Vice-President Nixon; internationally, its utility raised some doubts. As Adlai Stevenson correctly observed: "The fact is that the main effect of this embargo will be first to drive Cuba further into the Soviet orbit, second, to alarm our Latin American neighbors, whose memories of dollar diplomacy and American intervention are still fresh."[70]

The imposition of the embargo exhausted the arsenal of nonmilitary methods for controlling the domestic politics of Cuba. When the new President took office he had the choice of either allowing Cuba to go its own way or using the exile brigade that was being prepared in Guatemala. The choice he made is now history.

On the morning of April 17, the exile brigade was landed. Appropriately, the first man on the Cuban beach was an American frogman.[71] Within three days the invasion was stopped and the brigade cut to ribbons by a much superior Cuban force. The uprising against Castro upon which the success of the invasion depended remained no more than a figment of C.I.A. imagination. And U.S. sponsorship of an invasion that violated most of the legal commitments of the United States in the hemisphere stood openly admitted by the President, who eight days previously had declared that "there will not be, under any conditions, any intervention in Cuba by United States armed forces, and this government will do everything it possibly can . . . to make sure that there are no Americans involved in any actions inside Cuba."[72] The intricate chain of miscalculations, internal rivalries, misrepresentations by the intelligence agencies, and utter stupidities by which the fiasco came to fruition are of little relevance here. What is

[68] Schlesinger, *Thousand Days*, pp. 224–25.
[69] *New York Times*, August 28, 1960.
[70] *New York Times*, October 26, 1960.
[71] Schlesinger, *Thousand Days*, p. 274.
[72] *New York Times*, April 13, 1961.

important is the role played by the awareness of U.S policymakers of the nonintervention commitment.

Tactically there is little argument that the invasion failed for lack of effective air support. With superiority in the air, the Castro forces were able both to pin the exile brigade on the beaches and to destroy their supply ships. The only way that this disaster could have been averted was by providing the exiles with an overwhelming air support that would have been readily identifiable as U.S.-supplied. This Kennedy was unprepared to do in light of "his public pledge of nonintervention and his global responsibilities."[73] "That pledge, "says Sorensen, "helped avoid any direct American attack the following week, thus limited our violation of international law and—despite pressures from the C.I.A. and military—was never reversed or regretted by the President." A cynic might wonder if the Russian pledge to come to Cuba's aid against a direct American attack might not have had more to do with the decision not to launch an all-out assault; but it seems clear that in both planning and execution, U.S. political leaders were mindful of the expectations that had been created by the nonintervention commitment. That the line they drew between aiding an attack by Cubans and a direct application of U.S. military might is legally meaningless in light of hemispheric commitments does not diminish the fact that from a tactical point of view attention to the nonintervention commitment produced the military equivalent to being half-pregnant. The President's subsequent assertion of a unilateral right to intervene if O.A.S. countries failed to "meet their commitments against outside Communist penetration" is probably best understood against this background of frustration. And the subsequent rapid and full-scale occupation of Santo Domingo—with no concessions made to the nonintervention commitment—may likewise be traceable to the frustrating result of attempting to feign compliance with the nonintervention commitment in the Cuban case.

Indirectly the Cuban example was particularly revealing of the dubious underpinnings of the nonintervention commitment. Cuba was the first instance in which the domestic military forces of a country whose political configurations were not in synchronization with U.S. national security were not subject to manipulation—or, at least neutralization—by U.S. policymakers. In Guatemala it had been possible to make-do with a small proxy force, largely because the Guatemalan military—divided within itself and alienated from the civilian government—played virtually no role in the overthrow of Arbenz. Castro, on the other hand, had completely reorganized a military force loyal to the incumbent government. Consequently he could only be toppled by a major invasion. In short, if the

[73] Sorensen, *Kennedy*, p. 299.

goal was to throw out Castro, even visible adherence to the nonintervention commitment was impossible.

Thus the ability of the United States to maintain its commitment to nonintervention in the hemisphere, while achieving what was perceived to be a minimum level of national security, could be viewed as a spectrum: In those countries, such as Brazil, where the local military establishment was the dominant political force and was subject to manipulation through the bilateral military aid programs, visible U.S. involvement in local politics could be limited to the formalized channels of support to the local military. In those countries, such as pre-1954 Guatemala, where the local military—by virtue of its internal divisions or of the power of competing political groups—was not a major force in local politics, the United States was forced to resort to the construction of alternative military forces to exercise its proxy. But, where the local military establishment was prepared to support what the United States considered an undesirable regime with all the force at its disposal, it would be necessary to resort to direct armed intervention.

This growing conviction—voiced by President Kennedy and his legal advisers in the State Department—that the U.S. commitment to nonintervention might prove untenable in the Cold War context was greatly strengthened by events subsequent to the Bay of Pigs fiasco. The continued resistance of Latin American O.A.S. members to U.S. views on the dangers of communist infiltration and subversion and the Cuban missile crisis of 1962 served to increase U.S. disenchantment with multilateral alternatives to unilateral intervention, while seeming to confirm U.S. fears of foreign lodgment in the hemisphere.

In October 1961 Peru, apparently taking the State Department by surprise, requested the O.A.S. to reconsider the Cuban case. The time was hardly ripe for strong anticommunist measures. In Brazil President Quadros was moving toward closer trade relations with the Soviet bloc; in Argentina the Peronists and the Castroites had achieved a political alliance to exert pressure for liberal domestic reforms; similar left-wing groups were gaining power in Chile, Bolivia, and Ecuador; and Mexico had stated its intention of maintaining a neutralist position with respect to Cuba. On the other hand, the Kennedy administration was not in a position to reveal any lack of enthusiasm for anti-Castro measures. In May 1961 the House of Representatives had overwhelmingly passed a resolution calling for immediate O.A.S. sanctions against Cuba, and the Central American dictatorships—to which the United States was tightly wedded— were applying diplomatic pressure for such measures.[74]

[74] Douglass Cater, "The Lesson of Punta Del Este," *Reporter* (March 1962): 19–20.

The ambivalence with which the U.S. government viewed the attempt to impose sanctions on Cuba was apparent at the Punta del Este Conference held in January 1962. Initially the U.S. delegation backed a proposal for suspension of diplomatic relations and application of economic sanctions against Cuba, but it backed away in the face of strong opposition from Brazil, Argentina, Chile, Mexico, Bolivia, and Ecudaor. The move was a realistic one, since, as Adlai Stevenson had earlier remarked, collective action against Cuba could be meaningful "only if it is supported . . . by two of the three largest Latin American countries—Argentina, Brazil, and Mexico. This point is agreed upon by all concerned regardless of whether the legally necessary fourteen votes could be secured."[75] The contemplated diplomatic break and the imposition of economic sanctions would have required continued resolve on the part of even those countries favoring the move. The failure of major Latin American countries to comply with an O.A.S. directive would have dealt a severe blow to the prestige of the organization.

But even a compromise position was not without its cost. The proposal to exclude the present government of Cuba from O.A.S. participation had the great advantage of being instantaneous, but it was still able to garner only the bare two-thirds majority necessary for passage. The vote was similarly split on the establishment of a "Special Consultative Committee on Security against the Subversive Action of International Communism." In short, it was clear that the O.A.S. was not converting to the U.S. view of the "threat of International Communism."

Whatever its global effect, the famous "thirteen days" of the missile crisis changed little in hemispheric politics, except to give an outmoded hemispheric strategy of preventing foreign lodgment at all costs the appearance of continued validity. On September 11, 1962, Kennedy had reaffirmed the prevention of foreign lodgment and the protection of the Canal as part of U.S. strategic theology: "If at any time the Communist build-up in Cuba were to endanger or interfere with our security in any way, including our base at Guantanamo, our passage to the Panama Canal, . . . or if Cuba should ever . . . become an offensive military base of significant capacity for the Soviet Union, then this country will do whatever must be done to protect its own security and that of its allies."[76] When the threat finally materialized in the form of Soviet missiles in Cuba, Kennedy reacted in largely the same manner as his predecessors in the first three decades of the century.

---

[75] *Ibid.*
[76] *New York Times*, September 14, 1962.

Since the missile crisis was largely a confrontation between nuclear powers, its extended treatment in a study of civil strife is not warranted. Besides, the details of those fateful days are so well etched in living memories that they require little repetition here. For our purposes, all that need be noted is that the apparent hemispheric cooperation involved in the crisis neither diminished nor enhanced the possibilities for a multilateral approach to hemispheric security.

On October 23 the O.A.S. Council adopted a resolution recommending:

> that the member states, in accordance with Articles 6 and 8 of the Inter-American Treaty of Reciprocal Assistance, take all measures, individually and collectively, including the use of armed force, *which they may deem necessary* to ensure that the Government of Cuba cannot continue to receive from the Sino–Soviet powers military material and related supplies which may threaten the peace and security of the continent and to prevent the missiles in Cuba with offensive capability from ever becoming an active threat to the peace and security of the Continent (italics added).

But when the Council acted, it was perfectly clear that the United States was proceeding with the quarantine of Cuba regardless of the outcome of the vote. President Kennedy had already announced the initiation of the quarantine via television the night before the Council meeting. Under these circumstances a vote against U.S. action could have only weakened the organization's future leverage on the United States. Even so, Brazil, Mexico, and Bolivia made it clear that they did not consider the resolution as authorizing invasion of Cuba to remove the missiles.[77]

The missile crisis did have the beneficial result of bringing the efforts of the Kennedy administration to topple the Castro regime to an unforseen halt.[78] Part of the unwritten agreement through which the crisis was resolved apparently involved a pledge that no further action would be taken against Castro. But it was soon to become apparent that the U.S. resolution to live with Castro did not necessarily mean any change in a much older resolve to structure the configuration of hemispheric politics in the interests of U.S. security.

---

[77] *New York Times*, October 25, 1962.

[78] There was brief revival of these efforts under the Johnson administration, when the United States supported an O.A.S. resolution ordering a mutilateral break in diplomatic relations with Cuba; but this may be seen as a concession to rightist regimes in Latin America who had their own problems with Castro supporters. The four opponents in the 15–4 vote were the last American nations still maintaining diplomatic relations with Castro.

## Dominican Republic

With the landing of full-dress marine units in Santo Domingo at the end of April 1965, U.S. policy in Latin America had come full circle. With an almost refreshing absence of *apologia*, President Johnson ordered the occupation of the Dominican capital by nearly 20,000 U.S. troops in order to prevent a communist takeover, and the O.A.S. was utilized only after the primary objectives of the U.S. intervention had been accomplished.

As in the Cuban invasion, the roots of the U.S. involvement in the Dominican rebellion go back several years. For some thirty-one years, the dictatorship of General Rafael Trujillo had been one of the main beneficiaries of the U.S. policy "to tolerate and often to favor Rightist military dictatorships and to number some of the worst of them as among our 'friends'."[79] Trujillo had received strong backing from the Truman and Eisenhower administrations and in 1952 was being hailed by the U.S. ambassador, Ralph Ackerman, for his altruistic devotion to the welfare and improved living conditions of his people.[80] What Ackerman failed to note was that the General was mainly interested in his own welfare. By 1960 Trujillo and his family owned about 80 percent of the country's economy and were going after the remaining 20 percent. In large part, Trujillo's business acumen was dependent upon the government—which regularly expropriated properties for "resale" to Trujillo.

Of course, Trujillo's empire was dependent upon U.S.-supplied arms to maintain "order." Murder, torture, and prison were the regime's strongpoints almost from the beginning; but by 1960, under pressure from Castro-inspired guerrilla invasions, Trujillo reached new heights. A wave of domestic repression lost him the support of the Catholic Church—and with it the support of influential friends of the incoming administration in Washington. And in the summer of 1960 Trujillo henchmen botched an assassination attempt against Venezuela's popular President Betancourt. Venezuela brought the matter to the O.A.S. meeting at San José precisely at a time when the United States needed a strong anti-Castro resolution from the organization. The result, as previously noted, was that the United States reversed its policy of support for Trujillo.

Three months after the Kennedy administration entered office Trujillo was assassinated, and the new President was given the opportunity of structuring his own Dominican policy. What emerged is largely to be explained with reference to the President's proposed Alliance for Progress. After the Bay of Pigs fiasco and while the alliance was being elaborated

[79] *New York Times*, May 24, 1961.
[80] Department of State, *Bulletin* (July 14, 1952).

by the President's advisers, U.S. support for the pro-Trujillo groups in the Dominican government was unthinkable. The administration ultimately settled upon support for a regime headed by Joaquin Balaguer, who had been nominal President under Trujillo. Balaguer was considered as the administration's "only tool," since "the anti-communist liberals aren't strong enough."[81] If one considers that Juan Bosch, one of the anticommunist liberals referred to, subsequently won a free election by a 60 percent majority, the problem with the administration's thinking becomes clear.

The Balaguer administration pleased everyone except the Dominicans. On the right, it was opposed by the *Trujillistas* of the military and on the left by the Union Civica and the Partido Revolucionario Dominicano, both led by strong *anti-Trujillistas*. In addition there was a moderate-to-left-wing student movement called the 14 de Julio, but its numbers were insignificant.[82] The real danger to Balaguer came from the possibility that Ramfis Trujillo, the General's son, would be able to enlist support for a return of the Trujillo clan to power.

The threat became real in the fall of 1961 when two of Ramfis's uncles returned from Europe apparently having planned a coup with General Rodriguez Echavarria. The attempt was aborted by President Kennedy's dispatch of eight American ships with 1,800 marines aboard. In Schlesinger's euphemistic phrase, the presence of the fleet "encouraged" General Rodriguez to rise against Ramfis,[83] who, with his uncles, retired to Europe with a sizable percentage of the Dominican treasury.

However, General Rodriguez was not to be denied everything. At Kennedy's insistence, Balaguer and Rodriguez Echavarria agreed to the formation of a Council of State headed by Rafael Bonnelly, an old Trujillo henchman.[84] The Council, aided by a multitude of U.S. economic and military advisers, governed until January 1963, when Juan Bosch, the first popularly elected president in over thirty years, took office.[85]

Although Bosch's election came as a surprise for the Kennedy administration and Ambassador Martin considered Bosch "a destroyer," U.S. support for the freely elected regime was unavoidable.[86] The principal question was how far that support would carry him. The answer came in September 1963 when Bosch removed Colonels Imbert and Wessin y

---

[81] John F. Kennedy, quoted in Schlesinger, *Thousand Days*, p. 770.

[82] Edwin Lieuwen, *The United States and the Challenge to Security in Latin America* (Columbus: Ohio State University Press, 1966), p. 59.

[83] Schlesinger, *Thousand Days*, p. 771.

[84] *Ibid.*, p. 772.

[85] Some appreciation for the massive proportions of U.S. assistance to the Dominican Republic during this period can be gleaned from John Bartlow Martin, *Overtaken by Events* (New York: Doubleday, 1966).

[86] *Ibid.*, p. 329.

Wessin from the capital to prevent them from plotting against the government. The two lead a traditional army *golpe* ousting Bosch.

The initial reaction of the Kennedy administration was to break diplomatic relations with the new military regime, but the tragic events of November caused a change of attitudes. The Johnson administration quickly abandoned the policy of "punishing juntas."[87] On the same day that diplomatic recognition was extended to the junta Johnson appointed Thomas C. Mann as assistant secretary of state for inter-American affairs. The application of the so-called "Mann Doctrine" to the assessment of Latin American military regimes effected a return to the policy of the Trujillo era. As Mann was later to point out, the United States could not put itself into "a doctrinaire strait jacket of automatic sanctions" for all military regimes.[88]

The principal beneficiary of this new spirit of "neutralism" was Donald Reid Cabral, who assumed command of a reconstituted provisional government as a part of the arrangement for the re-establishment of economic and military aid. Reid Cabral, a businessman from the Dominican oligarchy, was Washington's man in Santo Domingo. With Mann at the helm in the State Department, that meant that a priority concern of the Dominican administration was to provide a favorable atmosphere for private U.S. investment. Consequently, an economic austerity program was in order.

At the time that Reid Cabral began tightening down on government spending, the Dominican military accounted for 38 percent of the national budget.[89] Austerity, therefore, meant hard choices between the three branches of the armed services for diminishing appropriations. The Dominican armed services were already plagued by intense rivalry between the air force, which had its own tanks and ground troops, and the army.[90] Hence, any funding of one was jealously regarded by the other. In the second place, given the oligarchical structure of the armed forces—a remnant from Trujillo days—it was inevitable that any cut in military spending would be felt first and hardest by the junior officer corps, which already tended to be sympathetic to the pro-Bosch opposition to the Reid Cabral government. Thus, with a single stroke Reid Cabral was able to throw his junior officers into the Bosch camp, to alienate the traditional military right which was highly dependent upon graft, and to pit the various branches of the service against one another. The result, as Draper

[87] *New York Times*, March 20, 1964.
[88] *New York Times*, June 18, 1964.
[89] Barnet, *Intervention and Revolution*, p. 169.
[90] Lieuwen, *Challenge to Security*, p. 75.

has pointed out, was to leave Reid Cabral "suspended in a political vacuum."[91]

"The political shambles created (in the Dominican Republic) in the spring of 1965 was a direct result of a falling out among the military who had previously held the political control mechanism together."[92] The first to go were the junior officers of the army. On Sunday, April 25, a pro-Bosch rebellion broke out in Santo Domingo. By late afternoon the air force had agreed to fight, but the navy and the senior officers of the army refused to participate.[93] Within three days it was apparent that the planes would not be enough to put down the revolt, and General Wessin y Wessin's ground troops were decimated by desertion and about to surrender to the rebels.

In the interval the U.S. embassy was a very busy place. All three branches of the Dominican armed forces rushed to the embassy to find out what they could expect from the United States. Within twenty-four hours of the first outbreaks they were told that they should oppose the rebellion with armed force.[94] Thus, as one writer has pointed out, the United States was actively promoting the antirebel fight "even though no responsible United States official was then ready to identify a single Communist in the rebel movement or to document the degree to which it might be subject to Communist influence."[95]

It was at this point—when the rebels were in firm control of the battlefield—that Johnson ordered 400 marines ashore to "protect American lives." By the next day when the marines were reinforced to 4,200 it was clear that it was the Wessin y Wessin forces that were being protected. Within a few days there were more than 20,000 U.S. marines and paratroopers ashore. From May 1 to May 3 they pushed into the rebel stronghold in downtown Santo Domingo. At this point President Johnson, who had previously hinted at Communist activities in the rebellion, gave up all pretense as to the purpose of the invasion and flatly declared in a nationally televised speech that communists were dominating the revolt.[96]

On April 30, with troops already occupying large sections of Santo Domingo, the United States went to the O.A.S. for the first time in the crisis.[97] But instead of requesting an inter-American peace force, the

---

[91] Draper, *Abuse of Power*, p. 10.

[92] Lieuwen, *Challenge to Security*, p. 75.

[93] *Ibid.*

[94] Geyelin, *Lyndon B. Johnson and the World* (New York: Frederick A. Praeger, 1966), p. 246.

[95] *Ibid.*

[96] *New York Times*, May 3, 1965.

[97] Apparently some informal warning had been given to prominent Latin American political leaders friendly to the United States, in order that they might anticipate domestic troubles from students and radicals protesting the invasion.

United States merely called for a cease-fire resolution in the manner of the Guatemalan affair.[98] The purposes of the U.S. move were twofold: In the first place, a cease-fire at this point would have worked against the rebels, since Wessin y Wessin was having serious difficulties with defection in his ranks. More importantly, by putting the matter in the O.A.S. in partial form the State Department made it possible for Ambassador Stevenson to argue the priority of O.A.S. jurisdiction in the U.N. Security Council against a Soviet request for Security Council consideration.[99] The first goal was not achieved, since the rebels never adhered to the cease-fire resolution. But the latter strategy resulted in a compromise where by the Security Council remained informed of the matter, but never went beyond sending a representative to the Dominican Republic and therefore took little part in the resolution of the crisis.[100]

On May 1 the United States submitted its proposal for a multilateral peace force, but formal presentation was delayed until May 3.[101] In the meantime President Johnson had formulated a curious blend of the "humanitarian" and the anticommunist justifications for U.S. intervention. Speaking before members of the House and Senate, he explained: "We are not the aggressor in the Dominican Republic. Forces came in there and overthrew that government and became alined (sic) with evil persons who had been trained in overthrowing governments and in seizing governments and establishing Communist control, and we have resisted that control and we have sought to protect our citizens against what *would have taken place* (italics added)."[102] The theory then was that communists were evil people who if given the chance would commit the atrocities that the original landing of troops was supposed to stop. In short, "humanitarian" intervention and anticommunists intervention became one and the same.

Early in the debate on the inter-American peace force proposal it became clear that the Latin Americans still did not share the U.S. view of the communist danger. Chile demanded that any such resolution renounce unilateral intervention by the United States; and Uruguay, one of the leading democracies in the hemisphere, refused to vote for the multilateral force until U.S. marines were removed. Ultimately the necessary two-thirds majority for the resolution could only be achieved by inclusion of the highly dubious vote of the Dominican representative. Even then the resolution did not clarify the status of the U.S. troops then occupying the

[98] Department of State, *American Foreign Policy: Current Documents*, 1965, Doc. X–18 and Doc. X–19.

[99] *Ibid.*, Doc. X–24.

[100] See Robert W. Gregg, *International Organization in the Western Hemisphere* (Syracuse: Syracuse University Press, 1968), p. 81.

[101] Department of State, *American Foreign Policy, 1965*, Doc. X–25.

[102] *Ibid.*, Doc. X–26.

country.[103] This was not done until May 22 when, by resolution, the O.A.S. requested Brazil to designate a commander of the force.[104] The first Latin American contingents arrived the next day.

But the multilateralization of the occupying forces was still not complete. Five days after the first Latin American troops arrived under the command of Brazil's General Hugo Panasco Alvim, Lt. General Bruce Palmer, the commander of the U.S. forces, stated that in a conflict of policy with the O.A.S. he would follow "the guidance" of the United States government.[105] The Latin American reaction made necessary a formal commitment by Dean Rusk that the U.S. forces would operate under the Inter-American Command.[106] Thus over a month after the occupation had begun the U.S. troops were finally placed under the theoretical direction of the O.A.S.

While the O.A.S. ministers and representatives negotiated and debated, U.S. marines and paratroops set about putting down the pro-Bosch rebels. From the beginning of the occupation the U.S. troops had established their "international zone" through the middle of the rebel sector—thus protecting the decimated troops of Wessin y Wessin from total annihilation. On May 4 the rebels proclaimed Francisco Caamano Deno "constitutional" president, raising the danger that the divided rebel groups would coalesce around a single leader. The marines then found that it was necessary to expand the international zone. Meanwhile the regrouped junta forces were launching attacks on the rebel sector and conducting bombing raids on known rebel positions. By May 19 U.S. troops were openly aiding junta forces in attacks on the rebels.[107]

Had the Dominican military been strong enough to produce a viable government the rebels would probably have been crushed before the arrival of the O.A.S. troops. But the military—already split by the rebellion itself—split again over the question of Wessin y Wessin's leadership. In a play for support, the three-man military junta resigned in favor of a five-man military-civilian junta headed by Antonio Imbert Barreras. Wessin y Wessin first held his ground but was ultimately forced to leave the country under pressure from the U.S. army attaché and the U.S. military commander, General Palmer.[108] This left Imbert facing the rebels, but by that time the O.A.S. force, along with the O.A.S. Secretary General Jose Mora, had arrived. Once the U.S. troops ceased to take sides a military stalemate ensued.

[103] *Ibid.*, Doc. X–29.
[104] *Ibid.*, Doc. X–39.
[105] *New York Times*, May 29, 1965.
[106] Department of State, *Bulletin* (June 21, 1965), pp. 1017–18.
[107] Tad Szulc, *New York Times*, May 20, 1965.
[108] Barnet, *Intervention and Revolution*, p. 175.

In the tenuous peace that followed, a three-man O.A.S. team dominated by Ellsworth Bunker, the U.S. member, created a provisional government under Hector Garcia-Godoy. Imbert and the junta were forced to resign by a U.S. threat to halt emergency funds.[109] With peace thus restored and the provisional government installed the U.S. troops began to be withdrawn. In the year following, "normalcy" returned, largely due to the help of massive foreign aid from the United States. Finally in June of 1966, in an election marked by intimidation and violence against the Bosch forces, Joaquin Balaguer, the former Trujillo president, again became President of the Dominican Republic.

The Dominican invasion in many respects parallels the pattern of U.S. involvement in the overthrow of Guatemala's Arbenz eleven years before. In both cases internal divisions in the military establishment rendered it ineffective as an instrument of contol over the internal political situation; in both cases the United States then resorted to unilateral military measures; and in both cases the justification was the necessity of preventing communist takeover.[110]

But the Dominican intervention differed in important respects from both the Guatemalan and the Cuban predecessors. Gone were the attempts of earlier cases to maintain at least the appearance of compliance with the nonintervention norm. Instead the U.S. intervention took much the same form as it had in the days of Roosevelt and Wilson. In part this may have owed much to the rapidity of events in the Dominican Republic—there was no time to prepare an "exile" force nor were there any exiles to prepare. But the form of intervention also owed much to a new-found "realism" with regard to both intervention and its alternatives. Just as the Johnson administration had expressed its willingness to support military regimes as a necessary concomitant of its anticommunist policy, it now seemed prepared to undertake armed intervention as a backup for the military regimes. But in the process, an important distinction had entirely shuttled to one side: Whereas the Kennedy and Eisenhower administrations had intervened against groups that they had conceptually identified as communist-dominated—implying some degree of control by extra-

---

[109] *New York Times*, September 5, 1965.

[110] I have chosen not to add to the voluminous debate on whether or not the fifty or so "communists" on the State Department's various lists could have taken over the rebel movement. In the first place, it is difficult to take the claim seriously in light of what is known about the strength of the Dominican communists and the political proclivities of the Bosch supporters. The State Department's attempts to prove the contrary never rose above the level of propaganda for home consumption. After May 5, even the press releases from Santo Domingo dropped all mention of the famous "54." Second, the Senate Foreign Relations Committee, invited to investigate the affair by President Johnson, found no evidence to substantiate the charge of communist infiltration. See 111 *Congressional Record*, No. 170 (September 15, 1965), pp. 22998–23005.

hemispheric powers—the Johnson administration was intervening to spike a condition of political instability that offered only a highly theoretical *possibility* of communist advances. This is the meaning of the President's Baylor speech and the resolution of the House of Representatives authorizing the unilateral use of force to forestall "subversive domination or any threat of it."

The problem with all this was and is that given the expansive U.S. view of the communist threat in the hemisphere, any active attempt—at least by the radical left—to alter the status quo, even when it consisted of a military dictatorship, was bound to produce the interdicted conditions of instability.

# X.

# Conclusions

THE PATTERN OF U.S. INVOLVEMENT in Latin American civil strife, from the wars of independence down to the present, can be described in one word: "pre-emptive." The first extension of recognition to the new Latin American republics was designed in large part to counteract British influence in the hemisphere. The Monroe Doctrine took up where Jefferson had left off in 1808, in the attempt to exclude the Europeans and the British from Latin America. Entry into the Spanish–American War was largely motivated by fear that a weakened Spain might cede or loose Cuba to a more formidable power. Time and again, between 1900 and 1929 the United States used armed intervention to foreclose the possibility of European lodgment in the Western Hemisphere. And this pattern was renewed in the 1950's and 1960's when the United States began to fear lodgment from another source—the Soviet Union and, to a lesser extent, China. That these latter fears were largely self-generated and resulted from naive and untenable views concerning the nature of the communist threat and the core nationalism of Latin American radicalism should not obscure an appreciation of the motive force of these views in American politics— domestic and international. Even American involvement in the Panamanian separation was pre-emptive, in the sense that American policymakers felt strongly the necessity of assuring (1) the construction of the trans-isthmian canal and (2) American control over such a route of communications before any rival power might gain it for itself. The canal was perceived as essential to American greatness, and control of the Caribbean area was perceived as essential to the security of the canal. The present hesitancy of the U.S. government to move toward internationalization of the canal

221

suggests that this perception has remained, even though the technological and geopolitical configurations that supported it have long since passed into history.

That nations, like people, are often possessed of irrational fears and proceed to action on outmoded assumptions is not a particularly revealing discovery. But what is striking about the tenacity of American "over-concern" with critical areas of Latin America is the degree to which national security interests in Latin America have been perceived as "essential," as opposed to merely instrumental. And the territorial area in which essential interests were thought to be at stake has progressively expanded. Adams, Monroe, and Madison, who carefully structured their attitudes toward the Latin American revolutionaries with an eye to European and British reactions, were, nevertheless, willing to go to war to avoid the transfer of either Cuba or Florida to another non-American power. In 1846 the nation that had undertaken "to abstain from entangling alliances" was willing to guarantee the sovereignty of the nation that con-trolled the Isthmus of Panama—and this in direct opposition to the British, who were then occupying several important territories of New Granada and Panama. By 1903 Roosevelt was willing to risk war to avoid a possible European occupation as far south as Venezuela. And while Cuba was only ninety miles off the U.S. coast, the nuclear logic that resulted in the confrontation of 1962—that the placement of Soviet missiles within an American state was a critical tip of the nuclear balance—would suggest that that nation's security perimeter now extends at least over the area in which ground-based missiles would be an advantage to a potential nuclear enemy.

Behind each of these expansions of the area of minimum security was a strategic doctrine that assured national leaders that the security of this or that area was indivisible from the security of the continental United States. And rightly or wrongly during both past and present periods of active interventionist policy American leaders were convinced that their inter-national rivals had hostile plans afoot in the Caribbean; that failure to act could result in serious injury to American security.

One consequence of this "external" orientation was that until the Cold War U.S. involvement in Latin American internal struggles was rarely related to the nature of the struggle itself. It was the fact of civil strife and the danger of foreign lodgment that accompanied it that were of concern to U.S. leaders prior to 1945. While U.S. intervention favored the incumbent government in the majority of cases, this effect was largely incidental. Where quick revolutions established new governments before intervention could be got under way, it was the new incumbent who benefited from the interventionary stabilization of the status quo. In

Nicaragua and Honduras, the United States, at different times, supported both of the contending factions.

In no instance before 1945 was the intervention-counterintervention phenomenon familiar in present-day civil strife apparent in Latin America. The act of intervention considered separate from its motives was a unilateral move by one power (the United States) designed to rectify political instability that might tempt a non-American power to intervention and possibly lodgment. The influence of international law upon this process was essentially destabilizing. Several times in the early twentieth century the United States indicated its willingness to circumscribe the use of armed intervention for the collection of pecuniary claims. The Drago Doctrine and other similar pronouncements of Latin American statesmen demonstrated the expectable Latin American concurrence in this desire. In 1889 and 1901 the possibility of establishing a multilateral commitment to compulsory arbitration of pecuniary claims in the hemisphere was discussed at inter-American conferences, with the United States supporting the commitment. Hence, quite early in the development of inter-American law there was a substantial foundation for the restriction of intervention in this limited area of pecuniary claims. General international law, on the other hand, not only continued to recognize the legitimacy of intervention as a means of enforcing international financial obligations but also tended to increase the attractiveness of armed intervention for this purpose. The Hague Court decision of February 1904 gave preferential status to the claims of intervening powers over those of states not participating in a given intervention. Had the United States gone forward in its project for a compulsory arbitration commitment, a completely asymmetrical situation would have been created, in which European powers would have continued their interventions while the United States would have been prohibited from intervening. Consequently in 1906 the compulsory arbitration idea was dropped completely.

The point cannot be overstressed that the involvement of other non-American powers in Latin American civil strike was usually an "external" rather than "internal" involvement. The rapid resolution of the characteristic *golpe* meant that in most cases European forceful presentation of pecuniary claims occurred long after the outcome of a given civil conflict had been determined. In contrast, American pre-emptive intervention was directed toward prophylactic correction of the conditions giving rise to the dangerous defaults on international debts. Both types of intervention, however, shared a common indifference to the actual domestic effects of the Latin American internal struggles upon the personnel and authority structure of the disrupted political systems.

This "non-ideological" attitude toward Latin American civil strife meant that the role of foreign countries in most civil struggles was virtually nonexistent, and where their influence was observable its impact was usually symmetrical. Personnel changes within the political elites were so frequent that standard diplomatic relations sustained for even a short period of time usually put foreign diplomats in touch with both the incumbents and the leaders of the "out-group" faction. These personal relationships with both sides in the short-lived internal struggles made for an easy continuity in diplomatic relations, regardless of the outcome of the civil conflict.

The Cold War, in common conception, changed all this. It is a popular theory that behind the Guatemalan enterprise, the Bay of Pigs, and the Dominican invasion lies a common conceptual premise that communism in any form, and particularly in locations close to home, is a kind of social malignancy to be treated with the antidote of military takeover if possible, or to be surgically removed if necessary. And there is much in the rhetoric of inter-American intervention to support the theory. But a closer view of recent interventionary practice raises the question of whether this view adequately explains the continuity apparent in U.S. interventions in the hemisphere. Guatemala was a communist state only in rhetoric and propaganda; Cuba was intervened only after turning to Soviet arms; and Santo Domingo was at most a prophylactic intervention. That is to say, the major interventions of the last twenty years have been directed more at the conditions that in popular conception favor communist advances than they have at established communist regimes.

The importance of this distinction becomes clear when one considers the claims made by both Kennedy and Johnson to the effect that intervention became necessary when the O.A.S. failed to fulfill its anticommunist obligations. Putting aside for the moment the issue of whether Latin American members of the regional organization have ever committed themselves to what U.S. leaders would consider an adequate anticommunist policy, they have certainly not committed themselves to the suppression of the social and political activities that U.S. leaders have considered synonymous with susceptibility to communist lodgment. This critical difference in perspectives between U.S. leaders and Latin Americans goes far toward explaining why the United States has shown an increasing disposition to by-pass the apparatus of regional organization in attempting to maintain the stability of the hemisphere.

As a regional security organization the O.A.S. faces problems not unlike those of its predecessors. The whole history of U.S.–Latin American relations from 1898 to the present can be broadly characterized as a search for some alternative to armed intervention that would still assure

U.S. security interests in the hemisphere. Dollar diplomacy was originally viewed as a laudable attempt to replace bullets with cash. Organizational alternatives, such as the Pan-American Pact and the Central American regional system, all failed. General economic instability, the hierarchical structure of Latin American society, and intra-Latin American nationalistic jealousies combined to make pacific resolution of internal conflicts unfeasible in the Latin American context.

Unilateral American intervention, on the other hand, suffered few natural restrictions in the international system. The doctrine of legitimacy made Latin America an important area for the maintenance of the concert-of-powers system of the late eighteenth and early nineteenth centuries. But when that system gave way to the balance-of-power configuration of the nineteenth century, the importance of Latin America to the non-American powers declined considerably. Until after World War II, Latin America remained far from the vital center of the international system of the day. On the other hand, the importance of the area to American security increased considerably in the two decades preceding World War I. This asymmetry in perceived interest in the area is important, for it goes far toward explaining the European ability to abide by its nonintervention commitments under general international law, while the United States has found itself incapable of abiding by a much more inclusive commitment under inter-American law.

Of course, armed intervention, though limited in its effects on the international system, has always carried its own economic and political costs. The concept of territorial sovereignty has been so embedded in the minds of international lawyers and diplomats that intervention to this day carries a high psychological cost to the people intervening. Second, Latin American diplomats have worked hard in the twentieth century to increase the price of American intervention in the hemisphere. These were the motivating factors for the American acceptance of the nonintervention commitment, when a freakish and short-lived condition of effortless hemispheric security made that acceptance possible between the wars. The general acceptance of similar commitments in international law, beginning with the Kellogg–Briand Pact and culminating with the U.N. Charter, was based upon the same antiquated spatial concept of territorial security that had become irrelevant to the American situation in the Western Hemisphere by the turn of the century.

The inter-American system does not appear to have provided for the protection of what are perceived as vital interests by U.S. leaders. The latest U.S. proposal for a standing inter-American peace force was rejected by the Rio Conference of 1965 for the same reasons that Latin Americans have rejected attempts to politicize the inter-American regional system since its creation: the myth of hemispheric community is simply not strong enough to overcome the very real nationalistic attachments of the member states. Yet the American commitment to nonintervention must rest upon the protection of those interests perceived as vital by other means. As Neal Ronning has pointed out:

> It is as useless to outlaw intervention without providing a satisfactory sub-stitute as it was to outlaw war when no satisfactory substitute was available. When the apparent "necessity" of intervention appears to outweigh any long-term advantages of preserving the principle of non-intervention, states will resort to the former. This holds true for small powers as well as great powers, and the record of the past two decades shows an increasing number of apparent "necessities."[1]

One such substitute would seem clearly unsatisfactory. The occupation by proxy through bilateral military arrangements that has characterized U.S.–Latin American policy both during and after World War II has already proven a bankrupt concept. Quite apart from the violence that such a policy does to traditional domestic values it has all too often proved the prelude rather than the alternative to armed intervention. Militarism is simply not an alternative to what U.S. leaders have insisted upon calling communist domination of Latin America in the way that it was an alter-native to American intervention in World War II. Those rare cases in which military leaders have undertaken a consistent program to institute needed reforms in the backward societies of Latin America are the exceptions that prove the rule. But it may well be that American policy cannot even afford the exceptions. Militarism in Latin America has become a prop-agandistic synonym for preservation of the status quo in an area where the status quo is generally perceived as intolerable. And there is ample evidence to indicate that military control of the internal politics of the Latin Ameri-can countries is actually playing into the hands of the radical left. Former President Manuel Ydigoras Fuentes of Guatemala—who was certainly not adverse to military dictatorship on ideological grounds—has suggested that the Castro-communists actually welcome military intervention into civilian politics, because intervention seems to prove that "democracy will not work, that it is a failure, that it is a joke."[2] Consequently U.S. support of military control in Latin America has its own radicalizing influence. Further dependence upon the military instrument means an automatic break in relations with the very parties that will ultimately con-trol the Latin American destiny. In large part, the collapse of U.S. policy

---

[1] C. Neale Ronning, *Law and Politics in Inter-American Diplomacy* (New York: John Wiley and Sons, 1963), p. 83.
[2] *New York Times*, May 10, 1963.

in Cuba was attributable to the long-standing U.S. link with Batista's military establishment. When Castro destroyed the military he effectively extirpated all U.S. influence over the course of Cuban politics. Finally, as Santo Domingo dramatically proved, the military link-up has its own momentum. The line between military control by proxy and direct intervention is one that neither Latin American nationalists or U.S. policymakers have been able to draw.

If the history of U.S. intervention in Latin America teaches anything, it is that the perceived "necessity" for intervention is not a new phenomenon. In truth, the United States has never faced the decision of whether or not to intervene in Latin America when its basic security interests were threatened, but only the question of when and how. Nonintervention was possible only in a brief period of hemispheric isolation between the world wars; and unless the general outlines of the international system are catastrophically altered in the near future, it seems doubtful that the strategic mutation that allowed the acceptance of nonintervention in the first place will ever be seen again.

It is, of course, appealing to argue as we have that whatever the strategic configuration underlying U.S. interventions has been, the basic problem with U.S. policy has been the misidentification of important political groups in Latin America as pawns or allies of the Sino–Soviet powers. Hence, it can be argued that a greater appreciation of the subtle complexities of Latin American politics should yield the conclusion that intervention was unnecessary, since even the success of the most extreme leftist groups in the area—if not opposed in such a way as to make inevitable subsequent dependence upon communist powers—is not a real threat to any essential U.S. interests. Once this is recognized, compliance with the nonintervention norm, at least insofar as it prohibits armed intervention, becomes the logical course for a nation concerned with the promotion of world legal order and with its international image as a law-abiding member of the international community. This position is rational and sound and suggests for the international lawyer a course of advocacy that is bound to prove more fruitful than the simple decrying of U.S. actions as clearly illegal under international law.

But the adoption of such a course requires an optimistic judgment as to the susceptibility of U.S. policymaking institutions to rational persuasion on the issue of anticommunism. This author does not question the legitimacy of that judgment; it is simply one that he cannot share. The anticommunist impulse, with all of its untenable identifications of devils, is so firmly embedded in the American psyche, institutions, and economic structure as to take on the impermeability of religious truth. And if the tragedy of Vietnam and the dissent that it has provoked has not served to temper the demonology of American anticommunism, how much more persistent that demonology is likely to be when the "communists" are but a few miles away.

For one who shares this pessimism there is a second judgment to be made as to whether liberalization of the nonintervention norm would not be preferable to the damaging effects of its continued violation. It is at least clear that the continuation of the American commitment to nonintervention in a context that as perceived in the United States makes nonintervention impossible is an hypocrisy that can only damage the prestige of the United States as a law-abiding nation and make a mockery of international law as a regulator of transnational interactions. In short, even for the advocate of legal order in international relations there may be times when retreat is the better part of valor. And at a minimum, reconsideration of the nonintervention commitment might serve to force reexamination of just what it is in Latin America that is thought to require the protection of the U.S. marine corps.

Even those who would oppose liberalization of the nonintervention norm should consider the extent to which the claim to a right of intervention for the protection of vital interests that lie beyond the national territorial confines has already been successfully promoted. The congressional resolution of 1965 quoted earlier seems to have already gone far in this direction. And Russian acquiescence in U.S. interventions in Cuba and Santo Domingo suggests that the principle has gained some support in the international system. Indeed, U.S. quietude over similar Russian intervention in Czechoslovakia might even suggest that intra-bloc intervention is fast becoming accepted international practice. In fact, the question is rapidly becoming, not whether the nonintervention norms should be liberalized, but how that liberalization should be circumscribed.

But to advocate the liberalization of the nonintervention norm is not to advocate unilateral means for its liberalization. It is doubtful that a unilateral assertion of a U.S. right to intervene in Latin American affairs would be politically acceptable in the present-day world. And given the degree of our involvement in other parts of the world it is even doubtful that unilateral intervention would be militarily feasible. What remains is the possibility of an effective regional organization that would preserve and protect those interests that the United States considers essential in the Western Hemipshere. In this area, the history of U.S.–Latin American relations is ambiguous. The O.A.S. has apparently not been effective for these purposes; but then the O.A.S. was never a completed structure. In its origin and present state it is a shell built upon a jurisprudential fiction that never had an actual chance for realization. Whether or not an effective and complete regional organization can yet be constructed is a question upon which the present study would imply much skepticism; but the present study is history. In the end, whether or not a successful alternative to unilateral intervention in this hemisphere is found will depend upon the identification of mutual interests in defending against what U.S. policymakers perceive to be vital threats in the hemisphere and a great deal of juridic realism with respect to the legal structure upon which such an organization must rest. But an assessment of the likelihood of these two elements emerging in the present-day context of hemispheric affairs is the subject for another study.

# Index

ABC powers, 82, 83, 86, 92

Adams, John Quincy, 24, 222; Cuban policy of, 28, 43; recognition policy of, 20–22

Agency for International Development (U.S.), police-training program of, 161

Airport Development Project, 145

Airpower, impact on U.S. hemispheric policies, 103–7

Anti-War Treaty of Non-Aggression and Conciliation, 122

Arãna, Francisco Javier, 186

Arbenz, Jacob, 186; overthrow of, 190–92, 195–96, 209, 219; Soviet arms for, 191, 193

Arbitration: inter-American conference on, 72, 120; pan-American pact on, 81; of pecuniary claims, 82, 223; special protocol for, 120; U.S.–Latin American treaties on, 72. *See also* Hague Court

Arevalo, Juan José, 186, 195

Argentina, 82–83, 134, 136, 162, 170, 210, 211; British investment in, 97, 122; challenge to U.S. by, 122–23, 192, 211; German influence in, 137, 143; under Peron, 150, 171, 197; during World War II, 139, 140, 142, 143

Arguedas, Antonio, 182

Armaments, limitations on: under League Covenant, 100; treaty on, 102; Washington Conference on, 101–3, 108

Armas. *See* Castillo Armas, Carlos

Arms, standardization of, 150, 158

Axis powers: airlines in Latin America, 130, 137; Havana declaration on, 141; hemispheric defense against, 8, 127, 142; infiltration in Latin America by, 128, 135, 137, 143; military missions of, 126, 131–32; relations with Argentina, 134; support of Latin American military, 132, 137; trade with South America, 97; U.S. plans for war against, 138–39

Ayacucho, battle of, 11

Balaguer, Joaquin, 214, 219

Barnet, Richard, 162, 168, 175

Barrientos, Rene, 182

Batista, Fulgencio, 171, 197; overthrow of, 198–202; U.S. support for, 160, 168, 200, 202, 227

Bay Islands, 25, 36

Bay of Pigs, invasion of: 174, 184, 208–10, 224; authorization of, 203–4; and OAS, 154; refugees from, 3, 197

Belize, 29

Bemis, Samuel, 43, 94, 124

Betancourt, Romulo, 167, 171, 175; attempted assassination of, 207, 213

Bliss, Tasker, 37

Bogotá Conference, 154

Bolivar, Simon, 15, 23–25

Bolivia, 174, 181, 213; in Chaco war, 122; and Cuba, 211–12; insurgents in, 172, 181, 210; U.S. aid to, 61, 145, 171, 182–83

Bonnelly, Rafael, 214

Bonsal, Philip W., 202–4, 206

Bosch, Juan, 181, 214, 219; U.S. attitude toward, 171–72, 181, 214–15, 218

Brazil, 82–83, 86, 162–64, 170, 172, 177; British interests in, 15; and Cuban crisis, 210–12; and Dominican intervention, 218; and Germany, 137; U.S. relations with, 6, 131, 144, 164; in World War I, 92; in World War II, 138, 140, 144–46

Britain, 65, 122; as dominant naval power, 10, 15, 31–32, 35, 37, 99–102; and Holy Alliance, 16, 19, 22; intervention in Mexico by, 25; intervention in Venezuela by, 38, 61, 78; Latin American investments of, 53, 59, 67, 97; Latin American trade with, 10–12, 14–16; naval competition with Germany, 36, 74, 99; naval competition

231